W9-BZQ-201

Repression, Exile, and Democracy:
Uruguayan Culture

A Book in the Series

Latin America in Translation / En Traducción / Em Tradução

Sponsored by the Duke–University of North Carolina

Program in Latin American Studies

REPRESSION, EXILE, AND

DEMOCRACY *Uruguayan Culture*

Edited by Saúl Sosnowski and Louise B. Popkin

Translated from the Spanish by

Louise B. Popkin

Duke University Press *Durham and London 1993*

Translation of the books in the series Latin America in Translation /
En Traducción / Em Tradução, a collaboration between the Duke–
University of North Carolina Joint Program in Latin American Studies and
the university presses of Duke and the University of North Carolina, is
supported by a grant from the Andrew W. Mellon Foundation.

This translation was assisted by the Joint Committee on Latin American
Studies of the Social Science Research Council and the American
Council of Learned Societies with funds provided by the William and
Flora Hewlett Foundation, the Andrew W. Mellon Foundation, and the
University of Maryland at College Park.

Originally published in Spanish with the title *Represión, exilio y
democracia: la cultura Uruguaya* (College Park, Md.: University of
Maryland; Montevideo: Ediciones de la Banda Oriental, 1987).

© 1993 Duke University Press. All rights reserved. Printed in the United
States of America on acid-free paper ∞
Library of Congress Cataloging-in-Publication Data appear on the last
printed page of this book

In memory of Angel Rama

Contents

❂

viii   Contents

Editorial Note

❂

The essays which follow contain interpretations of Uruguayan culture as viewed by their authors in March 1986. When the contributors to this volume were invited to revise them for the English-language edition, four of them chose to incorporate references to subsequent events: while Kaufman first updated his essay to reflect his views at a later moment, then added a postscript, Sosnowski and Weinstein did only the latter, and Achugar appended to his original comments a second article, written at a later date and reflective of a different state of mind. The remaining authors preferred to let their words stand as testimony to their states of mind at a particular moment in Uruguayan history, rather than produce updates which themselves were certain to be outdated by the time they appeared in print. So as to guide our readers with respect to the multiple chronological perspectives thus represented here, we have included at the end of each essay one or more dates of composition.

As Seen from the Other Shore: Uruguayan Culture (Repression, Exile, and Democracy)

Saúl Sosnowski

❁

I n early December 1984, a symposium entitled "The Repression and Reconstruction of Culture in Argentina" was held at the University of Maryland. The views expressed on that occasion—barely a year after the return of democracy—corroborated the need for further discussions on the impact of extreme repression on culture. Over and beyond the value of understanding itself, this was a topic of the utmost importance for the societies of the Southern Cone as they underwent transition from dictatorship to democracy. A review of what had happened over the last several decades—and especially a critical comparison of the many facets of cultural production both inside these countries and in exile—seemed as essential as it was bound to prove beneficial. To be productive, however, any such discussions would have to be true civil dialogues, extending beyond party slogans and pat phrases and seeking substantive answers to substantive questions. Even more, they would presuppose the ability to hear divergent opinions and use them as a starting point for collective reflection upon the multiple futures opening up for each country in question.

The experience with the symposium on Argentina led me to convene a distinguished group of Uruguayan intellectuals in an academic setting outside their national borders, in hopes of facilitating and encouraging dialogue (or compelling it, at the very least). From March 9 to 11, 1986, they came together at College Park, Maryland, in work sessions organized around five panels. The first of these, entitled "Contexts" and moderated by Azucena Berrutti, featured presentations by Martin Weinstein, Edy Kaufman, and Juan Rial. The topic "Culture and Power" was addressed by Mauricio Rosencof, Ruben Yáñez, Eduardo Galeano, and Leo Masliah, with Louise Popkin moderating. José Pedro Díaz, Amanda Berenguer, Teresa Porzecanski, Hugo

Verani, and Lisa Block de Béhar discussed "Literature and Repression" as participants in a panel moderated by Tomás Eloy Martínez. "The Shores of Exile" was the topic addressed by Hugo Achugar, Alvaro Barros-Lémez, and Jorge Ruffinelli, with moderator Hiber Conteris participating actively as well.[1] Since this symposium, like the one on Argentina, was part of a broader project aimed at examining the repression and reconstruction of culture in the entire region, there was also a panel entitled "The South: Comparative Aspects," moderated by Peter Hakim and featuring papers by Juan Corradi, Joan Dassin, Carina Perelli, and Bernardo Subercaseaux.[2] In addition to the formal deliberations that were part of the symposium, there were recitals by Amanda Berenguer and Leo Masliah and an exhibition of graphics by Uruguayans Luis Camnitzer, Antonio Frasconi, Naúl Ojeda, and Alberto Schunk, each of whose work embodies in its own way some of the concerns and experiences that figured in the discussions.[3] Those days in March also marked the first anniversary of the release of the last political prisoners from Uruguay's jails and military barracks.

The University of Maryland was thus a gathering place for Uruguayans who had suffered imprisonment and torture, for survivors of "insile" and exile (some of the latter having returned to Uruguay and others having settled abroad), and—although no one was invited specifically or formally as spokesperson for any group, party, or social sector—for Uruguayans representative of diverse political positions and generations. For three days, poets, writers of fiction, and playwrights shared the podium with literary critics and social scientists, all of them witnesses to the destruction of a mythified country now engaged in an arduous process of reconstruction.

And it was precisely in reference to the matter of myths (the topic of Juan Rial's presentation) that certain tensions arose. Notwithstanding the generals' (mis)uses and abuses, it was difficult to relinquish as formidable a political tool as an "official history" dominated by the central figure of José Gervasio Artigas had proven to be—especially since Uruguay's national hero was so genuinely superior to many caudillos of his day. Modified by successive governments and political groups to suit their own purposes (through careful emphasis on certain episodes and the downplaying of others), that official history was informed from the moment of its creation by a number of nationally recognized literary elements which were another major source of its ongoing appeal. A paternalistic state that offered both formal security and tangible forms of assistance was still an attractive model; as such, it favored a return to the old peace of averageness, even at the risk of consolidating an updated version of José Enrique Rodó's "mediocracy." Clearly, given the instability and terror afflicting other countries in the region, Uruguay's old liberal regime, which came to power by strictly legal means, was regarded as a sacred—and potentially retrievable—memory. That tends to explain why, so long after the ideals to which they corresponded were conceived, such stale expressions as the "Switzerland of America" (to refer to Uruguay) and its correlate, the "Athens of the River Plate" (to refer to Montevideo), the globalizing "There's no place like Uruguay" ("Como el Uruguay no hay"), and the foundational (and subsequently distorted) "model country" sought after by José Batlle y Ordóñez and his followers were heard repeatedly in the presentations and discussions. As they attempted to dismantle the ultimate myth, which held Uruguay to be different from its Latin American neighbors, well-known voices could be heard resisting the need—even for purely analytical purposes—to disavow their so-called alterity; yet that is precisely what must happen before the country can break definitively with a legacy that helped lead it down the path to its own destruction.

Having been born and raised in Argentina (and engaged both as witness and participant), I was struck by the fact that so many proven activists of so many political persuasions felt it necessary to safeguard Uruguay's foundational myths, whatever form the new political regime might eventually take. The presenters referred repeatedly to a Uruguayan core of values, whose existence was taken for granted; that common heritage, they argued (with few exceptions), might allow for "variants" of this or that form of government, but not—at least not yet—for the kind of radical transformation that would require abandoning what Uruguayan mythmaking held dear. This magnanimous reticence, which is echoed throughout the region, is understandable given the excesses of the most recent dictatorships: the first impulse was to protect "fragile democracy" from anything and everything that might threaten its existence—even a probing debate.

While calling for rigorous modifications, these Uruguayans seemed to regard a return to the best features of their liberal tradition as a sort of lifeline at a moment in their history when the first steps toward recovery were being taken. For that reason, deep soul-searching brought discomfort; question marks too sharply hooked might puncture or uproot what was defective and rotten without immediately offering new myths, fragrant and warm with nostalgia and the dream of Utopia regained. The familiar myths were comforting; they offered a moment of respite to a people faced suddenly with the task of rebuilding, perhaps even of redrawing within new parameters, a nation which was the product of political pacts, backhanded deals, and selected nineteenth-century foundational dreams. Fear for this new democracy, itself based on fear (which assessed its own worth, accordingly, from the perspective of fear), initially limited debate to certain agreed-upon areas, however short-lived these might prove to be: the so-called civil military regimes as a source of destructive elements, the matter of prison sentences for military personnel guilty of crimes and for their most obvious accomplices (a particularly conflictive topic), the concentrated power of certain elite families that form a local and international brotherhood, and the demographic deformities of a socioeconomically fragmented political order. The debate grew more heated as it once again centered on the need for pragmatic solutions based on the daily realities of reconstruction and the judicial and ethical problems posed by the immediate past. Here too, as Uruguayans scrutinized the decisions of their neighbors (especially regarding the matter of trials for the military), they were forced to come to grips with the nonexistent "alterity" by virtue of which they had considered themselves a privileged exception to the rule. By now it was obvious that Uruguay was not the only country afflicted by (or obliged to deal with) the painful realities of its Third World status.

The collapse of institutional life in Uruguay was neither sudden nor exclusively a product of the June 27, 1973, coup d'état. Recent studies have documented (and by this I do not mean necessarily to imply a cause-and-effect relationship) an increase in violence considerably before that date, as well as an increase in the power of the military—which was all too eager to go beyond its repressive and "strictly bellicose" responsibilities and take on a political role in the definition of the country while at the same time extending its own privileges. The existence of splits within the two traditional political parties made it virtually impossible for them to respond adequately as, from 1967 on, power was concentrated more and more exclusively in the hands of the president while democratic rights were restricted accordingly. As inflation spiraled increasingly out of control and labor unrest escalated, so did the activity of sectors opposed to dissent in a society long admirable for its tolerance of divergent views. To varying degrees, all these factors, along with others which pointed to serious divisions within Uruguayan society and shifts in international interests, led ultimately to the suspension of government by consensus and the installation of an openly authoritarian regime which ruled by force.

On a number of levels this violent, radical change replaced the vitality of voices with the silence of fear: legality gave way to terror, bewildering in its essential irrationality; freedom of expression fell prey to the tendentiousness of censorship; certainty as to the consequences of specific actions gave way to the unpredictability of arbitrariness. As the authorities proceeded to mutilate all elements perceived as "alien" to the body of the nation, the possibility of an honest debate about national reorganization vanished.

Obviously, in this climate and with education under attack at all levels, the isolation resulting from censorship, and the difficulties engendered by economic decline per se, cultural production suffered a setback. A further—and fundamental—aggravating factor was emigration: Uruguay, which already had a population too small for the demands of its territory, lost many of its intellectuals and highly trained professionals when conditions inside the country made exile the solution of choice for many. However, despite these numerous obstacles, and even with its access to the public limited (if not totally curtailed), culture as such did not go into remission. Nor, in the dispersion of the diaspora, with many of their works (and often their names) banned inside Uruguay, did the émigrés become the only bearers of Uruguayan culture. When the politics of repression and censorship succeeded in creating a virtual void, inasmuch as truly national voices of dissent could not be heard, the Uruguayan public transformed that void into a sonorous silence, filling it with alternative forms of music and an alternative literature of which international best-sellers were but a part.

In this connection—that is, given the dimensions of the cultural void and the fact that the dictatorship failed to obtain even the tacit backing of Uruguayan intellectuals for its attempts to create a new order—there does not seem to have existed in Uruguay the fierce, categorical polemic between exiles and nonexiles that was characteristic of Argentine intellectual circles. Nevertheless, distances and exiles were a source of considerable tension. As Hugo Achugar pointed out, residence abroad meant not just distance from Uruguay but also the acquisition of new homelands. Those who left did not simply undergo hardships; they were also enriched by new and broader histories, by access to new knowledge, by the awareness that their identity was not limited by nationality and the narrow confines of their respective hometowns. These were positive changes that, hopefully, repatriates would bring back with them as their contribution to the daunting task of rebuilding Uruguay. However, this would be possible only if they were welcomed back as fellow Uruguayans and if their different set of positive attributes was recognized by those who had stayed (with no criticism of the latter position implied) as a potentially valid instrument for the reconstruction of national culture. Hopefully too, a number of steps already taken in the interest of avoiding splits between the two groups would help expedite the process of reintegration into a newly redemocratized country.

The very coining of the term *insile*, analogous to *exile*, as a means of pointing to similarities between Uruguayans opposed to the regime—and thus marginalized—within the country and their counterparts abroad tended to diminish the importance of national borders as a means of distinguishing among attitudes toward the dictatorship. Insile took a variety of forms—active resistance, sonorous silence, or mere survival pending a new awakening. As presently regarded, the literature of insile encompasses an extraordinary group of texts by political prisoners who, while under detention, began (or went on) writing what has come to be called "prison literature." These texts offer the most direct and authentic testimony available concerning life in the prisons, the daily attacks on all aspects of human dignity, the brutal harassment by means of which the dictatorship, conscious of the far-reaching effects of its terror tactics upon third parties, attempted simultaneously to impose its rule of silence on the entire country. But perhaps more than that, in their frequent use of the first person ("I bear witness," as if to echo Zola's "J'accuse") they constitute one of the most eloquent literary statements we know concerning the impact of repression. They also underscore the double sense in which language is a lifeline: first, for those who grab onto it in the darkest of dungeons; and later, for those who seek in it—from the perspective of history or literature—the meaning, however incomplete, of their times. Given its uniqueness, prison literature belongs in a category by itself and should figure as such, alongside the literature of exile and insile, in any overview of the literary production of these past years.

Even before the return to institutional life in Uruguay, the displacement of so many intellectuals brought with it the realization that a break in cultural continuity might occur. This knowledge in itself generated the mechanisms necessary for undertaking the reconstruction of Uruguayan culture. Additionally, to the extent that cultural manifestations both in insile and in exile maintained some degree of continuity with the past—especially as regards adherence to certain national myths—the coming back together of insiled and exiled intellectuals after redemocratization seems free of permanent splits. At the same time, the very absence of individual and public freedoms inside the country led a small group of prose fiction writers to experiment with new forms. Even while subject to the punitive severity of the censors and the most asphyxiating kind of self-censorship (an asphyxia and a decadence prefigured in Juan Carlos Onetti's works of a few decades earlier), they managed to go on writing about the present through reference to certain previously codified and canonized events of the past; and, as Teresa Porzecanski argued, by dismantling literal meanings in their texts so as to lay bare the no less duplicitous nature of official discourse, they turned fantasy into a sphere of resistance. Also of interest are the concerns and loyalties of younger artists and writers—in particular, those who spent their formative years under the dictatorship—vis-à-vis the contemporary Uruguayan "classics" and more recent authors. Further analysis is needed of the artistic manifestations of this new generation, from such original cultural phenomena as *canto popular* and national rock to social practices as varied as street fairs and Carnival celebrations—all of them both responses to the limits set by the regime and means of documenting diverse aspects of Uruguay's social transformation.

Inquiry aimed at understanding the shifting social relationships surrounding culture customarily focuses on the multiple meanings of any text, the nature of its intended audience, the ways in which an initial message is echoed throughout its mut(il)ations, and, of course, especially, the texture of each page. Perhaps these approaches also allow us to gauge both distances between generations and possibilities for highly unpredictable futures. While generalizations are always risky, it can be said that older writers have tended, on the basis of their formal cultural baggage and personal experience, to seek a return to pre-1973 Uruguay by reclaiming the liberal values of the Batllista state, adapting them to meet current needs and accommodating them to political doctrines considered de rigueur.

Lacking comparable loyalties and responsibilities, forward-looking younger groups, on the other hand, are free to develop their views out of irreverence (not to be confused with irresponsibility), in an informal exercise of imagination not subject to social and cultural canons. Their attitude indicates, moreover, that a significant part of the cultural debate is occurring outside political parties and other formal arenas. Their questioning and tendency to challenge, their resistance to inherited formulas, and their criticism of easily predictable slogans and stereotyped forms are all clear manifestations of an experiential informality whose long-term ideological implications remain unclear.

Before a given generation can leave its distinctive mark on a country, breathing new life into culture and contributing to greater pluralism, its originality has to find a way into official discourse; otherwise, that generation will have no spheres of influence or even of transaction. In this instance, informality itself runs a risk of codification, or of becoming organized into fixed forms—whether these entail formulistic rejection of the status quo or a Utopian demand for perpetual renovation. In any event, in this new and foreseeably long stage of reconstruction, acts of rebellion against authority (including that of the established political opposition) have been informed by an imaginative power singularly and habitually lacking when manifestations of culture require extensive citing of influences, explanations, or other such concessions to established norms to be regarded as legitimate. It is clear that too many areas of cultural production have been adversely affected by this kind of obsequiousness. Striking examples are the literary forms recently emerging from, and dealing with, Uruguayan society and the manifesto-like nature of certain texts from this symposium.

In the fiction, poetry, and theater of these years—whether of exile, insile, or the unique category represented by prison literature—polarizations and splits (or repetitions) have not occurred strictly along generational lines, nor do they fit comfortably into the geographical categories of "inside" versus "outside." Rather they fall for the time being into a vague and disquieting area that encompasses diverse attitudes and styles of openness, of apprenticeship, of constant reflection, of unrelenting and unobjectionable self-criticism, of availability—all nourished by a pragmatic impulse that allows for even the surprisingly Utopian perspective characteristic of some survivors.

❂

The choice of participants for this symposium implied knowledge of their respective careers and points of view. In certain cases it was possible even to predict titles, frames of reference, and, to some extent, the contents of position papers. Nevertheless, a symposium of this nature—which could not have been held in Uruguay—was obviously not going to be an occasion for passive receptivity; rather, the organizers anticipated critical self-searching, frank dialogue, and a candid exchange of opinions, whether restrained because of the general setting or inflamed by differences and the lack of a large audience ready to react immediately to every opinion expressed. Being neither a zealot nor unrealistic, I did not expect the sessions to bloom with joyful bliss; I simply hoped for some degree of collective analysis, even if accompanied by silence, reticence, or outright contempt, condescending looks or perfunctory greetings, temporary tolerance (barely skin-deep) or transparent animosity toward an enemy close at hand.

For some participants, certain presences and absences themselves sufficed to aggravate tensions and escalate existing conflicts. With the historical, social, and political analyses of the first panel (whose purpose was to provide a context for later discussions) came the inevitable recovery of historical memory, precise information, an incisive compendium of errors committed by the democratic forces in response to the first onslaught of authoritarianism, a list of political measures that were called for now that the electoral process had been restored, and, as already mentioned, criticism of uncritical adherence to national myths. Descriptions of Uruguay's decline and its causes (both mediate and immediate) and rigorous analyses that gave rise to tacit accusations and led some participants to question the behavior, lifestyles, and ways of thinking of others were sufficient to heighten initial feelings of discomfort, relief, and sometimes ill-contained rage. Hardhead-edness, open-mindedness, veiled references to third parties, ideological clarifications, animosity, punctilious calls to action, vindications, and at-tributions of blame were all increasingly in evidence as the meetings pro-gressed and political tactics were refined, principles were reexamined, new knowledge was acquired, and old knowledge was validated. This admittedly partial account of attitudes and actions can be assumed in differing degrees to characterize panelists and public alike, since the problems under scrutiny were of deep concern to all and visceral involvement seldom (if ever) allows for detached reflection.

In the many—and welcome—presentations involving direct testimony, the first person naturally predominated. But individual presences and unin-hibited egos were also very much in evidence when this or that interpretation of a political course of action was impugned, or when participants stated their differences in terms sometimes far too emotional for the issues under discussion, even while attempting to reach a temporary understanding. Not-withstanding their shared willingness to engage in the deeply felt soul-searching without which no progression from the level of "I, protagonist/I, witness" to the plural meaning of our objective analyses would have been possible, some participants proved incapable of contributing significantly to an understanding of immediate history, offering valuable access to the realm of the private instead. In other cases, a well-polished demeanor and a smooth bearing accustomed to pontificating from prestigious national and interna-tional public platforms—while no less sincere—were equally unable to enhance our understanding of the issues under discussion.

In its varied emphases and cadences, the predominantly dramatic dis-course of those days in March—which ranged from eloquence to occasional shrillness to the urgent silence imposed by our shared awareness of the significance of the occasion—echoed both the drama of live experience and personal conduct that spoke for itself, thus requiring no other comment. In the great majority of cases (for reductive arrogance was not totally lacking), that conduct ran the gamut from humility to resignation, from the acceptance of partial victories and old defeats to tempered pride and satisfaction with survival, from a somewhat embarrassed self-belittlement at not having paid as high a price as some others to rejoicing in the reality of repatriation. A fundamental agreement as to the unquestionable importance of redemocra-tization frequently tempered the noisy disagreements that burst forth on the surface, then promptly gave way to an apparently agreed-upon commonality of interests.

Some excesses and rebuffs may have been the result of generational splits or pale patricidal impulses, clashes in temperament and social demeanor, and recent or remote recollections of events inside Uruguay or in the vaster reaches of exile, which today might best be forgiven and forgotten. However, there also were (and continue to be) basic disagreements concerning the reactions of the political parties and their permeability to change; the role played by armed organizations and their influence on the course of events; the role played by Uruguay in the region and the hemisphere; the extreme ideologizing of certain episodes in the historical process; educational policies, particularly at the university level; the meaning of certain cultural products for audiences with different memories and dissimilar futures; the restrictiveness of certain modes of expression characteristic of limited sectors; the ability of Uruguay's youngest citizens to recover what they lost as a result of the dictatorship; generational differences which extend beyond the sphere of cultural expression; and what it means for certain Uruguayans to have returned, and their ability to recapture the tone and rhythm of a systematically devastated country.

So extensive, yet partial, a list of areas of friction should not be taken as proof that this gathering of Uruguayan intellectuals was rife with discord and irreconcilable differences. It was precisely around some of these issues that a certain consensus was reached—albeit at times restricted explicitly to the limits of the specific point under discussion. There were also moments when it was impossible to disagree. The delivery of Mauricio Rosencof's paper—in a sober (but in no way neutral) voice that underscored the gravity of its contents, by someone who had paid so heavy a price for his activism—brought one such moment. Leo Masliah achieved the same effect in another register, with his observations and songs, which in their very hilarity demolished (deconstructed?) the disasters of recent years (and of Uruguay's entire history) while at the same time raising new questions. Even as Uruguayans rejoiced justifiably over the retreat of the military and the return of the electoral process, there was uncertainty: might this be just one more transitional stage toward a democracy that had yet to encompass all of Uruguayan society, bringing with it the corresponding benefits and civic responsibilities? From behind prison bars and the suppler bars of a song, that same hooked symbol emerged, challenging all to reexamine their faith in the good myths of salvation.

This outstanding collection of essays delivered during those memorable days should give the reader (as they did the audience at the time of their presentation) a sense of the dynamics of the symposium and, more important, of the range of issues still to be resolved. They represent vital and radically different sets of experiences and projects for participation in the reconstruction of Uruguay. As such, they are linked to other inquiries, both individual and collective, to analyses unavoidably remote or deeply committed by dint of personal involvement, to more formal proclamations, and to the litanies of losses which, these days, tend to give way to new hope.

Any listing of partial conclusions would be futile and would only detract from the multiple meanings of that singular event. For those who are still open to new experiences and proposals for change, sensibly and sensitively disposed to examining and taking into account the opinions of others (notwithstanding the aforementioned doses of irony and cynicism), and aware that survival in the fullest sense implies renewal and an ability to break with old rules and practices so as to build a new order, those days in March and these essays will provide a broad spectrum of experiences—restoring memories and relating events that must be understood if grievous new errors and the futile repetition of old ones are to be avoided. At the risk of sounding elliptical, let me add that much of what is to be found in these pages also points to the uncertainty of any future; but however uncertain the future may be for the countries of the Southern Cone—still controlled by foreign investors and alien to their own inhabitants—it may be slightly less so now that the (re)construction of democracy has begun.[4]

College Park, November 1986

A 1991 Postscript

As I reread the essays that constitute this volume, their dual significance becomes apparent. On the one hand, their content may appear somewhat dated. More than five years after the fact, the symposium at which they were presented must be viewed in historical context—as one event among many in Uruguay's process of democratic recovery. On the other hand, inasmuch as they constitute a compendium of the thoughts and feelings of Uruguayan intellectuals at a crucial juncture in their history, they can serve as a point of reference, allowing us to gauge the significance of subsequent changes.

A key event during these past years—both as a pragmatic and programmatic expression of opinion regarding the dictatorship and as an indicator of how Uruguayans perceived their own future—was the national referendum on the granting of impunity to military personnel guilty of human rights violations. Whatever other implications that vote may have had, it was clearly a reaffirmation of the Uruguayan people's desire for security and their belief in their country's uniqueness. Notwithstanding that (perceived) uniqueness, Uruguay has participated actively in planning for the regional common market known as MERCOSUR.

Given the results of the referendum and with these plans for increased regional cooperation under way, it might seem that the central issues for Uruguay and Uruguayans today are essentially different from the ones discussed in many of these essays. And yet, the clashes (commendably covert, to be sure) between voices which in a not-too-distant past represented exile and insile continue to exist, while the perception of a homogeneous Uruguay remains virtually unchanged—as if it were still possible to speak of a national culture (in the strictly singular sense) without even mentioning the heterogeneity that nation's cultural map may contain. Can Uruguay really move forward unaware of changes that have taken place in the production of symbolic goods? Or perhaps I should say, Can Uruguayans go on as they always have, simply taking it for granted that "there's no place like Uruguay"? That the answer to these questions is still affirmative is yet another measure of how much history has gone by and how much myth survives— veiled but nonetheless informing Uruguay's national project.

I know that the destruction of myths is too ambitious an undertaking for one symposium, or even one generation, however swiftly state apparatuses have been dismantled in other respects and other latitudes. I also know how tempting it is to build the future by sweeping the remnants of the past under a rug, even though sooner or later those buried remnants are bound to reappear. In my view, what is at issue is the integration of memory and future, honesty when what the mirror reveals is not what we would prefer to see, and ethics. The words *memory, ethics, knowledge,* and *culture* seldom figure in the technocratic design of political models; yet without them, no rubble will ever be sufficiently textured or vital to be anything else. To face the recent past by saying "This is a new ball game" is to deny the weight of history. It is also an attempt to take on another history, someone else's history, a history conveniently written beforehand by those who designed the institutional breakdowns of the past. The dominion of politics is impatient; time, always scarce, requires the swift design of quantifiable legacies. In that connection, culture is a perennial nuisance, as is the memory that can and should dispel myth, reminding us that—as always—we are in a new stage of reconstruction. But precisely because we are on our way back from a more than metaphorical darkness, we are all the more obliged to work with materials of the highest quality. Only thus, I believe, will we spare ourselves that return to the past whose inevitability certain parties never cease to proclaim from the depths of their ever temporary defeat.

A final note: Few people have been as devoted to Uruguay, its recent history, and its culture as Louise Popkin has been for many years. Her work on this book has been not a purely professional undertaking but a rarely found expression of love and commitment to its subject as well. I am grateful to Louise for her dedication and honored to have her as translator and coeditor of the English-language edition.

College Park, 1991

Notes

1   The editors have included Professor Conteris's comments as part of the discussion on "Literature and Repression" because of their thematic focus.
2   Whereas all the papers from this last panel (including Subercaseaux's, which was read at the symposium in his absence) appear in the original Spanish-language edition of this volume, only Perelli's, dealing with Uruguay, has been included in this edition, as part of the discussion on "Culture and Power" [TRANS.].
3   Also invited to participate in the symposium were a number of distinguished Uruguayans who, for different reasons, were unable to attend, among them Mario Benedetti, Hugo García Robles, Juan Carlos Onetti, Cristina Peri Rossi, and Idea Vilariño. Another, Carlos Martínez Moreno, died in Mexico, D.F., a few weeks before he was to have joined us. In his last letter from that city, dated January 2, 1986, he announced:

> My paper, which is already half-written and should reach you shortly, will be called "The Death of the Critics." It proposes an allegorical interpretation of the fact that the three most distinguished critics of the Generation of '45 (Ruffinelli belongs to a later generation) all died without reaching old age: Real de Azúa was born in 1916, Emir [Rodríguez Monegal] in 1921 and Angel [Rama] in 1926. I relate the political crisis of the country and the exile of its two active literary critics (Real was principally an essayist on political and social topics) to the rest of the debacle [that characterized] the years of military rule and I reach several conclusions. That is formally more original than going back over old ground [by talking about] this or that exile and the diaspora.

Martínez Moreno never got to finish his paper. We deeply regret his passing.

In a letter from Madrid dated October 19, 1985, Onetti wrote that he would be unable to attend the meeting because the trip to Maryland was "too long for [his] health and age." To this he added: "Regarding the problem of exile, I send on a synthesis of my hypothetical paper:

What nature withholds, exile cannot offer.

What nature offers, exile cannot take away.

That is my experience, after being obliged to observe the trajectory of exiled writers."

4   The people who helped make this gathering a reality are many. Among the authorities at the University of Maryland, special thanks go to William E. Kirwan, then Vice President for Academic Affairs and currently president of the university, for his ongoing support for activities related to Latin America; Richard D. Brecht, then Dean of Arts and Humanities; and our colleagues in the Department of Spanish and Portuguese and the Latin American Studies Center.

I am grateful to Naúl Ojeda, whose poster for the symposium provided the cover for this volume. I also thank him for his help in organizing the exhibition of graphic art.

Juan Rial and Carina Perelli deserve our special and deep gratitude for their many organizing efforts on our behalf in Montevideo. Their attention to the manuscripts for the Spanish-language edition of this volume hastened its publication considerably, making of it yet another manifestation of the urgency with which Uruguayans continue to seek an understanding of their recent history.

Finally, our thanks are due the Joint Committee for Latin American Studies of the Social Science Research Council and the Graduate School of the University of Maryland for their generous financial support, which made the symposium possible.

I
Contexts

The Role of the Political Parties in the Redemocratization of Uruguay

Edy Kaufman

❁

Introduction

The first dilemma I encountered in the preparation of this essay was what to call it: can we talk about "redemocratization"? At the level of intention the consensus is affirmative, although any claim that the supremacy of the civilian political forces over the military is again what it was before the *autogolpe*, or "self-coup," of 1973 would be premature. The Uruguayan military had spent most of the twentieth century in virginal seclusion from political life. And once they tasted power, they may have learned a lesson and developed a new appetite for it. The extent of their return to the barracks is an important matter for analysis here.

With that in mind, we will also have to take up a second question related to the dynamics of the process of liberalization which the Brazilians have called *descompressão,* or "decompression": in the Uruguayan case specifically, to what extent was the decompression known as *apertura,* or "opening," a victory of the political parties and other social groups over the Armed Forces? Is the situation in Uruguay comparable to that of Argentina, where, according to one expert, the military government which collapsed in December 1983 had invited its own defeat? "Far from being overcome by a formidable opposition, the armed forces, through their own blunders and inadequacies, opened up a political space which their adversaries gladly occupied" (Pion-Berlin 1985, 71).

A third point: it would also be possible to reject a "zero sum" concept in which the weakening of the military could be either the result or the cause of the strengthening of the political parties. Many other variables may have played a role, and it would be important to identify them. Even more, instead of concluding after the fact that such a bivariate relationship may have existed, perhaps it would be feasible to explore in greater depth the impact of circumstantial factors—developments unforeseen by either group that may have surprised both and affected the subsequent stages of the process. In that connection, the results of the 1980 plebiscite will serve as an appropriate and revealing example.

This observation brings us to our fourth topic: what can the dynamics of the military's transition to power teach us about their return to the barracks? In my book concerning the first part of that process (Kaufman 1979) I saw it as occurring in three stages, culminating with the closing of Parliament on June 27, 1973. To these a fourth stage, lasting a few months longer, could be added: after the political parties were stripped of their deliberative faculties, the pressure groups controlled by the Left were repressed—especially the labor unions and the University (Lerin and Torres 1978, 19–23). Either way, the process that later returned civilians to power appears to have been slow and gradual and to have featured some of the same dynamics as the stages leading up to their earlier demise.

While I am wary of artificial symmetry, I believe that what happened in Uruguay can be seen as a kind of "replay in reverse"; this is important inasmuch as it both enables us to establish the moment at which military intervention was at its peak and allows for analysis by stages of events inside and outside the country which determined the outcome. By 1980, it was already clear that the process would occur in stages rather than suddenly (Kaufman 1980). From a continental perspective, it was obvious that the fall of the Somoza regime in Nicaragua (and, later, the fall of the Duvalier regime in Haiti) was not to be repeated in Uruguay. Neither was the quick call for elections and return of power to the civilian authorities that has occurred in countries where military intervention has been more the rule than the exception (for example, the Dominican Republic, Ecuador, Honduras, and to a certain extent Bolivia).

One option for a gradual process was that of a transitional military government under a general acting in a peacemaking capacity (such as General João Batista Figueiredo in Brazil, or the fourth military junta in Argentina, and to a certain extent General Mejía Victores in Guatemala). Another possibility was a period of cogovernment, where civilian authority would evolve within the framework of a constituent assembly alongside an executive branch under military control (as has been the case in Peru and El Salvador). Given the peculiar characteristics of Uruguay as a *partidocracia,* or "partidocracy," a transitional phase may in this case have involved the internal elections held by the traditional political parties in 1982, after General Gregorio Alvarez had come forth as "peacemaker."

Fifth and last, there is some doubt as to whether Uruguay has returned to the two-party system of the past, or whether a political space has opened up on the left for a third force, by now a relatively constant factor in the balance of power in that country.

To facilitate discussion of these matters, I have divided this essay into the following sections: first, a brief review of theories relevant to the rise to power of the military in Uruguay; second, a more detailed examination of recent theories regarding demilitarization in Latin America in general, and Uruguay in particular. Once the theories have been presented, their validity will be tested through an analysis by stages of the process of demilitarization in Uruguay.

I undertake this analysis from two perspectives. The first views demilitarization as a consequence of a decision on the part of the military to return to the barracks. This perspective, which highlights the importance of "intramilitary" arguments (i.e., the "barracks mentality" that is created as officers are socialized into specific roles; Janowitz 1964), suggests that in the more than ten years of military rule in Uruguay, decompression occurred through decision-making in the political, economic, and military-repressive spheres. On the other hand, it is possible to argue from an opposing perspective (Huntington 1957) that "intramilitary" factors do not explain military intervention, and that civilian society, with its many contradictions, allows its competitors to seize and hold on to power. This second interpretation suggests that primary responsibility for the demise of the military regime in Uruguay may lie with the political parties and other groups. In this connection, the dynamics of the process of demilitarization will be discussed in relation to events both inside and outside Uruguay.

Following an updated account of events occurring between 1985 and 1989, I will conclude by returning to the topics mentioned here in an attempt to clarify the factors that have strengthened civilian control over political institutions in Uruguay. The definitive democratic reconstruction we all hope for is neither a simple nor a preconceived matter. Specifically regarding the central theme of this symposium, the sociocultural framework through which criticism of military rule was voiced during the eleven years of the dictatorship has been a powerful force for redemocratization. In the long run, the failure of the regime to co-opt these forms of popular expression has served as a guarantee that today's possible solution would eventually appear. The strengthening of such cultural patterns, over and beyond legitimately existing ideological differences, is essential to the health of democratic institutions. For that reason, what follows is to be taken as no more than an analysis of infrastructural political conditions for the defense of democracy—conditions which must be viewed, in turn, within a broader frame-work of social and cultural realities.

Theories of Military Intervention

One legacy of an extended period of military regimes in Latin America has been a great number of theories that attempt to explain military intervention. Given the different realities to which they apply, it now seems obvious that no one of them is totally and universally valid. As a starting point, we might distinguish between explanations that rely on external factors and those that consider particular coups to be domestic in origin.

Within the first category, the direct or indirect role of the United States has been given great importance—as, for example, in the overthrow of President Salvador Allende in Chile (Petras and Morley 1975). U.S. interference proba-bly was not a major factor in the Uruguayan *autogolpe*. While increasing military intervention in Uruguay had the backing of Washington and the U.S. ambassador in Montevideo, that fact was probably of minor significance. The role of the processes of militarization occurring simultaneously else-where on the continent cannot be discounted. Given that no fewer than fifteen of the twenty Ibero-American countries were governed by generals, it is not surprising that President Juan María Bordaberry considered it "neces-sary to allow the military greater participation in the country's affairs, as [was] the case elsewhere in the world" (*Keesing's Contemporary Archives,* January 22–28, 1973, 25691). The military pay close attention to what happens to their colleagues in other countries, especially when they see resemblances to their own situation (Barros-Lémez 1980, 73).

External and internal factors are connected in Guillermo O'Donnell's theory (1988, 1–38) that the "bureaucratic authoritarian" model appears when the state responds with repression to the escalating demands of the popular classes. These demands arise as a result of unfulfilled expectations once a previous "easy" stage of industrialization via import substitution has ended. As part of the same process of modernization, the dominant groups side with the only force capable of stemming the ensuing social unrest, the armed forces, finding in them a long-term substitute for a weak civilian regime.

An even more determinist argument considered the Uruguayan Armed Forces "basic to the refurbishing of the bourgeois project of domination" (Torres 1985, 163–64). As part of their critique of the "bureaucratic authori-tarian" model, K. L. Remmer and G. W. Merkx (1984, 3–51) detailed the difficulties involved in generalizing from it with reference to Mexico, where the expected failed to occur. Nevertheless, the correlation between economic crisis and military coup would seem to have been very high in the past, creating the strong impression that authoritarian regimes are in a better position than elected presidents to impose policies involving austerity.

Another way of looking at the problem is to stress the deeply rooted and long-term nature of the processes involved: "The breakdown of institutions in 1973 in Uruguay is seen as the culmination of a long process of wear and tear; as little by little, the democratic system lost its capacity for renovation, it grew less and less able to transform a negative sum game system into one capable of developing policies consistent with the affirmation of democratic order" (Filgueira 1985, 57).

Stressing the final stages of that process, a popular explanation of military coups relates to the breakdown of democratic regimes (Linz 1978, 50–74). When a representative government has so lost legitimacy that it faces a disloyal opposition and is unable to function, the result is polarization and a confrontation between the middle sectors. In the case of Chile, this situation is characterized as "the failure to structure a viable Center in a highly polarized society with strong centrifugal tendencies" (Valenzuela 1978, 59). The importance of ideological radicalization as an element of polarization is considerable in the segmented systems in Brazil and Chile (Dos Santos 1982).

An attempt to apply the same analysis to the Uruguayan process describes the weakening of civilian power through confrontations between and within Bordaberry's Colorado party and Wilson Ferreira Aldunate's Blanco party (also known as the Partido Nacional, or National party); to a large extent, both groups found an alliance with the military preferable to an alliance with each other (Gillespie 1984a, 33–34). In at least one instance, a comparison with the polarization which occurred in Chile is considered invalid (Gonzalez 1983), and all the more so since the last act of Parliament was the refusal of a broad majority to comply with the demand that one of its members— Senator Enrique Erro, an ex-Blanco who at the time belonged to the center-left coalition known as the Frente Amplio (Broad Front)—be stripped of his parliamentary immunity. Having accused him of collaborating with the subversives, the Armed Forces were eager to bring him before the military courts. It was precisely the confrontation of the military by virtually all the representative political forces that led to the closing of Parliament.

Generally speaking, it is difficult to regard a single variable as decisive in bringing about military intervention while overlooking others or considering them to be secondary. Even at the risk of presenting too long a list (and as the saying goes, losing sight of the forest for the trees), I prefer to enumerate other factors I consider no less important. In my book on Uruguay (Kaufman 1979,

93–101) I included twenty-five possible bivariate correlations, which are also listed briefly in another work (Gillespie 1984b, 133).

We should not underestimate the impact of the Tupamaros—also known as the Movimiento Nacional de Liberación (MLN), or National Liberation Movement. The role of this armed opposition group in accelerating (if not bringing about) military intervention was highly significant, not only because the Tupamaros provided the Armed Forces with a serious excuse for confronting an increasingly chaotic situation, but also because their presence was a source of trauma and insecurity in a country where (except for the notorious duels still fought over questions of honor) political violence had all but disappeared in the course of the twentieth century. In resorting to "revolutionary violence," the Tupamaros legitimized the use of equally illegitimate methods by the Armed Forces. In making illegal use of the mass media, they may have legitimized the practice of forcing military communiqués on the press. Their actions also led to the declaration of a state of emergency under which the civilian government called the Armed Forces out of the barracks and into the streets. Once they have gotten out and accomplished their mission, generals have often preferred to advance toward the seat of power and replace the authorities who, paradoxically, first called on them for assistance (Klieman 1980).

The presence of a weak and essentially antidemocratic figure in the presidency was another factor of paramount importance in the creation of a vacuum conducive to the seizure of power by the military (which, nevertheless, kept Bordaberry as a figurehead until 1976). In this connection, it would suffice to ask what would have happened if the ballot count had awarded the Blanco candidate another eleven thousand votes. It is inconceivable that Wilson Ferreira would have yielded to pressure from the military. This argument raises the question of the impact of the Uruguayan electoral system, which in the 1971 elections proved insufficiently resilient to corroborate the will of the people. Concretely, the fractionalization that system produced within the political parties helped to weaken civilian power and made the formation of stable coalitions difficult (Gonzalez 1983).

It is also important to point out that the Bordaberry government enjoyed little popular support. On the whole, the Uruguayan public was apathetic toward it and thus somewhat accepting of greater participation by "honest" officers in national life. This is not an uncommon phenomenon; when the governing authority is considered to lack legitimacy, a group with greater coercive powers often gains the upper hand. And in this case, the inhibited and indecisive Uruguayan military could not help but be encouraged to do so by the favorable results of certain public opinion polls.

Finally, a number of scholars have studied the internal factors that lead to the formation of a "coup mentality," among them, S. E. Finer (1962) and M. Janowitz (1984). One of these factors is the "new" professionalism that develops when the military begin to see themselves not just in their traditional role of defending against external enemies but also (and primarily) as responsible for the struggle against internal subversion (Stepan 1976, 248). All these factors contributed in Uruguay to the transition from civilian to military rule. Scholars have advanced hypotheses involving multiple variables. For example, the collapse of democracy has been seen as the combined result of (1) a tendency to resort inappropriately to unprecedented extralegal means of political expression, (2) a breakdown in the cohesiveness and hegemony of the elites, and (3) the diminished capacity of the state to secure resources and implement policies (Schmitter 1982, 288).

In my own view, the process was highly complex and multicausal. Military intervention in Uruguay derived from a decision by the High Command to gradually increase their political participation, and they were influenced in that decision by what they perceived to be favorable external conditions as well as by the formation of attitudes and images conducive to greater participation. Theirs was not a premeditated choice, arrived at systematically over a long period, but rather the result of a process of apprenticeship reinforced by their success at each of the three stages leading up to the *autogolpe*.

At the same time, the values characteristic of a military mentality were reaffirmed once the military perceived their role in the defense of the country as a patriotic mission (obviously in the only context possible at the time— namely, the struggle against internal subversion). International attitudes, above all that of the regional superpower, and pressures from neighboring Brazil and Argentina motivated them in their subsequent advance toward the seizure of power. And inside Uruguay itself, the weakening of the civilian political system and the perception of significant support encouraged the generals increasingly to demand a decisive role in governing the country. It is not the purpose of this essay to go over that part of the process in any depth. What does concern me is whether the return to democracy, or *apertura*, can be explained in more or less inverse terms.

Theories of Demilitarization and the Uruguayan Case

Only in the past few years has there been widespread scholarly interest in what characterizes the military's return to the barracks; and rarely have the factors identified in the previous section been "replayed," as it were, in an effort to determine whether this process is the reverse of the one which brought them to power. Before attempting such a "replay," I should stress the total nonvalidity of theories which invest the military with an exceptional aptitude for political leadership in developing countries. In the early sixties, this view was held by a sizable number of U.S. sociologists and political scientists, who both influenced and were influenced by the Pentagon in its advocacy of the Doctrine of National Security as the ideological cornerstone of the struggle against subversion. For example, J. J. Johnson (1964, 261) wrote of the armed forces: "For the next decade or more, they will on occasion be the most reliable institution to ensure political continuity in their countries. They will, in certain instances, stand as a bulwark of order and security in otherwise anarchical societies."

Regarding the armed forces as the most efficient type of organization for combining maximum rates of modernization with high levels of stability and control, L. W. Pye (1962) presented them as the only elements truly capable of competing for political power and formulating public policy. Edward Shils (1962) saw the military in developing countries, in situations where constitutional governments were very weak, as the principal force for modernization in technology and administration. M. J. Levy, Jr. (1971) stressed the relative virtues of military organizations as vehicles for a type of planning specifically and essentially related to the complex problems of modernization.

These theories were not taken up only by policymakers in Washington. Stressing the middle-class origins of the majority within the officers' corps, some communist analyses from the same period also view the armed forces in Latin America as "engines of social change rather than . . . mere servants of the landed oligarchy, the local businessmen and the big foreign companies" (Woddis 1978, 85). In fact, one way to explain the process of demilitarization on the continent in general, and in Uruguay in particular, is to view it as the inevitable outcome of dashed hopes; when military rule failed to produce the expected results, a crisis necessarily ensued, forcing the armed forces back to the barracks.

Most recent analyses of the processes of redemocratization in Latin America have not sought systematically to invert the equations pertinent to military interventions. Peter Calvert (1985, 37–38) sees the return to democracy in relation to five factors: (1) the long-standing traditions and norms of republican government; (2) the armed forces' experience with power, which makes them conscious of the danger of politicization; (3) the implicit threat which such politicization poses to their primary role as defenders of the state; (4) reconsolidation of the fragmented civilian opposition as a consequence of military rule; and (5) the fact that despite their expertise in the running of complex organizations, their performance in government has been mediocre, particularly as regards management of the economy.

To these last two factors Paul Cammack (1985, 42–43) adds the argument that the failure of the military has restored the appeal of reformist civilian leaders, whose respect for public liberties makes them popular even when their economic programs are austere and their reformism is cautious. This phenomenon is related to what Juan Rial (this volume) calls "inverse Hobbesianism." After the hard times of the dictatorship, he observes, "we are no longer expected to sacrifice individual liberties for the sake of social and economic security; instead, we are urged to lay aside certain socioeconomic aspirations . . . [for the sake of] the individual liberties consecrated by liberalism and coined in the bourgeois revolutions of the North Atlantic."

To Calvert's first and third explanations should be added the absence of a single strongman in the Uruguayan Armed Forces and the total disappearance of the subversive threat—allegedly the justification for the military takeover (Handelman 1981, 3–6). The principal obstacle to the creation of a "military project" was a lack of agreement within the military leadership.

Yet another factor, along with the failed policies of the military and the people's refusal to accept their visions and behavior, was the persistence within the Armed Forces of elements of a democratic liberal ideology, vestiges of Uruguayan political culture which led them to seek legitimacy for their programs through the ballot box (Torres 1985, 22). J. Otero Menéndez (1985) also stresses the appearance of splits among the military leadership once they were faced with a real civilian alternative—that is, once the political parties and other social groups began to mobilize to demand a change of regime. Of exceptional importance is the fact that both sides were aware of the limits of political change and both viewed the transition as a zero-sum-game situation.

Finally, external conditions favored a transition (Otero Menéndez 1985, 109–17). Otero Menéndez's essay contains one of the few explicit references in this connection to the international isolation of the military regime. Specifically as regards the United States, the pressures on behalf of democratization were very great, above all during the Carter administration (1976–80). Also relevant is the fact that developments in South America revealed a tendency toward the democratization of political institutions; the scales tipped markedly in favor of democracy, and by 1986 only two authoritarian military governments remained—in Paraguay and Chile. Redemocratization in Argentina has been singled out as a decisive influence, together with the collapse of the economic model and the strength of democratic sentiments and traditions (Finch 1985, 599–600).

A sort of reversal of J. J. Linz's position (mentioned earlier) was suggested by C. Filgueira (1984, 25), who considers the most striking aspects of the Uruguayan experience to be "the vitality with which the political parties were reconstituted" and the unity exhibited by civilian groups in opposing the regime. Finally, the decision of the military to withdraw gradually from power may have been due not so much to the successful unified functioning of the political parties as to the pronouncement of the Uruguayan electorate, which, when consulted by the High Command, expressed its negative opinion of them (Rial 1984). The outcome of the 1980 plebiscite has been referred to as an "unexpected opening."

The frame of reference I have chosen for this discussion of demilitarization in Uruguay is Finer's (1985, 23), since it includes the elements I consider essential to understanding what happened. Finer's analysis combines into a single matrix both the dispositions of the military and surrounding societal conditions, on the one hand, and the motivations and conditions necessary for a return to the barracks, on the other. In his view, in any given situation the military are motivated to hand over power to civilians by their own belief in civilian supremacy, a perceived threat to their cohesiveness, and/or a lack of self-confidence in the presence of whatever combination of internal challenges and external factors may pertain. In order for them to withdraw, there must be internal consensus, guarantees that their corporate interests will be adequately protected, and, of course, a civilian organization to yield power to.

The Military Retreat

The return to democracy in Uruguay can be regarded as primarily the result of a decision by the regime, notwithstanding the important role of popular mobilization and political action in bringing about that decision. According to this view, the transition, which was initiated from above, appeared as the authoritarian regime underwent a crisis and a process of deterioration (weakening of its social bases of support, failure of its economic policies, international isolation) (De Riz 1985, 19–21).

The task of dividing the process of return to the barracks into stages is complicated by the fact that often, but not always, different dates signal different stages in the political, economic, and repressive spheres. Filgueira (1984, 23–25) divides the process of political opening into four stages: (1) from the autogolpe of June 1973 to the resignation of President Bordaberry in June 1976, (2) from June 1976 to the plebiscite of November 1980, (3) from November 1980 to the internal elections held by the traditional parties in

November 1982, and (4) from the beginning of political discussions in May 1983 to the replacement of the military president in February 1985. I will examine the military retreat over the first three of these stages; my subsequent analysis of the civilian advance will focus primarily on the dominant strategy of the political parties during the fourth stage and will cover the postelection period as well.

June 1973–June 1976

The first stage of military rule over civilian life began on June 27, 1973, when, with the backing of the president of the republic, the generals of the Armed Forces occupied the Parliament building. Bordaberry created the fiction that there was still a deliberative body by appointing a Council of State consisting of twenty-five civilians. Among them were individuals from different sectors of the Right—majority groups in the Colorado party and minority groups in the Blanco party. The retirement of Lieutenant General H. Chiappe Posse and the appointment of General Julio César Vádora strengthened the hand of the coup-minded sector. A new cabinet, made up primarily of civilians (the exception being Colonel Hugo Linares, who was minister of the interior), included Alejandro Vegh Villegas as minister for economic affairs, and the outlines of a specific economic program took shape with the appointment of high-ranking officers to head the large state monopolies known as *entes autónomos* (i.e., fuel and energy, communications, and fishing) and the Central Bank. The landed interests allied with the president lost influence and important positions.

By defining itself as a *régimen cívico-militar,* or "civil military regime," the new government both cynically implied subordination of the military and guaranteed itself a significant amount of civilian support. However, the autonomy of the office of president was severely circumscribed once the Armed Forces made known their opposition to proposals advanced by Bordaberry in two secret memoranda. In these he suggested that the military reappoint him as part of an attempt to do away completely with the political parties and thus prevent their being used as "Marxist fronts" (Maggiolo 1976, 81); he also urged that the parties be replaced by a corporatist form of representation. Upon making public the contents of these memoranda, the Armed Forces emphasized: "Such discrepancies, nuanced by minor but conflictive arguments and stemming from rashness and failure to consult on the part of the former Chief Executive, also involved a lack of tolerance toward fundamental aspects of the political process currently under way and as such, basic to the future of the definitive ideology of the national revolution, as regards the electoral system, institutional reorganization, the role of the Armed Forces, economic policies, the system of education, social programs, etc." (Junta de Comandantes 1978, 381).

The rejection of Bordaberry's proposals led to his removal from office and sparked an internal debate within the military regarding both the appointment of his successor and their own long-term plans. The appointment of a well-known civilian was ruled out (among the candidates were Foreign Minister Juan Carlos Blanco and Vegh Villegas, who was apparently backed by the United States). In a memorandum responding to Bordaberry's (*Carta Política* [Buenos Aires] 34, July 8, 1976), the notion of coparticipation of civilians and the military was accepted within the parameters of the model then in force in Brazil; as we shall see, this model provided for "limited" or "guided" democracy, with a president elected indirectly and restricted participation by the political parties, in elections to be held in 1981.

For a period of two months Alberto Demichelli, the octogenarian president of the Council of State, replaced Bordaberry. That the members of the council had been appointed by an elected president supposedly gave legitimacy to that body, which was in turn to legitimize its selection of his successor; of course, this totally circular process allowed for no direct representation of the aspirations of the citizenry (Torres 1982, 15). In any event, the Council of State together with the twenty-one-member Junta de Comandantes (Senior Officers' Council)—later expanded to include twenty-eight generals—set themselves up as a self-styled Council of the Nation, and at the suggestion of the commander in chief of the army chose Aparicio Méndez to take over the presidency. The new president was a mediocre individual who acknowledged publicly that he owed his position to the "confidence and collaboration of the Armed Forces" (Kaufman 1979, 74).

In the economic sphere, an analysis by stages suggests that after some initial confusion, a clear model emerged between 1974 and 1978, under the influence of the Chicago school, of which Vegh Villegas was a devotee (Macadar and Barbato de Silva 1985, 14–15; Finch 1985, 595). In keeping with a neoliberal model, an attempt was made to adapt the Uruguayan economy to the characteristics of the international market by stressing the comparative advantages of that market and generating exports in nontraditional sectors; with meat in crisis internationally, the latter measure seemed especially auspicious. A special effort was made to promote manufactured exports derived from leather and wool, with credit incentives and a fiscal policy which favored those sectors by eliminating financial controls.

At the same time, the economic situation inside Uruguay impacted heavily on the majority sectors of the population, drastically reducing their buying power. The decline in real wages affected the level of consumption in such a way that "in the final analysis, the income-producing capacity of exports depended on the transfer of surpluses from the primary sector and the reduction of salaries. The latter contributed to the shrinking of the domestic market, generating an extra margin of capacity for exports" (Macadar and Barbato de Silva 1985, 15).

With relatively liberal policies at the domestic level, selective price controls, and some success in controlling the inflation rate, Uruguay could look forward to continuing economic growth through the beginning of the next decade. The resignation of Minister Vegh Villegas in 1976, in response to the high level of repression, was a sign of existing pressures within the military; these would result in a change in economic planning in 1978. Eventually the military's economic program failed, due in part to the world recession and the ascent of protectionism and its negative effects on the level of exports (Weinstein 1984, 12).

The high level of repression to which I have referred reached its peak in late 1975. After the *autogolpe,* the military systematically outlawed all groups with leftist affiliations. The labor unions, the University, and the left-leaning press all became targets of the regime. Meanwhile, new laws were added to the flagrantly repressive ones already contained in the military penal code. Many of these included severe retroactive penalties for participation in organizations that subscribed to "an ideology of violence," especially Marxism.

Although the government claimed to have wiped out subversion by 1974–75, large numbers of prisoners were detained without trial under the Medidas Prontas de Seguridad (Prompt Security Measures). The extensive and systematic use of torture was documented in testimony presented to the U.S. Congress (Kaufman 1976) and in a number of reports prepared by Amnesty International. All Uruguayan citizens were classified into three categories, A, B, and C, according to their *grado de peligrosidad,* or "degree of dangerousness." In 1975, hundreds of members of the Communist party were arrested and sentenced to long prison terms. By 1976 Uruguay had the highest per capita level of political prisoners in the world. The figure cited by Amnesty International was five thousand, meaning that one in every five hundred citizens was confined to prison; at the same time, it was claimed that one in every fifty Uruguayans had been interrogated and one in every five was living abroad (Amnesty International 1975).

Uruguayan exiles began to disappear in Argentina in 1975, and May 1976 brought the abduction and subsequent assassination of two parliamentarians—Senator Zelmar Michelini of the Frente Amplio and Hector Gutiérrez

Ruiz of the Blanco party, formerly president of the Chamber of Deputies. On that occasion, Blanco leader Wilson Ferreira Aldunate narrowly escaped assassination by entering the Austrian embassy in Buenos Aires.

The reactions of some groups and individuals within the Armed Forces to this generally repressive situation led to a cleansing of their ranks. In many cases high-ranking commanders who did not support the escalating military intervention were forced into retirement. Several officers sought asylum in foreign embassies, and scores were arrested between 1973 and 1976 (Amnesty International 1983a, 3). This last group included sympathizers with the Frente Amplio and the Frente's own leader and presidential candidate, General Líber Seregni. Through internal purges and intimidation within the ranks of the Armed Forces, the most repressive elements eventually gained the upper hand. Yet by 1976, an eventual retreat could be foreseen—both because the military had achieved their goal of virtually destroying their internal enemies and because they faced growing international pressures.

June 1976–November 1980

The hallmark of the second stage of authoritarian rule was the military's decision to seek long-term legitimacy for their political program. First they promulgated Institutional Act Four, which rescinded the right of fifteen thousand citizens to participate in politics for the next fifteen years. As General Gregorio Alvarez put it: "New men will have to rebuild the political parties under new laws. . . . In the past, the parties infiltrated by subversive propaganda were unwilling or unable to stop it; and their demagogical politics . . . brought results familiar to all" (Junta de Comandantes 1978, 369). Then they announced their own plan, known as the *cronograma*, or "chronogram." When the term of President Méndez expired in 1981, elections would be held involving a single candidate agreed upon by both traditional parties; his candidacy would require the backing of the Armed Forces as well. His five-year term of office would provide a transition to the 1986 elections, in which two candidates—one Blanco and the other Colorado—would be allowed to run; participation by the Left with its own candidates would still be illegal.

On the one hand, this plan could be regarded as the military's attempt to consolidate a high degree of political control while leaving the presidency— a purely decorative office—in the hands of a civilian out of deference to the country's strong tradition of respect for civilian government. Nevertheless, when the *cronograma* was proposed, both General Alvarez and General Julio César Vádora were considered possible presidential candidates for the 1981 elections (Handelman 1981, 4). Although some of the rivalry between the two was a matter of personal ambition, it was felt that each represented a different position regarding the extent to which the parties should take part in the structuring of new forms of political power. Vádora was the spokesman for a faction of hardliners, also including Generals Esteban Cristi, Alberto Ballestrino, and Manuel Núñez, who favored greater restrictions on civilian participation. This group saw its power wane from 1977 to 1981 as, one after another, those officers retired (Torres 1982, 17).

In the draft constitution which would be voted down in the 1980 plebiscite, military participation was institutionalized by means of permanent organisms—especially the already existing National Security Council (Consejo de Seguridad Nacional [COSENA]), which was invested with broad new powers. The period 1977–80 also brought the establishment of the National Directorate of Public Relations (Dirección Nacional de Relaciones Públicas); the Secretariat of Planning, Coordination, and Dissemination (Secretariado de Planificación, Coordinación y Difusión); and, as earlier noted, an attempt to give the military a legitimate legislative role by incorporating the Junta de Comandantes into a "second chamber" which together with the Council of State made up the Council of the Nation.

After much activity and internal deliberation, and with the cooperation of some civilians from the Council of State, four days of intense debate in late October 1980 resulted in a decision to submit the draft constitution to a plebiscite a month later. The desire to legitimize it was absolute. On the one hand, an intense propaganda campaign was launched in favor of ratification. At the same time, General Raimúndez, chair of the military's Commission on Political Affairs (Comisión de Asuntos Políticos [COMASPO]) announced that voting would be mandatory and that there would be sanctions for those who failed to comply (El Día [Montevideo], July 27, 1980). As the date for the plebiscite approached and negative reactions from civilian political leaders grew more numerous, the extreme right sectors of both traditional parties also called for ratification and, to quote Vejo Rodríguez of the minority Herrerista faction of the Blanco party, for a "Uruguay in full civil military accord" (El País [Montevideo], October 17, 1980).

The defeat of the military's proposal by a vote of 57.2 percent to 42.8 percent—that is, by a margin of 14.4 percent—came as a total surprise to the High Command. Absolutely confident that the public was on their side and reinforced in this belief by their own intimidatory tactics and manipulation of the controlled press, they were badly shaken by the results. So began a period of confusion and mutual recriminations in the ranks of the Armed Forces.

The "free market" (i.e., Chicago school-based) economic policies of the military remained in effect until late 1978. Then there began a second phase, in which greater emphasis was placed on controlling inflation and the balance of payments suffered as a result. Inflation declined from 83 percent in 1979 to 21 percent in 1982. Real growth, which had reached an extraordinary 8.4 percent for 1979, entered a period of negative growth, the most dramatic decline being −9.7 percent for 1982 (Gillespie 1985, 102). Currency controls resulted in an overvalued exchange rate vis-à-vis foreign currencies, which brought an influx of Argentine capital and an initial boom in the construction industry (Finch 1985, 596). The money that entered the country was largely speculative in nature, and the financial system that should have offered monetary stability destabilized the productive sectors, leading to a wave of bankruptcies. Unemployment rose, the fiscal deficit grew, and foreign indebtedness increased as a result of capital flight. Toward mid-1978, after a significant increase in international reserves had been achieved, the authorities decided that problems of external imbalance had been overcome and greater emphasis was placed on price stabilization (Macadar and Barbato de Silva 1985, 16). All sectors of Uruguayan society deemed the military's economic program a failure.

In the area of human rights, the wave of repression that occurred in 1976 was followed by a new exodus, particularly of communist activists in flight from the almost systematic arrest of all their cadres. Other leftist groups were also persecuted—for example, the Partido por la Victoria del Pueblo (PVP; People's Victory party). Amnesty International continued denouncing the death of prisoners under torture (GRISUR, March 31, 1977); and in a departure from its traditional policy of confidentiality, the Red Cross allowed publication of a report highly critical of the situation of the political prisoners (Desde Uruguay, November 15–30, 1980), whose numbers had fallen to some 2,800 (Amnesty International 1978) or 3,000 (Informaciones y Documentos, November 14, 1979, 31) by early 1979. During the first three months of 1979, there were some 1,500 additional arrests, with 300 or more detainees remaining in jail (Desde Uruguay, July 11, 1979). What little freedom of the press remained at the beginning of this period was further restricted through temporary or definitive shutdowns (Grisur, September 30, 1977).

November 1980–November 1982

The third stage began with the appointment of retired general Alvarez as president and ended with the holding of internal elections by the political parties. For the Armed Forces, losing the plebiscite was, to quote General Luis Queirolo, a "historical red flag" (Torres 1982, 22). They saw it not just as a miscalculation on their part but also as a catalyst for popular aspirations, expressed freely for the first time since the *autogolpe*. Initially, their frustration was expressed through abstruse rationalizations; for example, they claimed that the people had really voted to support them—that is, that many who voted against their draft constitution were seeking to stop the clock and keep things exactly as they were at the time. However, after the summer (which traditionally brings Uruguayan political life to a grinding halt), the consensus among the military was that the *cronograma* would have to be replaced by a new plan. A president would be elected from among the military and given responsibility for overseeing internal party elections by November 1982. The idea was that the transition not be a brusque one and that normalization occur slowly (*New York Times,* December 7, 1980).

Some generals still argued that whoever replaced President Méndez, whose term of office was about to expire, should be elected for a period of five years (*Miami Herald,* April 6, 1981). Finally, a struggle within the Armed Forces involving accusations of corruption led to the appointment of General Alvarez by the Council of the Nation. When he took over the presidency in September 1981, General Alvarez laid out the course to be followed over the next three years: 1982 would be "the year of the political parties"; 1983, "the year of the Constitution"; and 1984, "the year of general elections," with a return to civilian government in 1985.

During the following months the regime took a carrot-and-stick approach toward the civilian political leaders. Their preferred strategy was the creation of a "party of the process" to support Alvarez. When this idea proved unpopular, they sought instead to shore up those sectors within the traditional parties that had collaborated with the military. With that in mind, they introduced changes into the by-laws governing the internal elections. For their part, the party leaders accepted those changes; they were convinced that eventually a victory by opposition candidates would prove decisive. Conscious of their weakness, the military also began to clamp down on the emerging free press. Finally, as the date for the internal elections approached, the deteriorating economic situation was felt even more.

The military interpreted the outcome of the plebiscite as a rejection, a threat to be overcome. Accordingly, they attempted to muzzle the jubilant opposition by means of a new wave of arrests and escalated their mistreatment of political prisoners (Handelman 1981, 9). This time they accused 120 inmates at the Libertad prison of engaging in subversive activities. Denunciations of torture by Amnesty International continued (Amnesty International 1982). A letter from that organization to President Alvarez, dated December 4, 1981, includes references to the great number of prisoners of conscience, the practice of torture, and the cruel, inhuman, and degrading treatment of the political prisoners. A reply from the Uruguayan government, dated January 5, 1982, and signed by Colonel Dr. Carlos Maynard, contains no detailed discussion of the issues raised.

At the same time, the opposition press, which was allowed to function in the last few weeks before the plebiscite, was again shut down—temporarily in some cases and definitively in others—and a number of journalists were detained or otherwise persecuted. During the two years that preceded the visit of an investigating team in April 1983, no less than thirty-five punitive acts against the mass media were documented (Committee to Protect Journalists 1983, 6). The military continued its policy of compression and decompression vis-à-vis opposition activities until 1982.

The Civilian Advance

My second scenario presents the same process discussed above as an instance of redemocratization—that is, of the imposition of representative civilian rule on an authoritarian military government. Let us now go back over the stages described thus far and view them in relation to opposition initiatives, both inside Uruguay and in exile.

The reaction of the political parties to the autogolpe was not unanimous. Jorge Batlle, head of the Lista 15 fraction of the Colorado party, issued a declaration against the dictatorship that had no major consequences; but otherwise the Colorados, who held most of the civilian posts in the government, did not mobilize against it. For their part, the Blancos circulated a written message in the capital criticizing Bordaberry harshly and calling upon all citizens to prepare to "defend the Republic" (Miami Herald, July 3, 1973). In any case, with substantial sectors of the traditional parties providing the new regime with technocratic expertise, the formation of a pro-military party was at this stage superfluous.

The parties of the Left emerged from their lethargy. Under the influence of the Communists, the National Workers Convention (Convención Nacional de Trabajadores [CNT]) called for a general strike the day after the closing of Parliament. Some legislators from the outlawed Frente Amplio had to flee into exile, and others were arrested. The military ordered the workers back to work, and the CNT responded with a list of five demands: (1) trade union freedom and freedom of the press; (2) reinstatement of constitutional guarantees and rights; (3) a series of economic measures aimed at healing the economy—in particular, the nationalization of banking, foreign trade, and the meat-packing industry; (4) price controls and restoration of the buying power of salaries and pensions; and (5) the elimination of fascist groups at the National University (Lerin and Torres 1978, 20). When negotiations with the military broke down, the CNT was declared illegal; the strike fell apart two weeks later. Its leaders were arrested and taken to the stadium known as El Cilindro.

The University fell a few months after that. In July, university authorities and the Uruguayan Federation of University Students (Federación de Estudiantes Universitarios Uruguayos) proclaimed their opposition to the regime but protested within the institution itself. It was only when the Frente Amplio triumphed in the September election of university authorities that the rector and the deans were declared responsible for "Marxist infiltration" of the University and the intervention and subsequent purge took place.

On July 9, a demonstration of between five and ten thousand people organized by the CNT was violently suppressed, with about thirty participants seriously wounded. The wave of arrests of leftists intensified. A year after the coup, a declaration demanding the legalization of political activity and signed by one hundred leaders of the traditional parties appeared in the principal Uruguayan dailies; the regime responded with an order for the capture of some of the signers. The press was heavily censored, and the leftist press was shut down by the end of 1973. All the groups in the Frente Amplio except the Christian Democrats and a group known as Lista 99 (made up of former Colorados) were declared illegal and had their assets seized.

Buenos Aires now became the principal center of opposition activity for Uruguayan exiles. In 1975, Senator Zelmar Michelini (Lista 99) of the Frente Amplio, Hector Gutiérrez Ruiz, a Blanco and former president of the Chamber of Deputies, and Senator Wilson Ferreira Aldunate, leader of the majority fraction of the Blancos, launched a public campaign against the military. On the one hand, they established contacts with Minister for Economic Affairs Vegh Villegas, who represented the civilian wing of the regime. On the other, they began to mobilize in search of international solidarity, a task already undertaken by communist activists, Tupamaros, and other leftists exiled in major European capitals.

Thanks to the efforts of a group of exiled legislators, the European Parliament voted to condemn repression in Uruguay; that same year in Luxembourg, Amnesty International launched a major international campaign against human rights violations in Uruguay, especially the widespread and systematic practice of torture. This activity led to more intense contacts with the opposition, inside Uruguay (particularly with Communists working underground) as well as outside the country. A first attempt at conversations between Uruguayan parliamentarians and members of the U.S. Congress went awry in May 1976 due to the capture and assassination of Gutiérrez

Ruiz and Michelini. As earlier noted, it was thanks to a successful last-minute bid for asylum in the Austrian embassy that Ferreira Aldunate was spared the same fate. He settled in London, and his speech before a subcommittee of the U.S. Congress contributed to the decision to suspend U.S. military assistance to Uruguay.

○

The removal of Bordaberry from office may also have been a reaction of certain sectors within the military to the assassinations of legislators and other leftist political activists in Buenos Aires (*Latin America Regional Report: Southern Cone,* June 18, 1976). Civilian opposition to the *cronograma* was widespread, but this did not stop the military from attempting to initiate a dialogue with the political parties through COMASPO early in 1978. Among the Colorados both Jorge Batlle's sector and that of José María Sanguinetti expressed their willingness to "break the silence." Both major parties were opposed to the drafting of new party by-laws, a subject that had come under discussion even by this early date. The Blancos responded to the military's project for constitutional reform by demanding that the task be undertaken by an elected constituent assembly, as called for by Article 331 of the old constitution (*Informaciones y Documentos,* August 12, 1979, 7); they also insisted that any real return to democracy would have to involve the rehabilitation and full functioning of all the political parties (*Por la Patria* [Madrid], November 1979, 14).

Preparations for the 1980 plebiscite galvanized the opposition. Enrique Tarigo, a leading Colorado, spoke out against the military's proposal in a carefully worded column in *El Dia* (*New York Times,* November 30, 1980). Jorge Batlle also declared his opposition to the military's project (*El Dia* [Montevideo], June 12, 1980), and his followers in the party's youth sector actively disseminated his message. At the same time, the followers of former president Pacheco Areco came out in support of the Armed Forces. For their part, except for the minority Herrerista sectors, the Blancos were categorically opposed to the *cronograma*. The Christian Democrats also expressed their total opposition (*Miami Herald,* June 14, 1980). The rest of the Left, severely repressed, carried out their clandestine activities with great difficulty and undertook their principal actions from outside the country.

With the seizure of power by the military junta in March 1976, Argentina became a dangerous place for Uruguayan exiles, many of whom fled following the May killings of Michelini and Gutiérrez Ruiz and the capture in June and July of a group of activists from the Student-Workers Resistance (Resistencia Obrero-Estudiantil), the organization that later formed the PVP. The principal centers of exile activity in Latin America henceforth were Mexico City and Caracas. As a result of an incident at the Venezuelan embassy in Montevideo on June 28, 1976, a 1975 declaration of the Venezuelan Parliament severely censuring the Uruguayan dictatorship turned into a break in diplomatic relations. On that day, a prisoner named Elena Quinteros attempted to gain asylum on the embassy grounds and was forcibly removed by her captors; she subsequently disappeared and is presumed dead.

Madrid, Paris, Stockholm, and London became important centers of opposition activity in Europe. From London, Wilson Ferreira sent taped messages to his followers in Uruguay, established close relations with European social democratic and Christian democratic circles, and made frequent visits to the United States and Latin America. With his father's encouragement, Juan Raúl Ferreira began his political career by opening an office in Washington to lobby the U.S. Congress.

Juan Raúl Ferreira also paved the way for the formation of an opposition front, the Union for a Democratic Convergence (Grupo de Convergencia Democrática). The parties of the Left (Communists, Socialists, and pvp), which in a public statement issued in 1977 in Mexico City had joined forces to oppose the regime, now agreed to unite with the Blancos within this common framework. The July 1980 press release announcing this new initiative read in part: "The basic purpose of the Convergencia is to contribute to the reestablishment of Uruguayan democracy by collaborating in the preparation and implementation of a responsible political project, as an alternative to the official *cronograma*, which is an attempt to institutionalize the dictatorship" (Grupo de Convergencia Democrática [Mexico], July 1980, 5). The Colorados, only scantily represented in exile, preferred not to ally themselves with the Convergencia. Given the limitations on political activity inside the country, the Convergencia became the principal voice of the Uruguayan opposition (Handelman 1981, 5).

Both the Interamerican Commission on Human Rights of the Organization of American States and the Human Rights Commission of the United Nations led their respective organizations to undertake a vigorous campaign against repression in Uruguay, while a number of parliaments contributed to that international effort with motions of censure.

❂

The surprise of the opposition at winning the November 1980 plebiscite brought activities to a standstill for the next several months. At the same time, the military faced internal rivalries in their search for a presidential candidate.

Inside Uruguay, the Left circulated clandestine pamphlets and held flash demonstrations in different parts of Montevideo on May 1, 1981. A matter of intense debate within the traditional parties was what to demand of the military. There were further calls for the election of a constituent assembly. Although the position of Colorado leader Enrique Tarigo vis-à-vis the *cronograma* implied acceptance of certain conditions laid down by the generals, including proscription of political figures and parties of the Left, he was clear in his support for a return to elected government. "While the first steps should not be too rapid, in any case they have to be taken," he said (*Informaciones y Documentos,* June 15, 1981, 55). As for the Blancos, from Mexico Juan Raúl Ferreira demanded the lifting of all proscriptions and the unrestricted functioning of all the political parties: "We want democracy. Democracy either exists, or it doesn't. There is no such thing as half-way democracy" (*Informaciones y Documentos,* June 15, 1981, 15).

Despite the fact that the Blancos, the Colorados, and the Unión Cívica (Civic Union, a center-right splinter group originally affiliated with the Christian Democrats) had all submitted proposals for the conduct of the internal elections, the COMASPO decided to hold them in keeping with its own limited agenda. In July, the choice of General Alvarez as the presidential candidate was legitimized in a meeting attended by emissaries of the Commission of Ten from the Blanco party (a group which did not represent the majority sectors and which later resigned), the Group of Six from the Colorado party (representing the party leadership), and the Unión Cívica. After the new president took office in September 1981, the parties allowed to function legally faced a double threat: first, that their co-opted sectors might prove to be majorities within their ranks, and, second, that a new pro-military party might defeat them in the public elections.

Announced the following January, the plans for the November 1982 internal elections explicitly excluded parties with "international connections" (thus the Christian Democrats) as well as those which "advocated violence." Voting was not mandatory as it had been in the 1980 plebiscite; nevertheless, a significant 60.5 percent of the electorate took part. The Blancos received the most votes (49.44 percent of the total, including 44.25 percent for opposition lists), followed by the Colorados (42.30 percent of the total, including 30.29 percent for opposition lists). Part of the Left, especially the Communists, supported the sector led by Wilson Ferreira; other leftist groups preferred to express their opposition to the partial *apertura* by calling for a blank ballot (7.06 percent of the votes cast). The Unión Cívica figured in the tally with 1.2 percent.

The results of the internal elections expressed more categorically than those of the plebiscite the increasing unpopularity of the military's program. In the two largest parties, opposition factions were clearly a majority. This was especially significant within the Colorado ranks, where dwindling support for former president Pacheco Areco netted his sector only three of the fifteen seats on the National Executive Committee. In the Blanco party, the opposition groups known as Movimiento por la Patria and Movimiento Nacional de Rocha, both of which supported Wilson Ferreira, won nine seats out of ten.

From exile, the leftist sectors of the Convergencia had urged support for Wilson in response to the Blancos' ongoing struggle inside Uruguay for an end to proscriptions and the holding of free elections by 1983. The Convergencia also carried on an international struggle on behalf of political and trade union prisoners by calling for an unrestricted amnesty. At the same time, international and regional organizations kept Uruguay on their agenda, and criticism of human rights violations continued. As was to be expected, the inauguration of President Ronald Reagan brought an attitude of greater tolerance toward the regime, but that more permissive attitude was balanced by the repeated refusal of the U.S. Congress to renew military aid.

❁

The internal elections strengthened the hand of the opposition; henceforth, their negotiators would be more unanimously critical in discussions with the military over subsequent steps to be taken. Nevertheless, the parallel occurrence of three processes—liberalization, transition to democracy, and the electoral campaign—made for conflict as well as cooperation among the three main opposition forces.

In May 1983, shortly after negotiations with the military began at the Parque Hotel on the Montevideo beachfront, the Blanco representative withdrew, alleging censorship of Blanco publications and spokespersons—especially the weekly La Democracia, which was shut down for six months (New York Times, May 30, 1983). A hardening of positions on both sides led to a temporary interruption of the talks. Seeking ways to appease the generals, Sanguinetti (then secretary general of the Colorado party) called for a partial end to proscriptions, which would still exclude the Communist party on the grounds that political realities precluded their participation (Desde Uruguay, June 1–15, 1983).

During this stage, popular mobilization became the opposition's principal weapon. Mass demonstrations occurred regularly. In a show of truly peaceful resistance Uruguayans took to the streets chanting slogans about the fall of the regime; turning off their lights, they banged on empty pots and pans.

Especially significant were demonstrations held on May 1, and at the Obelisk in downtown Montevideo in November 1983, in support of free elections. Among the organizers of the latter event were old social organizations which reappeared under different names. The University students regrouped under the banner of the Social and Cultural Association of Students in Public Education (Asociación Social y Cultural de Estudiantes de la Enseñanza Pública), and the trade unions under that of the Interunion Workers' Plenary (Plenario Intersindical de Trabajadores [PIT]); the principal human rights organization was a branch of the Peace and Justice Service (Servicio de Paz y Justicia).

At this point the Intersectorial was created as a forum for the political parties and other social organizations (including the unions, student groups, cooperatives, cultural collectives, human rights groups, and others). "This arrangement played an important role in the transition, perhaps not so much because of concrete agreements reached but simply because it provided a much-needed occasion for real participation and . . . a common ground where different political actors . . . could meet and interact" (Filgueira 1985, 67). Taking the form of an informal multiparty and intersocial coalition, the Intersectorial was really a means of consolidating opposition to the regime.

In a joint declaration issued on November 27, 1983, right after the huge public demonstration in which a full 10 percent of the population is said to have participated (New York Times, January 16, 1984), the political parties called for a new round of talks aimed at "restoring the democratic institutions of the Republic" in keeping with the constitutional principle of unrestricted pluralism and at the removal of proscriptions against citizens and political parties (Desde Uruguay, December 16, 1983). The unity thus expressed proved more apparent than real, however, given the Colorados' desire to reopen talks with the military even before the latter could meet these demands and the existence of a coalition between the Blancos and the Frente Amplio in exile.

Things came dramatically to a head with the return to Uruguay and subsequent arrest of Wilson Ferreira and his son, Juan Raúl, on June 16, 1984. The censors forbade mention of the episode and attempted to head off popular demonstrations. Wilson's party had named him as their presidential candidate the previous December, and a stalemate had occurred when the military stubbornly rejected his candidacy. For their part, the Colorados had conveniently insisted that the political future of a single candidate should not be allowed to block the return to democracy (Washington Post, June 17, 1984).

On June 27, just a few days after the Ferreiras' arrest, a new round of talks began between the Armed Forces and the parties—this time on the grounds of the Club Naval. With the Blancos refusing to participate unless Wilson was freed and with the elections drawing nearer, the Colorados and the Unión Cívica brought the Frente Amplio to the negotiating table (although the Communist party was still officially proscribed, the Frente had by now regained its legal status).

While Jorge Batlle expressed his opposition to continuing popular mobilization, which he considered "highly disadvantageous" (*Jaque*, July 20, 1984), popular demonstrations calling for Wilson's release continued. So did the Blancos' indecision and their internal differences over strategy. The decision as to whether to participate in the upcoming elections with Wilson still in prison was a weighty one, and their leaders would have to make it. "The Blanco majority is standoffish about the dealings of the other opposition forces with the military," said the weekly *Búsqueda* at the time (July 25, 1984). "Meanwhile, the [party's] minority sectors continue to criticize the Blanco directorate for its refusal to negotiate, go right on with their electoral campaign and announce new candidacies."

Tensions also mounted between the Blancos and their opposition ally, the Frente Amplio, which had been quick to join the negotiations and seemed little concerned about the situation of the Ferreiras. Although the Frente did not consider the continued imprisonment of many of its own leaders to be any more of an obstacle to the transition to democracy, its stand on this matter was viewed as an expression of the bitter partisan differences present throughout this stage. Meanwhile, an overwhelming majority of the population thought Wilson should be freed (only 4 percent expressed the opposite view) and should not be tried by the military courts (*Jaque*, July 20, 1984).

Finally, the decision to participate in the elections prevailed among the Blancos. Wilson renounced his candidacy, and his replacement, Alberto Zumarán, promised that if elected, he would grant amnesty to all the political prisoners and organize new elections in which Ferreira Aldunate and other proscribed politicians would be free to participate (Amnesty International USA, *Newsletter Uruguay*, November 1984, 1). This offer does not seem to have been well received; apparently reluctant to throw the country into a new campaign, public opinion favored stability for the eventual winner of the elections.

In August, the Pacto del Club Naval (Club Naval Accord) was approved by the Armed Forces and the parties participating in the talks. The Blancos returned to their places in the Intersectorial, and that opposition coalition began to function again, demanding amnesty for the political prisoners and stressing the need to proceed with the lifting of proscriptions (*Últimas No-*

ticias [Montevideo], August 16, 1984). General Líber Seregni, former presidential candidate of the Frente Amplio, was released from prison and the secretary general of the Communist party returned from Moscow—albeit after the November elections. Recognition by the traditional parties and even the Armed Forces of a formal political space for the Uruguayan Left has been a key factor in the present political panorama (De Sierra 1985, 154); for their part, the Marxists have agreed to play by the rules of the game (Pérez 1985, 129).

In the final analysis, the election of a Colorado president on November 25, 1984, was not surprising. The joy most Uruguayans felt at seeing eleven years of military government come to an end exceeded their discomfort over restrictions and the lack of fair play. In Sanguinetti's view, if an agreement with the military had not been reached, there would have been no elections (*New York Times*, August 29, 1984).

Given the high level of domestic activity, international pressures on the Uruguayan military during the final stage of redemocratization were less visible than they might otherwise have been. In a sense the return of Wilson Ferreira was symbolic; the center of opposition activity seemed overtly to shift back inside the country. Not only was Wilson accompanied by an entourage of illustrious political leaders and journalists from all over the continent, his arrest also set off a wave of international protest of the highest order. Presidents and legislators from Latin America and Spain demanded his release and reaffirmed his right to participate in the elections, as did editorials in the U.S. press (*Washington Post,* June 20, 1984; *Miami Herald,* June 18, 1984, June 23, 1984).

In fact, there were strong international pressures on the military throughout this stage. The Alfonsín government in Buenos Aires and its ambassador in Montevideo offered ongoing support for redemocratization in Uruguay. Human rights organizations continued to concern themselves with that country. In April 1983, for the first time in over ten years, Amnesty International sent an investigating team to Uruguay. Its report, issued several months later, documented the continued existence of a sizable number of prisoners of conscience, the continued use of torture, and a lack of information concerning persons who had "disappeared" following arrest (Amnesty International 1983b).

Update: 1985–1989

Bringing the military to justice for human rights violations has been one of the principal topics under discussion by the political parties since the democratic government took over. Negotiations on this topic began when the first complaints involving such serious crimes as torture, disappearances, and abductions were lodged with the judiciary on April 19, 1985. The Armed Forces reacted by claiming that the March 1985 Amnesty Law, under which the political prisoners were released, applied to military personnel as well. This law provided "amnesty for all political offenses, whether common crimes or military crimes related to them, committed on or after January 1, 1962"; however it explicitly excluded military and police officials responsible for, or party to, "cruel, inhuman, or degrading treatment, or the detention of persons, later disappeared, for the purpose of concealing any of these behaviors." Also explicitly excluded from the amnesty were "all crimes, even if politically motivated, committed by persons acting under the protective power of the state in any form, or from government posts."

The negotiations centered on the possible granting of amnesty to the military, and on the nature of trials of military personnel if amnesty were denied. The Colorados proposed a blanket amnesty out of fear that any other alternative would mean conflict, a sure confrontation between the Armed Forces and the civilian government, and thus the weakening or collapse of democratic institutions. At the same time, President Sanguinetti tried to assure the Armed Forces that in the area of human rights, he would not risk compromising their integrity.

The Blancos and the Frente Amplio rejected the Colorados' proposal, and the Blancos then advanced one of their own, according to which no trials would be held under existing laws. Instead, the law would be changed so that the military could be tried only for serious crimes such as homicide, disappearance, torture, and *supresión de estado civil*, or "stripping of legal status" (a charge brought against the abductors of children whose identity was subsequently altered). The Blancos' proposal also established that no crimes committed before November 1973 or after March 1985 would be subject to prosecution; and it provided for prompt action by the Supreme Court, so as to wrap up the matter of trials for the military as quickly as possible. The position of the Frente Amplio fluctuated between acceptance of existing laws as a basis for trials of the military and advocacy of changes similar to those proposed by the Blancos.

The Blancos' proposal was also rejected by a parliamentary majority, and the eventual solution was a Blanco-Colorado accord which led in December 1986 to passage of the Ley de Caducidad de la Pretensión Punitiva del Estado (Law Declaring an Expiration of the State's Punitive Authority). According to this law, the state could not "exercise . . . punitive authority . . . with respect to crimes committed before March 1, 1985, by military and police officials."

The Blancos considered the Ley de Caducidad a necessary means of preventing the weakening of democratic institutions; in their view, what most Uruguayans have come to refer to as *impunidad* ("impunity") for the military was all but implicit in the Pacto del Club Naval. The Colorados saw it as a logical consequence of the Pacto del Club Naval, even though that document contains no clause tacitly or explicitly promising *impunidad*. For its part, the Frente Amplio opposed the Blanco-Colorado accord, insisting that all that was agreed upon in the Pacto del Club Naval was the establishment of the democratic system; they denied that anything was implied regarding *impunidad,* or that the topic of human rights had even been discussed.

Early in 1987, in response to the enactment of the Ley de Caducidad and with the backing of the Frente Amplio, the Movimiento Nacional de Rocha (which broke with Wilson Ferreira on this issue), a tiny sector of the Colorado party, and a number of human rights organizations and other social groups, the Comisión Nacional pro-Referendum (National Commission for a Referendum) was formed for the purpose of overturning that law. According to the Uruguayan Constitution, the signatures of 25 percent of those who voted in the previous election must be gathered in order for a referendum to be held. The campaign for a referendum went on for over two years. By December 1987 the Comisión Nacional had already obtained more than the requisite number of signatures.

The referendum was held in April 1989. Those who wished to see the Ley de Caducidad upheld claimed that a vote against *impunidad* for the military would lead to an institutional crisis and endanger the new democracy. They also argued that the civil courts would be in no position to conduct the necessary trials, given the complexity and dilatory nature of the judicial process. Those who voted to overturn the Ley de Caducidad did not believe that bringing members of the military to justice would result in a clash between the Armed Forces and the civilian government. In the end, the Ley de Caducidad was upheld by 53 percent of the voters, with 41 percent in favor of overturning it and 6 percent of the ballots blank or otherwise invalid.

❂

In summary, during the first years of the new democratic government in Uruguay, the political parties devoted their energies to a matter presumed settled when that government took office—namely, a solution to the "military question." In the process, which encompassed first the passage of the Ley de Caducidad and then the campaign leading up to the April 1989 referendum, they neglected other problems—for example, the budgetary process and implementation of the Gran Acuerdo Nacional (Great National Accord), a political pact between the Colorados and the opposition intended to facilitate the task of governing the country. Negotiations between the parties led to the formation of different coalitions. Although the return to democracy was the direct result of an agreement between the Colorados and the Frente Amplio, alliances changed during discussions about the fate of the military. Initially, the Frente Amplio and the Blancos joined forces to reject the amnesty proposed by the Colorados. Later, the Blancos and the Colorados reached an agreement which excluded the Frente Amplio. The polarization between the traditional parties and the Frente grew more intense during the campaign for the referendum. However, neither the formation of these different coalitions nor the outcome of the referendum has weakened democracy thus far.

Another topic of concern has been the economic situation. The new government has had to deal with the crisis it inherited from the dictatorship. One of its top priorities in this area has been negotiating with its creditors in hopes of reducing the foreign debt. The government has not had the full backing of all the political parties in these efforts. The Frente Amplio has opposed the plans proposed by the creditors (for example, the Baker Plan), preferring to advocate nonpayment of the foreign debt.

The Sanguinetti government has achieved positive results in the economic realm. Together with favorable external factors (a rise in domestic consumption in Brazil, realignment of the dollar, a decline in international interest rates on the foreign debt, a decline in the price of oil), on the whole its sensible economic policies have brought improvement since the beginning of the democratic period. Sanguinetti has succeeded in halting the growth of the foreign debt, increasing exports and placing them in regional and international markets, increasing the efficiency of tax collection, reducing public expenditures, and reducing unemployment. Nevertheless, inflation has remained high. The problem with the Uruguayan economy is that it uses up almost 100 percent of its installed capacity. Therefore, an increase in investment is needed before economic growth can occur (La Democracia, December 31, 1986).

A third problem the Sanguinetti government has had to face is labor unrest. Despite higher salaries, the unions have continued to press for changes in economic policy. The government's position has been firm and aimed at avoiding disorder and chaos. The unions have accused the government of authoritarian tactics. The government has been willing to resort to any means legally at its disposal in dealing with labor or union disputes. Popular confidence in the effectiveness of mobilizations proved excessive during rede-mocratization, and this might explain why the unions have failed in their efforts (*Búsqueda,* December 6, 1986).

Until now this update has focused on the new government and the political parties. What follows is a brief look at the attitudes of the Uruguayan Armed Forces toward democracy in the period from 1985 to 1989, so as to make it clear that their willingness to transfer power to a civilian president has not necessarily meant total acceptance of the concept of civil supremacy.

Democracy is regarded by the military as "a complex form of social equi-librium, which is difficult to sustain unless certain prerequisites are met" (*El Soldado* 10 (109):8). In their view, a democratic regime is possible only in the presence of certain economic, social, and cultural conditions rarely present in Third World countries. While democracy is rooted in high ideals of social justice and freedom, its practice poses grave problems. By allowing freedom of thought and expression, democratic regimes invite infiltration by commu-nism; it is here that the military has felt compelled to act. The Uruguayan Armed Forces have always regarded themselves as responsible for maintain-ing order and preventing subversion by Marxist infiltrators. Theirs is a Man-ichean world, where good struggles constantly against evil (Perelli 1987). The evil is communism, the USSR, and that country's goal of subverting the entire world through the spread of communism. The good is the West, represented by the other superpower, the United States. In this struggle between good and evil there are often "conflicts between civilian and mili-tary authorities which culminate in coups d'état. . . . [This occurs when] the democratic opening is so broad that enemies of the nation become en-trenched in parliaments, the mass media, the church, the universities, and the government itself, in collusion with outright subversives. . . . That liberal bunch is so open-minded they even make room for Communists; and obvi-ously, that provokes the wrath of many officers" (*El Soldado* 10 (100):16–17).

Conclusions

Returning now to Finer's model, it is not certain that the motives of the military changed upon leaving power, or that the political parties are doing much to limit the possibility of a new military intervention. With regard to the first point, the nature and magnitude of the commitments contained in the Pacto del Club Naval have yet to be fully clarified. President Sanguinetti has agreed that the signing of that pact was negotiated with the Armed Forces as a means of reaching consensus among the signers, and that therefore it should be respected. The legacy of the Pacto del Club Naval is apparent to the extent that attention has remained focused on the "military question" that was presumed settled in March 1985. The passage of a law granting *impunidad* to the military also reveals a certain feeling of responsibility toward the Armed Forces on the part of the civilian Parliament. Nevertheless, the outcome of the April 1989 referendum demonstrates that the Ley de Caducidad was not just a concession to the military; clearly, there was popular support for the government's action.

In the view of one researcher writing early in 1985, the Pacto del Club Naval failed to change much. By leaving in place a series of laws and institutional acts that had served previously to strengthen the hand of the military, it granted them a certain continuity in power while doing little to encourage renewed acceptance of civil supremacy on their part. According to this view, what occurred when the elected government took office was less a "democratic breakthrough" than a reform of the existing regime (Torres 1985, 179). Among the vestiges of authoritarianism surviving at the time C. Torres cites (1) the continued existence of the COSENA as an advisory group; (2) the ongoing possibility of declaring a state of insurrection, thus giving the military jurisdiction over "suspicious civilians"; (3) the fact that while the president was responsible for appointing the High Command, he was obliged to choose from among the military's own candidates; (4) the military's unqualified refusal to investigate or hold accountable those allegedly guilty of excesses against civilians during the "belligerence"; and (5) the continued incarceration of political prisoners who resorted to violence.

In practice, some limits have been set in these areas, at times due to circumstances which have kept the government from acting. For example, an article entitled "A COSENA That Has Nothing to Do with That Other COSENA" stressed the ways in which the original functioning of that group has been restricted; it is now comprised mostly of civilians and has a limited mandate (*Opinar*, August 16, 1984). Similarly, the government's lack of a parliamentary majority and the opposition's resistance to certain provisions in the pact have sometimes effectively circumscribed the president's authority. This was clearly the case as regards the immediate release of all the political prisoners, even those identified as Tupamaros; the measure was enacted before the president could formally head it off.

The same was true of the Chamber of Deputies' appointment in April 1985 of a parliamentary investigating commission on the "disappeared," and of the three commissions formed to investigate, respectively, the assassination of parliamentarians Gutiérrez Ruiz and Michelini and of other Uruguayans in Argentina, the abduction and disappearance of Elena Quinteros from the Venezuelan embassy in Montevideo, and the fatal poisoning of the wife of opposition leader Mario Heber. Similarly, over fifty civil suits have come before the courts—some of them even before the elected government took office. For the leftist opposition, to quote Senator Hugo Batalla, "there can be no acceptable democracy without some trials. . . . We have to set an example, because nobody will have any faith in democracy if we simply turn the page and act as if nothing happened here" (*El Dia* [Montevideo], January 17, 1986, "La Semana" section, 11).

Nevertheless, as General Líber Seregni put it, "society cannot banish the Armed Forces from its midst" (*El País* [Madrid], September 23, 1985); the president himself has sought to involve the military leadership in situations where they would feel called upon to reaffirm their loyalty to republican institutions. Although there is a consensus among civilians that military participation must be severely circumscribed, the degree of circumscription and the way to proceed have yet to be defined.

At the same time, the political parties have taken on their roles both for and against the government with such a vengeance that there has sometimes been concern that the fledgling return to democracy might collapse. However, with the active cooperation of the Blancos, after a year in office the president succeeded in working out the above-mentioned Gran Acuerdo Nacional by means of which the government and the opposition joined forces, reaffirmed their commitment to democratic institutions, and agreed to a coherent, stable economic and social policy for the next three years. With multiparty support for the adoption of a hundred initiatives, forty of them to be enacted as laws (*Latin America Regional Report: Southern Cone*, April 18, 1986), expectations have turned out to be higher than the level of agreement finally reached. Overall, as the end of Sanguinetti's term approaches, the Acuerdo appears to have been more a hope than a reality—though again, democracy is none the weaker for that fact.

In conclusion, we can categorically reject the predictions of those researchers (Johnson, Pye, Shils, Levy, et al.) who consider the military uniquely suited to govern developing countries. The failure of the Armed Forces in Uruguay has been obvious, and the most convincing explanations for this are offered by colleagues who have looked specifically at the Uruguayan case. Citing anywhere from one to five causes, they tend to underscore collapse of the economic model, a lack of popular support, disappearance of the violent opposition activities that originally provided the justification for military intervention, consolidation of a civilian opposition front, a strong popular tradition of respect for civilian government, and the military's lack of patronage mechanisms with which to garner favor among their civilian clients.

Chief among the external factors habitually cited is Uruguay's uncomfortable isolation within the international community. To explain transformations occurring within the military itself, repeated mention is made of their sense of frustration in their role as experts, particularly in the economic domain; polarization within the High Command; the lack of a strong figure capable of promoting internal cohesion; the danger of politicization and the corresponding fear that the Armed Forces would no longer think of themselves primarily in terms of national defense; and, finally, the prevalence of liberal and democratic values among a substantial number of Uruguayan military personnel. Once more we are dealing with multiple variables. The reader can judge to what extent any or all are valid on the basis of the preceding discussion.

As I observed earlier, an important question in relation to the theories previously summarized is whether anything can be predicted from "replaying in reverse" the factors that brought the military to power in Uruguay. A certain skepticism seems warranted if we apply this idea literally and ask ourselves whether the same melody could be replayed in its original form after twelve years. Even assuming that we were dealing with the same piano, the same concert hall, and the same performer (and obviously the same audience to judge the quality of the performance), it would be virtually impossible to produce a perfect copy of the original. The piano might or might not be in tune, and the performer might have practiced a lot or lost much of his former virtuosity. As a result of biological changes, his playing might be more or less energetic; his mood at the time would affect the rhythm and the intensity of the sound, and so on.

The point here is that no process can be predicted automatically and simplistically. In general terms, we can state that the melody has a beginning and an end, but any replaying of it will result in marked variations. As to the stages of the transition to and from military rule in Uruguay, the power of the military peaked at the end of the first stage and diminished progressively thereafter. What the processes at issue have in common is their linear nature and the fact that they occurred in stages. At this moment, a new status quo between civilians and military has not yet been reached.

From today's perspective, it can be said that external pressures have been of greater significance in the return to civilian rule than they were in bringing the military to power. The role of the United States—of the U.S. Congress in general and the executive branch during the Carter administration—was paramount. International and regional groups (both governmental and nongovernmental) also played a key role in wearing down the military, who found themselves continually under fire from abroad. Finally, the impact of developments in neighboring countries, first Brazil and later Argentina, must be considered.

Among internal factors, we should consider the inactivity of sectors such as the Catholic church and the late and meager functioning of Uruguayan human rights groups, compared with those of other countries in the area. The high level of repression precluded the functioning of popular organizations, trade unions, and the University, which only reemerged as sources of organized opposition around 1984. The mass media have also lacked independent critical voices; on the whole, the opposition press has been closely linked to initiatives of the political parties.

What I have said underscores the conflictive nature of the confrontation between the military and the parties as a dominant factor in the transition. Demilitarization or redemocratization? This is more or less for the reader to decide after examining the two scenarios presented here. In either case, the answer to this question involves two sequences of events. The first extends from the *autogolpe* in 1973 to the 1980 plebiscite. During this period, and notwithstanding their acute awareness of their international isolation, the Armed Forces dictated the dominant strategy, and the return to greater civilian participation was a result of an autonomous decision within their ranks.

The plebiscite itself was an important dividing point. The outcome, which came as a surprise to all concerned and shows just how important contingencies can be in political processes, was a major source of discouragement for the military and encouragement for the civilians. After a brief hiatus of astonished immobility, both groups began to reassess their positions. From then until the 1984 elections, civilian initiatives gained in strength and momentum. At the same time, the military found themselves increasingly at the mercy of the civilian political leaders; however, the latter were also undeniably cognizant of the existence of a considerable residue of military power.

In short, it can be said that the Uruguayan Armed Forces accepted certain limitations, taking it upon themselves to implement a "Brazilian" form of military control with significant civilian participation. Still, they undertook the second half of their journey very reluctantly, in reaction to pressures from the population at large and civilian opposition groups. Moreover, the return to civilian rule in Uruguay involved the retreat of the military from a position of authority, notwithstanding a split in the opposition front over the negotiated terms of that retreat (Filgueira 1985, 54).

The term *redemocratization* can be misleading if what is understood is a return to the situation that existed before the *autogolpe*. The characteristics of that process are "a matter of degree, rather than an absolute" (Calvert 1985, 33). Once the military knows the taste of power, it is unrealistic to expect it and society to return automatically to the status quo ante. Some have viewed the "triumph of democracy in Uruguay" as little more than the imposition of conditions of political and social regimentation only acceptable after twelve years of repression and state terrorism (Torres 1982). While the military themselves now extol the virtues of republican democratic institutions, they still think of themselves as guardians of Uruguay's "moral and material foundations" and describe their role as the "preservation of sovereignty" and the "maintenance of internal peace." Throughout most of the twentieth century the Uruguayan Armed Forces played virtually no role in the country's history; but unless there is a coherent and planned commitment to both demilitarization and redemocratization, they will never again be as aloof from politics as they were until 1973. The "Argentinization" (Finch 1985, 608) of the process and their eventual return to power cannot be ruled out.

In an interview published in Montevideo (La Democracia, March 8, 1985), I wondered aloud whether Uruguay might not go the way of Costa Rica and decide to dispense with the Armed Forces altogether, leaving police and judicial functions and the policing of borders in the hands of smaller specialized and decentralized groups. Clearly, Uruguay's military potential would be worth little if the country were ever seriously threatened by its great neighbors to the north and south; only by means of international pressures and prior guarantees could an attack be averted. Paradoxically, one reason why guerrilla movements have not prospered in Costa Rica—a region where such activity is common—is that guerrillas have had no military to confront; civilian opposition to that type of illegitimate option has therefore been unanimous. In other words, just as it takes two to tango, it takes two to make war. However, when Vice President Tarigo mentioned the possibility of eliminating the Armed Forces as in Costa Rica, adding that "in . . . countries that don't need to defend themselves because they have no enemies or territorial ambitions, the army serves only as a repressive apparatus," his statement sparked a heated exchange of letters in the local press (Búsqueda, February 14, 1986, March 6, 1986).

Obviously, the civilian forces do not now have the political power to make such a risky decision—or even to discuss it formally in the now refurbished Legislative Palace. Also worth remembering in this connection is the growing economic importance of the phenomenon known as clientelism, in which the military provides employment and services to a vast sector of the population (Rial 1986, 107). Although in the long run the possibility of doing away with the Uruguayan Armed Forces altogether should be discussed calmly and dispassionately, for the time being it is more important to strengthen civilian control over the military.

This could be achieved by giving the president a primary role in the selection of the military leadership, revising military training programs so as to eliminate discussions of "national security" that might lead to "coup-mindedness," inserting a human rights component into those programs and encouraging future officers to take courses at the University in subjects that are not strictly military—or better yet, granting scholarships for university study. The possibility of university study, combined with a decent retirement plan after twenty-five years of service, would encourage officers to consider another twenty years of active professional life in the civilian domain. These are only a few suggestions for demilitarization, my understanding of which is based on the situation in Israel, where a "citizen army" exists within a highly militarized society (Horowitz 1982).

At the same time, there is little doubt that these measures are of limited effectiveness. Real consolidation of democracy will be attained not so much through time and the restoration of democratic traditions as through a true transformation of the metaethos which justifies the role of the Armed Forces within Uruguayan society—that is, by making it clear that they are super-fluous if their sole or primary purpose is to participate in international wars against neighbors with infinitely superior military capabilities, and by trans-forming them into a popular defense force. Groups like the artillery and the air force should be replaced by analogous groups trained in civil defense—perhaps even in techniques of nonviolent resistance to invaders—making of each Uruguayan citizen a potential defender of his sovereignty. Norway and Sweden have been preparing such plans, and they might agree to share them with interested parties. The existence of the Armed Forces in Uruguay might be justified in the eyes of the people if, as is suggested here, the citizenry could remain intrinsically involved with their civilian traditions within the institution itself.

Equally important is the need to ensure that competition between political parties and social groups does not escalate to such a degree that mutual wear and tear wins out over cooperation and a sense of common purpose. The economic situation after the military left office was truly tragic. Without a willingness to work together, no government program for economic recovery can be developed or implemented to the point where it can be judged on its own merits. The experience of the opposition during the two last years of mil-itary rule was characterized by a spirit of cooperation on behalf of redemoc-ratization, but also by the competitiveness of the electoral campaign. The lack of equal opportunities for the three major sectors, and especially for the Blancos, undoubtedly left a bitter taste; and it is to be hoped that in the interest of consolidating democracy, a spirit of unity will prevail over party rivalries.

With this in mind, we can attempt yet another evaluation of the notion of "replay in reverse," treating events in Uruguay from 1973 to 1985 as two parallel but inverse processes: on the one hand, the "breakdown" of democracy as a result of polarization, the paralysis of governmental institutions, and confrontation between the middle groups in Uruguayan society; on the other, the "reconstruction" of democracy through the efforts of the political parties. It might turn out that the variables mentioned were significant but not critical in the process of militarization. Neither of the two traditional parties was split down the middle, and eventually only a minority of collaborationists confronted the immense majority in the Parliament opposed to the military. But in the return to democracy, it is clear that cooperation between political parties took different forms inside and outside the country. Whereas inside Uruguay there was a consensus between the Colorados and the Frente Amplio concerning the terms of the transition, in exile the coalition was between the Frente Amplio and the Blancos. In both cases a weakening of the link between the traditional parties was apparent, especially as regards their moderate sectors. As I have said, during the first two years of democratic government still other alliances appeared—initially a Blanco–Frente Amplio coalition against *impunidad* for the Armed Forces, then a Blanco-Colorado coalition in the drafting of the Ley de Caducidad.

From that point of view, it can be argued that the political parties failed to join forces as fully as they might have for the purposes of rebuilding democracy. In retrospect, however, it can also be said that this very fact made it easier for them to accumulate power and carry out a relatively rapid transition between 1980 and 1984; for an excessive show of force by the civilians might well have proven counterproductive, frightening the military and delaying rather than hastening their return to the barracks. That is, too much unity on the part of the civilian opposition might have been perceived as "overkill," and as such could have produced a backlash.

For his part, Wilson Ferreira perceived the outcome differently—as a surrender of sorts. In his opinion, by backing down on key demands the civilian opposition lost "the historical opportunity to end the dictatorship with a real retreat of the military from power" (*Guambia* 2 (28):39). However, there is some question as to whether in 1984 the military would have accepted unrestricted participation in the elections by all the parties with their respective candidates; an ultimatum of "con Wilson o nada"—that is, "elections with Wilson or no elections at all"—might have delayed considerably the transfer of power.

Another important feature of the Uruguayan political scene is the growing presence of the Left both inside and outside the Frente Amplio. Organized into a coalition which is particularly favored by the Uruguayan system of "unified fractionalism," the Left seems to have established itself as a third force in electoral politics. Whether as a swing vote between the traditional parties (whose percentage of the vote declined from 81 percent in 1971 to 76 percent in 1984) or even a second force in some future election, the Frente Amplio is now considered an integral part of political accords and alliances. By virtue of its consistently strong showing during the transition to democracy, its role as coparticipant in the formulation of unitary policies is well established; it would not be surprising if this were to translate into positions of power.

That the Frente agreed to join the Gran Acuerdo Nacional—albeit with reservations—bespeaks a willingness to share responsibility for governing. At the same time, the outdated internal structure of that coalition gives insufficient control to its more moderate sectors; it is therefore possible that it will continue to function as a traditional opposition force. As Martin Weinstein (this volume) has pointed out, another danger for the Frente is that of continuismo, or "continuism"—that is, of uncritical and ultimately divisive dogmatism based on orthodox beliefs.

Last but not least, the process of redemocratization has shown how deeply respectful Uruguayans are of their democratic political traditions; the Uruguayan people chose to express their opposition to the military even before the political parties were fully able to channel it. The great number of demonstrators, the countless artistic and cultural expressions of opposition to the regime, the festive atmosphere at the inauguration of President Sanguinetti, the flags emblazoned with the words "¡Viva la democracia!" in the hands of children, all bear living witness to the strength of such feelings. These expressions fall within what Juan Rial calls the "myth of a country of cultured citizens" (this volume). It should be remembered however, that in the early seventies, disenchanted with party politics, the economic crisis, and the lack of physical safety that resulted from the escalating use of violence as a means of political expression, a majority of the population chose in their despair to give military rule a try. To quote a popular saying, "Democracy is like your mother; it's only when she's gone that you feel just how much you loved her" (Guardian Weekly, August 23, 1981, 4). At a certain point, the electorate can take on the role of "legitimate arbiter" between civilian and military rule (Gonzalez 1983, 73).

What the Uruguayan political parties should have learned from the lessons of the past is that Uruguay can still avoid falling into a cyclical pattern of alternating civilian and military governments; and that a large part of the responsibility for the future is in their hands.

Postscript

In retrospect, the results of the referendum may have been the best anyone could have hoped for. On the one hand, there is no longer a possibility that a majority pronouncement in favor of punishing the military for their violations of human rights will reveal the existence of a civilian power vacuum—that is, make it clear that "the emperor has no clothes," or that the president is unable to do the people's bidding. On the other hand, the fact that almost half the electorate expressed its opposition to *impunidad* for those responsible for repression should serve as a strong reminder to the Armed Forces that their transgressions were serious and must never be repeated.

Tensions and more or less serious crises notwithstanding, Uruguay has emerged from its transitional stage and begun to consolidate civilian power. Undoubtedly much remains to be done; but if we gauge the extent of military authority at the beginning of the transition and at present, we can see that it has diminished. While this is certainly important, the famous "Switzerland of Latin America" will be a reality again only after the Uruguayan Armed Forces have become an integral part of civil society.

March 1986/May 1989

Works Cited

Amnesty International. 1975. *Annual Report*. London: Amnesty International Publications.

———. 1978. *Annual Report*. London: Amnesty International Publications.

———. 1982. *Annual Report*. London: Amnesty International Publications.

———. 1983a. *Briefing: Uruguay*. London: Amnesty International Publications.

———. 1983b. AMR (Internal Circular) 52/29/83. August 8.

Barros-Lémez, A. 1980. "Clase media; el falso modelo uruguayo." *Nueva Sociedad* 49:30–43.

Berger, S. 1981. *Organizing Interests in Western Europe: Pluralism, Cooperation and the Transformation of Politics*. Cambridge: Cambridge University Press.

Bienen, H., ed. 1971. *The Military and Modernization*. New York: Aldine.

Calvert, P. 1985. "Demilitarization in Latin America." *Third World Quarterly* 7 (1):31–43.

Cammack, P. 1985. "Democratization: A Review of the Issues." *Bulletin of Latin American Research* 4 (2):39–46.

Committee to Protect Journalists and the PEN American Center. 1983. *Uruguay: Does Democracy Include the Freedom of the Press?* New York.

De Riz, L. 1985. "Uruguay: la transición desde una perspectiva comparada." In *Uruguay y la democracia,* ed. C. Gillespie et al., 1984–85, 3:121–38.

Desde Uruguay. Underground Bulletin of the Uruguayan Communist Party. Montevideo.

De Sierra, G. 1985. "La izquierda en la transición." In *Uruguay y la democracia,* ed. C. Gillespie et al., 1984–85, 2:149–60.

Dolkowitz, R., and A. Korbonski, eds. 1982. *Soldiers, Peasants, and Bureaucrats.* London: Allen and Unwin.

Dos Santos, W. G. 1982. "Autoritarismo y Apos: convergencias y divergencias entre Brasil y Chile." *DADOS* 25 (2):151–63.

Filgueira, C. 1984. *El dilema de la democratización en el Uruguay.* Cuadernos de ciesu, no. 46. Montevideo: Ediciones de la Banda Oriental.

————. 1985. "Mediación política y apertura democrática en el Uruguay." In *Uruguay y la Democracia,* ed. C. Gillespie et al., 1984–85, 2:53–76.

Finch, H. 1985. "Democratization in Uruguay." *Third World Quarterly* 7 (3):594–609.

Finer, S. E. 1962. *The Man on Horseback.* New York: Praeger.

————. 1985. "The Retreat to the Barracks: Notes on the Practice and the Theory of Military Withdrawal from the Seats of Power." *Third World Quarterly* 7 (1):16–30.

Gillespie, C. 1984a. "From Suspended Animation to Animated Suspension: Political Parties and the Reconstruction of Democracy in Uruguay." Department of Political Science, Yale University. Photocopy.

————. 1984b. "Desentrañando la crisis de la democracia uruguaya." In *Uruguay y la democracia,* ed. C. Gillespie et al., 1984–85, 1:109–40.

————. 1985. "Uruguay's Return to Democracy." *Bulletin of Latin American Research* 4 (2):99–107.

Gillespie, C., L. Goodman, J. Rial, and P. Winn, eds. 1984–85. *Uruguay y la Democracia.* 3 vols. Montevideo: Banda Oriental.

Gonzalez, L. E. 1983. "Uruguay, 1980–1981: An Unexpected Opening." *Latin American Research Review* 18 (3):63–76.

GRISUR. Bulletin published in exile by the Grupo de Información y Solidaridad Uruguay. Geneva.

Handelman, H. 1981. *Politics and Plebiscites: The Case of Uruguay.* Latin American Working Paper, no. 89. Washington, D.C.: The Wilson Center.

Horowitz, D. 1982. "The Israel Defense Forces: A Civilianized Military in a Partially Militarized Society." In *Soldiers, Peasants, and Bureaucrats,* ed. R. Dolkowitz and K. Korbonski, 77–106.

Huntington, S. 1957. *The Soldier and the State.* Cambridge: Harvard University Press.

Informaciones y Documentos. Bulletin published in exile by the Partido por la Victoria del Pueblo. Paris.

Janowitz, M. 1964. *The Military in the Political Development of New Nations.* Chicago: University of Chicago Press.

Johnson, J. J., ed. 1962. *The Role of the Military in Underdeveloped Countries.* Princeton: Princeton University Press.

———. 1964. *The Military and Society in Latin America.* Stanford: Stanford University Press.

Junta de Comandantes en Jefe de Uruguay. 1978. *Las Fuerzas Armadas al pueblo oriental: el proceso político.* Vol. 1. Montevideo.

Kaufman, E. 1976. Testimony before the House Committee on International Relations, *Hearings on Human Rights in Uruguay and Paraguay.* 94th Cong., 2d sess., 36–74.

———. 1979. *Uruguay in Transition: From Civil to Military Rule.* New Brunswick, N.J.: Transaction, 1979.

———. 1980. "Uruguay in Transition: From Military to Civil Rule?" Washington, D.C.: Washington Office on Latin America.

Keesing's Contemporary Archives. 1973. Vol. 19. Bristol: Keesing's Publications.

Klieman, A. S. 1980. "Confined to Barracks: Emergencies and the Military in Developing Societies." *Comparative Politics* 12 (2):143–63.

Lerin, F., and C. Torres, 1978. "Les transformations institutionnelles de l'Uruguay (1973–1978)." In Sécretariat Général du Gouvernement Français. Directions de la Documentation Française. Notes et Etudes Documentaires, nos. 4 485–4 486. *Problèmes d'Amérique Latine* 49 (November):7–57.

Levy, M. J., Jr. 1971. "Armed Forces Organizations in Societies Undergoing Modernization." In *The Military and Modernization,* ed. H. Bienen, 41–78.

Linz, J. J. 1978. *The Breakdown of Democratic Regimes: Crisis, Breakdown and Reequilibration.* Vol. 1 of *The Breakdown of Democratic Regimes,* ed. J. Linz and A. Stepan. 4 vols. Baltimore: Johns Hopkins University Press.

Lowenthal, A. F., ed. 1976. *Armies and Politics in Latin America.* New York: Holmes and Meier.

Macadar, L., and C. Barbato de Silva. 1985. "Fracaso y expectativas de la economía uruguaya." In *Uruguay y la democracia,* ed. C. Gillespie et al., 1984–85, 2:9–17.

Maggiolo, O. J. 1976. "Uruguay: tres años de dictadura." *Nueva Sociedad* 27:74–84.

O'Donnell, G. 1988. *Bureaucratic Authoritarianism: Argentina, 1966–1973 in Comparative Perspective.* Trans. James Mcguire and Rae Flory. 1978. Berkeley: University of California Press.

Otero Menéndez, J. 1985. "La transición política hacia la democracia: el 'naipe de dos palos' y los 'campos minados.'" In *Uruguay y la democracia,* ed. C. Gillespie et al., 1984–85, 2:99–127.

Perelli, C. 1987. *Someter o convencer: el discurso militar en el Uruguay de la transición y la redemocratización.* Montevideo: Banda Oriental.

Pérez, R. 1985. "La izquierda en la fase post-autoritaria." In *Uruguay y la democracia,* ed. C. Gillespie et al., 1984–85, 2:129–47.

Petras, J., and M. Morley. 1975. *The United States and Chile: Imperialism and the Overthrow of the Allende Government.* New York: Monthly Review Press.

Pion-Berlin, D. 1985. "The Fall of Military Rule in Argentina: 1976–1983." *Journal of Interamerican Studies and World Affairs* 27 (2):55–76.

Pye, L. W. 1962. "Armies in the Process of Political Modernization." In *The Role of the Military in Underdeveloped Countries,* ed. J. J. Johnson, 69–91.

Remmer, K. L., and G. W. Merkx. 1984. "Bureaucratic Authoritarianism Revisited." *Latin American Research Review* 19 (1):3–49.

Rial, J. 1984. "Los partidos tradicionales: restauración o renovación." In *Uruguay y la democracia,* ed. C. Gillespie et al., 1984–85, 1:193–227.

————. 1986. "Las FF. AA. como partido substituto: el caso uruguayo. 1973–1984." *Nueva Sociedad* 81:106–16.

Schmitter, P. 1986. "Interest Intermediation and Regime Governability in Contemporary Western Europe and North America." In *Organizing Interests in Western Europe,* ed. S. Berger, 285–327.

Shils, E. 1962. "The Military in the Political Development of the New States." In *The Role of the Military in Underdeveloped Countries,* ed. J. J. Johnson, 7–69.

Stepan, A. 1976. "The New Professionalism of International Warfare and Military Role Expansion." In *Armies and Politics in Latin America,* ed. A. F. Lowenthal, 244–60.

Torres, C. 1982. "Uruguay: l'échec de la tentative d'institutionnalisation du régime." In Sécretariat Général du Gouvernement Français. Directions de la Documentation Française. Notes et Etudes Documentaires, nos. 4 663–4 664. *Problèmes d'Amérique Latine* 64 (April–June):8–34.

————. 1985. "Las Fuerzas Armadas uruguayas en la transición hacia la democracia." In *Uruguay y la democracia,* ed. C. Gillespie et al., 1984–85, 2:161–81.

U.S. Congress. House Committee on International Relations. Subcommittee on International Organizations. 1976. *Hearings on Human Rights in Uruguay and Paraguay.* 94th Cong., 2d sess.

Valenzuela, A. 1978. *The Breakdown of Democratic Regimes: Chile.* Vol. 4 of *The Breakdown of Democratic Regimes,* ed. J. Linz and A. Stepan. 4 vols. Baltimore: Johns Hopkins University Press.

Weinstein, M. 1984. "Uruguay's Election: A Prolonged Transition to Democracy." *NACLA Report on the Americas* 18 (6):12–15.

Woddis, J. 1978. *Armies and Politics in Latin America.* London: Lawrence and Wishart.

The Social Imaginary: Utopian Political Myths in Uruguay (Change and Permanence during and after the Dictatorship)

Juan Rial

❂

The Social Imaginary and Political Myth

Can the concept of a social imaginary be successfully applied to a rationalist, secular society such as Uruguay's? Every society has its basic institutions. In capitalist systems (and with minor modifications, in socialist systems), the "public" sphere is currently viewed as comprising such institutions as economics, law, politics, religion, art, science, and technology, while in the "private" sphere, the principal institution continues to be the family. It is possible to "construct" the time and space of a society by joining to each of those institutions a whole series of others on successively descending levels. Thus, for example, the principal economic institutions have come to be known as work, capital, business, wages, profit, value, and so on. From each of these in turn, another set of institutions derives. These are created through a process of externalization, objectivation, and internalization that leads us to "experience" the process of institutionalization as an objective reality.[1]

Institutions, then, appear as symbolic constructs, in accordance with the referents "natural" and "real" offered us by both society and reason.[2] Real acts are not symbolic. Working, making war, making love, and living are not symbols, but we cannot conceive of these activities except as subjective exchanges on a symbolic level. Thus, society "constructs" reality through language and the creation of institutions—that is, by organizing systems of symbols capable of conferring social legitimacy or by assigning to its symbols (signifiers) given meanings (signifieds).

The concepts that must be developed in order to arrive at the notion of a social imaginary, which assumes the existence of a symbolic universe and the construction of a social reality "by society," bear on the problem of alienation. Used first by Hegel and then successively by Feuerbach, Marx, and Freud—to cite only the best known figures—this concept has been the object of much discussion. On one level, alienation refers primarily to the estrangement of man from his work. But here I am interested in another meaning; namely, a feeling of estrangement on the part of a society from the institutions it constructs as a means of referring to *its imaginary world* and treating that imaginary world as *the real world*.

Alienation does not just assume the existence of institutions. It appears as a way of relating to them, and through them, to history (development through time and space). This last aspect is what I will focus on. In contemporary societies, alienation appears internalized in class structure and in the domination by a minority in keeping with their theoretical view. But here again, these classes can be regarded as socially constructed institutions. Alienation appears when a society becomes estranged from its institutions—when those institutions become autonomous vis-à-vis the society that created them.

Relating to institutions and their creation and development through time and space implies relating to a symbolic world. But the symbolic presupposes the existence of a capacity for creating images. Behind the "good order"[3] created by society, which we come to know through symbolic exchanges, is the social imaginary. In commonsense terms, we consider to be imaginary *that which is invented or that which has changed meaning*—that which exceeds the limits of "normal" meanings. It exists both separate from the "real" and "in place of the real," enabling us to apprehend that which cannot be seen but is thinkable in another dimension, that which can be imagined. The symbolic and the imaginary are closely related, but in an obscure way. It is through the symbolic that the social imaginary can exist and be expressed; on the other hand, the symbolic presupposes the capacity to imagine—to see things that "do not exist" or to see them with a different meaning. The symbolic has a "rational-real" element: that which is indispensable in order to "think it" or accept it, the referent in those factual events that can be perceived. But this element is colored by the imaginary.[4] Everything that can be reduced to functional terms refers back to this social imaginary. Institutions constructed by society through history but now existing independently are doubly grounded, in both functional and imaginary elements. The latter both treats *the world as its world* and turns *its world into the world*. The social meaning which is constructed and expressed symbolically eventually becomes primary, irreducible to the sociohistorical even though it was originally a product of the passage of time and the ordering of space—an image of society which is not society but makes it possible to recognize society and fill the void between *the* world and *its* world.

Institutions make up a symbolic universe,[5] but one which cannot be interpreted in the purely symbolic terms that exist through language. How to interpret them then? One way is to reconstruct social meanings in a style similar to Max Weber's; that is, as "ideal types," related in this case to culture, to cultural history.[6] On the other hand, talking about "collective social images" or a "collective unconscious" entails a high risk of hypostatization. Thus, we prefer to talk about *political myths* not just because of our specific interests but also because we think this will facilitate identification of the social imaginary we are after. Leszek Kolakowski has pointed out the presence of myth in realms of thought and experience which, in principle, do not seem mythical: "Myths give a meaning to empirical realities and to practical activities via relativization. A mythical organization of the world— that is, the rules of understanding empirical realities as meaningful—is permanently present in culture."[7]

The principal theorizer on political myths is Georges Sorel.[8] In referring to the general strike as a social phenomenon, he labels it a myth, "a set of images capable of evoking instinctively all the sentiments which correspond to the diverse manifestations of the war waged by socialism against modern society." What Sorel defines is not an abstract analytical act, a product of the intellect, it is an act of will, grounded in an intuitive, immediate perception of a Bergsonian nature, linked to a truth which refers to "the strongest tendencies of a people, a party, a class." Sorel saw in this truth the most appropriate support for mass mobilization as well as a means of avoiding intellectualized forms that are both manipulative and subject to manipulation.

Myth seeks to give material form to that which has "duration," and meaning to the fruits of experience, so that the world appears as a *continuum*. It does not do this by looking for justifications; these follow within the bounds of experience and practice. Rather, myth appeals to the emotions by seeking an awareness of universality and identity (Friedrich Schelling used to speak of a "system of identity"). Myth should be lived collectively with no possibility of distinguishing subject from object. Individuals are "possessed" by myths, not myths by individuals. Although myths were originally connected to religion and are ways of consolidating values, most secularized societies are based on myths constructed in an effort to reconsolidate those inherited values under new conditions. This requires a constant search for "atemporality" (even though myth assumes a vision of time) that can easily result in Utopian constructs (see Sorel).

Mythopoeia has led to the resignification of old forms of mythical consciousness as part of an ultimately futile attempt to incorporate the conscious and rational into that process of consolidation. Organizational myths such as sovereignty, the social contract, revolution, and the division of powers have long been cloaked in that "rationality." The most intense effort in this connection involves the "scientific" versions derived from Marxism or those that seek a justification for democracy (as does McPherson's).

Mythopolisis, a permanent process which repeatedly recasts archetypes in new images and symbols, is aimed at that consolidation of values. The values in question are not always the same. The myth of Protagoras for example, is the basis for all myths about democracy. Nevertheless, how that myth is interpreted and how new *mythologemes* are constructed depend on how an egalitarian distribution of the virtues of decorum and justice (for which Hermes was responsible) is to be achieved. Myth can be—and is—manipulated. In secularized societies, the process of mythopoeia is constantly cloaked in "rationality." Myths consist of a "bundle" of symbols; they constitute part of that symbolic world and express meanings of a poetic but also a political nature in a given society.[9]

The notion of "political myth" has come under harsh attack; in this connection we need only recall the critiques of Ernst Cassirer and Georg Lukács.[10] Although he did not deal directly with the subject, Lukács would consider these views on political myth to be irrational—as much on account of their philosophical as their political content—because they point up the negative dialectic component of history, which ultimately expresses "false consciousness" of an ideology (in the "weak" sense of the word). In reference to Nazi Germany, Cassirer wrote about the persistence of myth as a means of facing desperate situations and described the process (in his view, negative) which led to the exaltation of the Führer, the Aryan race, and the Nazi regime. This doubly convergent criticism seemed to limit discussions of the subject to the matter of rationalist forms, whether liberal or Marxist.

However, the growing body of theory regarding the problems of language and, more generally, the symbolic universe has reawakened interest in political myth as a reality to be analyzed rather than simply exorcised.[11] As Murray Edelman argued,[12] every political act can be examined both in terms of its effects on power and as a means of condensing hopes, fears, and repressed and unconscious emotions. It is through the symbolic sphere that mythical elements converge on politics and fix onto specific points and moments. Myths are stories that have been structured symbolically and are therefore "overdetermined," linked emotionally to real situations and destined to channel behavior toward certain preferred forms of action. The point of departure for establishing the "truth" of the mythical story is a social construct of reality related to a social imaginary.

Myth is an underlying principle of social consciousness, which gives rise to the structure of thought and action. It sets forth and delimits a series of possibilities—a realm of the possible—even while it is also ambiguous, since the order it constructs is constantly threatened by the possibility of disorder. For that reason it has to be reconsolidated and perpetuated through periodic *rites*. Myth is the place beyond which it is impossible to look. Liminarity is one of the meanings of myth, since it is from liminarity that myths function. Thus myth, which in large measure is the symbolically structured form taken by the social imaginary, is a void which consciousness cannot reach. Nevertheless, it is from myth itself that the very structure of consciousness is born. Myth is not simply a representation of man's irrational or primitive moments, but rather a consequence of his way of being which emerges as a means of facing problems. For that reason, even though traditional societies have disappeared (at least for the most part), and even though the old mythologies as a global form of cultural organization have been destroyed, myths themselves are still with us. Here we have the beginnings of an answer to our initial question. Myths also exist in a society like Uruguay's, even though that society is tugged at constantly by liberal rationalism from one side and Marxist rationalism from the other. Also present are beliefs rooted in faith, whose social imaginary is therefore based on myths (Judeo-Christian myths, for example).

Obviously, according to traditional Marxist analysis, appealing to those beliefs implies depending on a "weak" meaning of ideology; that is, using neutral concepts that protect the circumstantially mystifying character of political beliefs and mask the power relationships between classes. Nevertheless, I am referring in this instance not to ideologies in the "weak" sense but to a series of ideas connected to action and manipulable with relative ease—a process of degradation and reduction of symbols to the positivity of signs. To be sure, the point of departure for the mechanisms of ideology is likewise myths torn from their structure and functioning in a void; but the former should not be confused with the myths themselves or with the social imaginary. An analysis of the social imaginary and its symbolic expression through the symbolic world in the form of myths is therefore perfectly compatible with the existence of these other versions of ideology, which can also be studied, albeit on another level. Last of all, what follows is not intended as a kind of history of mentalities à la Pierre Chaunu, or as the type of study that might be undertaken by the Ecole des Annales. These might also lead to hypostatization. Accordingly, my focus will be on that imaginary and those political myths of which I have spoken.

From the Creation of the Social Imaginary to the
Elaboration of a Social Counterimaginary

In keeping with the preceding, let me describe what I consider to be the fundamental, foundational myths behind the social imaginary which ordered the time and space of Uruguayans. Note that Uruguay was a "new" society, created over a spatial and temporal void—an "alluvial" society of immigrants that by the late nineteenth century was trying to establish its own profile, process the construction of a state and a nation, create a culture, and consolidate its values and its faith in its existence as an entity. For all that, this society needed myths.

Uruguay was once known as the "Switzerland of America," and its capital, Montevideo, as the "Athens of the River Plate." These terms were used commonly in the "happy Uruguay," the prosperous Uruguay of the years just preceding and following World War II. The "invention" of that Uruguay and the creation of those images took half a century of real action in the areas of economics, politics, and law. The process took the particular form it did thanks to the symbolic universe created through the successive intersubjective contacts of members of that society, who had a social imaginary as their point of reference.

I will refer to the myths that were consolidated in that happy Uruguay, the predominant myths in existence during the 1950s. These myths, which form a "system of identity" with integrating and elucidating functions, permit identification of the individual with the content of the myth and give meaning to the vague, unconscious desires of each member of the society.[13] I will discuss four of those myths.

Averageness as a Prerequisite for Security

Averageness was to be the basis of a happy Uruguay.[14] From the beginning of the century on, a "welfare" state was created to protect the subordinate sectors of society. This state very clearly favored the creation of middle strata by stressing the cultural values typical of a group that exercises no leadership and occupies an ambiguous place on the social ladder. While receiving benefits from the upper classes and aspiring to be their equals, such a group has more in common with the subordinate sectors, to which it also belongs. The social stability that emanates from a situation of this type is very great. The imaginary to which it gave rise strongly emphasized a vision of predominant middle sectors standing out clearly against the sum total of the subordinate strata—especially those who lived in Montevideo. The mediocrity inherent in their position of nonleadership was at the same time a promise of security; that is, acceptance of the existing sociopolitical frame of reference guaranteed these groups a relatively "easy" existence. Uruguayan life, whose inertia is so apparent today, has been governed largely by this myth of hope.

At first glance, one might argue that this was not a myth but a rational construct. First and foremost, however, such constructs are themselves based on the myth of reason, which holds that the diverse forms of human thought or knowledge (e.g., reasoning and logic) exist independently of the means of expression allowed us by our biological conformation, including language. As Kolakowski said, this basic notion allows us to overcome the contingency of existence; science can be practiced without rejecting myth.

In this case, the mobilizing function of myth is *not* present. As part of the process of secularization, the new social myth created was not aimed at the destruction of an order. It did not seek to maintain the hope that the system would collapse and did not require mobilization of forces to that end, as Sorel argued.[15] Nor is there a clear connection with the redemptionism present in many myths. In fact, although it has all the characteristics of myth, this is really a kind of antimyth.

Mythologemes characteristically view as absolute the value they seek to impose on a given society, whatever that value may be; in this case, mediocrity. They simplify by viewing the values of every sector of society as part of that absolute, even if small groups within the society have values of their own.[16] They also marginalize certain attributes (for example, the selfishness and pettiness resulting from that mediocrity) and add others. Especially when it placed security as a value in direct relation to mediocrity, the myth of averageness as a prerequisite for security in Uruguay added the belief that remaining inconspicuous would ensure a way of life free of surprises and relatively predictable. Mythologemes also "atemporalize"; with their faith in averageness, Uruguayans thought themselves safe from the cyclical ups and downs characteristic of any society in its diverse contingencies. The desire to suspend the effects of time and events—to make a good situation last indefinitely—led to the incorporation of a mythical dimension into time. The past was to be preserved, not transformed. In practical terms, the prevailing averageness translated into strongly quietist attitudes, and that underscored the conservative nature of Uruguayan society.

This entire mythical statement, which is a combination of various stories making up a mythologeme, is obviously subordinate to other higher-level myths constructed much earlier and expressing values related to the kind of life considered desirable. A mixture of myths of Judeo-Christian origin with others of a rationalist-spiritualist nature informed this construct that crystallized toward the fifties, when an attempt was made to "seize the moment."

Uniqueness

In a sense, this second myth relates to whether there is such a thing as *uruguayidad,* or "Uruguayanness."[17] The issue is not one of identifying Uruguayans with any characteristic in particular, but of examining the probable differences between Uruguayans and others. Uruguay is a highly Europeanized country, but this is not to say that Uruguayans are Europeans. For a long time the myth regarding the difference between Uruguayans and Europeans pointed to Uruguay's presumed "superiority" vis-à-vis a continent faced with constant wars, problems of integration for many of its citizens, and a high degree of inherited inequality. A number of European countries, at least those with which Uruguayans were most familiar, even lacked "progressive" legislation of the type which favored Uruguay's subordinate classes by means of a welfare state. Uruguayans were not Latin Americans either. How could we be, compared to our "backward" neighbors with highly illiterate indigenous populations and governments which could not provide the same mantle of security we enjoyed? And we were not North Americans. Already in José Enrique Rodó's day, we looked askance at a people we regarded as motivated purely and exclusively by a desire for power, both in economics and in international affairs. For Uruguayans, the great myth was to be different—Europeanized, but not in any European way.

In this case, mythical consciousness seeks to awaken a sense of obligation and belonging, but not through a mythologeme about a mission or a chosen people. Nor do we have here an image that would traditionally be considered mythological. A rationalist-spiritualist antimyth functions this time to define the uniqueness of Uruguayans in basically negative terms. According to the perceived and reinforced prototype, a Uruguayan is *not* European, or Latin American, or North American. He has lots of the European in him, but *not* the characteristics deemed negative. Owing to simplifications, only a few types really qualify as Europeans (the French, the English, and, to a lesser extent, the Germans). Absent from the myth are considerations about how those Europeans arrived at their identity. Wars were part of the process by which European societies and states were constructed. So were strong uniqueness and social conflict. On the other hand, some attributes that were not part of the process were added in the case of Uruguay. It is assumed that European culture is the common heritage of all Europeans and that contrasts play no part in the definition of identities. The myth does *not* aim at highlighting the "strong" characteristics of Uruguayans (and I am not referring here to a possible "oriental" identity that can take on different meanings),[18] but rather blends with the myth of their mediocrity and lack of outstanding features.

Consensus and the Rule of Impersonal Law

I might also present this third great myth in another way, as a myth of democracy; however, in the strictest sense, this would be inaccurate, for it was more a myth of order, of respect for rules, of support for the rule of law. When symbolic construct and reality are compared, we see that this myth depended for its functioning on another type of factor. Nobody doubts that a high degree of clientelism existed in Uruguay. And nobody doubts that the considerable benefits of the welfare state were only available to the urban strata (although it is true that most of the population was gradually incorporated into those strata, as a result of which a smaller and smaller percentage lived in rural settings).

Democracy was treated basically as a rule in a game—to be respected, of course. But there was no myth about the need to support that society or to strive for equality. The essential thing was that there be security; and if that security entailed being mediocre, then mediocrity was essential as well. To that end certain inequalities were acceptable, although on other levels (fundamentally the imaginary ones) it was considered that they did not really exist. While law can be justified by historical evolution and/or a theory of a social contract, the notion of law as an obligation follows from Hobbesian or Kantian premises regarding man's intrinsically evil nature, which responds only to the threat of coercion. But in this case, the formulation of this myth of consensus and the rule of law presupposes a clear contractualist notion expressed as a set of rules to be followed in playing the game. This myth assumes no transcendence beyond respect for dates, norms, procedures, and the rights and guarantees that accompany these; but it is grounded in a belief in the myth of the contract.

Culture of the Great Mass of Citizens

Uruguay is a country of *culturosos*.[19] When the welfare state was launched, one of its prime objectives was total literacy for the subordinate masses; Uruguay was to be distinguished by the high cultural level (mediocre, but appropriately leveling and equalizing) of its middle strata. This was an "economical" way to raise the self-respect of the middle classes and consolidate their values while working toward a society totally permeated by those values.

The myth of the country of *culturosos* really sought a negation of its mythical status. In keeping with the principal ideological currents (ideological in the "weak" sense),[20] rationalist conceptions predominated; in this case, they were obviously of liberal vintage. Rationalist spiritualism was the basis for Batllismo,[21] and it was Batllismo that inspired this process of constructing a universalizing, but at the same time appropriately average, culture. Hoping for change was presumed to involve not the destruction of an order but rather the construction of a transcendent myth encompassing a large part of the masses. The notion of an intelligentsia comprised of *culturosos* was highly compatible with the idea of security-producing mediocrity. This myth was fully accepted because each individual felt that the rest of society shared it.

The constant search for a higher cultural level was the particular form taken by the myth of progress[22] in Uruguay. This form was extremely rational. The Uruguayan concept of progress rejects social conflict and centers on achievement by the masses of a high cultural standard—so much so that the Uruguayan Constitution includes among its articles a provision making secondary education mandatory. Although other provisions concerning health care and housing might also be considered part of the myth of progress, they refer more to material necessities. Faithful to the rationalist-spiritualist tradition on the one hand, and to the view of culture promoted by José Pedro Varela, Rodó, and Carlos Vaz Ferreira, on the other, the ideal of the country of *culturosos* was aimed at a less tangible asset (even if positivist interpretations tended to see in it a justification of the search for social ascent). This myth had as its goal a twentieth-century version of the old Artiguista slogan, "May Orientals be as enlightened as they are brave."[23] The idea was not so much to make available a tool with which to improve the material social reproduction of society as it was to impart "transcendent rational knowledge" in a secular country where religion has as its referent the state.

The four myths mentioned—*averageness* as a prerequisite for security and the attainment of a happy Uruguay; the *uniqueness* which enabled us to feel strongly Uruguayan; *consensus and the rule of law,* of respect for the rules of the game which ultimately laid the foundation for Uruguay's democratic regime; and a *country of cultured citizens,* appropriately *culturosos* with a minimum standard far above average—were the basis for the imaginary of Uruguayans during the period of the happy Uruguay. These myths were set in motion by elites in order to "modify," unify, and, especially, adapt a variety of social imaginaries, ideas, and ideologies (in the "weak" sense) to this new society.[24] The key point here is that a project of the elite which governed Uruguay (Uruguay's political community), meshed with the desires and aspirations of the subordinate classes. The success of this effort to solve the problems of the citizenry through internalization of a set of myths placed Uruguay apart from the rest of Latin America, where those problems persist. The price of success, however, was averageness.

The structuring of a symbolic order useful for understanding Uruguayan identity generated another series of "naif" myths dependent on the earlier ones—for example, the claim that "there's no place like Uruguay" ("como el Uruguay no hay").[25] These are myths for "believers," for all the Uruguayans who use them to reconsolidate a belief in their uniqueness, their status as *culturosos,* and as "proof" that Uruguay, the country of consensus, is very different from other countries. Another second-level myth is that of the importance of the state, which is regarded as a father, responsible for the lives of his children[26] and guilty of negligence if he fails to take proper care of them.

The ordering of time was accomplished chiefly by means of an official history, which was created gradually beginning in the late nineteenth century; its point of departure was a persistent revisionist tendency that repeatedly gave rise to and incorporated new naif myths. Thus, the "black legend" of Artiguismo eventually gave way to the "blue legend," and at a later stage, to a sort of "red legend."[27] Collective memory assimilated this official history, soaked up these myths, and created a symbolic universe; in other words, it transcended the sociohistorical boundaries of life in the here and now and enabled these myths to be expressed. The ordering of time afforded glimpses of a "possible" future—secure, mediocre, and notably lacking in messianic tendencies; for young people, a kind of Utopia of mediocre good order was opening up. In reality, it was a *topia* of decidedly conservative tenor.

The idea of Uruguay as a "model country"[28] persisted as a systematic construct—rigorous, to some extent logical, and characterized by advance planning. The term *model country* implies the creation of a "perfect city," which in this case, in its spatial version was virtually a model country as well. What was envisioned was a country full of cities, strong municipalities whose ultimate goal was to have more citizens—that is, individuals all equal in the eyes of the state. These citizens were to be guaranteed access to culture, the greatest asset the state could offer them. This vision of a small model country, as embodied both in the orderliness of its lesser municipalities and in the Montevideo which successive city governments embellished in times of plenty and transformed into the "Athens of the River Plate," was becoming a symbol of Uruguay's greatness. The greatness of this Utopia of good order was to be sought in averageness, in the existence of democratic institutions, and in the widespread availability of public education. Finally, Uruguay's traditions figured in this Utopia—traditions which in reality were recent creations endorsed by the power elites. This symbolic universe expressed the fundamental myths through which our social imaginary appeared. The foundational myths that gave rise to this imaginary—that made us cosmopolitan, transcended nationalism, and differentiated us from other Latin Americans—established our identity as Uruguayans. The possibility of creating new myths in order constantly to reconsolidate that identity assured its continued existence.

To a considerable extent, the secondary myths were cloaked in rational, Utopian forms. As Sorel observed, Utopian visions are complex and can be broken down into a number of component parts. The characteristic notion of an ideal "island," cut off from the world ("There's no place like Uruguay") and atemporal ("Uruguayans, champions of America and the world"),[29] was articulated in the form of naif myths. These in turn encouraged the kind of social reforms that were embodied in the Batllista welfare state. In time, these Utopian visions were superimposed on the basic myths as well, obscuring them and accentuating their potentially pragmatic, positivist aspects. This constituted an attack on those myths, and gradually, old existential attitudes involving a faith grounded in the Hebraic idea of truth were displaced by more rationalized forms. However, the latter generated Utopian visions in response to repeated frustrations and disappointments. Eventually, this led to the unraveling of the basic myths and the emergence of movements that were less messianic than they were counter-Utopian.

Some of the rituals that sought to consolidate Uruguay's social imaginary reveal the existence of these Utopian visions. For example, Uruguay's Carnival[30] celebration contrasts dramatically with its Latin American counterparts, especially the Brazilian version. In Uruguay, no attempt is made to turn social conventions completely on end. Carnival is nothing but a means of expression for certain subordinate sectors (generally belonging to the lower strata rather than the middle classes) who seek to exercise their right to be critical or simply, while appearing to be critical, to perpetuate the myth that "there's no place like Uruguay."

Uruguay's reputation as Olympic and world champion soccer players contributed notably to the perpetuation of that myth. The world championship won in 1950, when the "happy Uruguay" was at the height of its glory, brought renewed expressions of confidence in the country and underscored the importance of that mediocrity singularly driven by hope.[31] To a large extent, what these rituals did was to emphasize, not subvert, reality; in no way did they alter the usual order of things. A strong hyperreality was present, in the sense in which Jean Baudrillard uses that term.[32] The important thing was to avoid an imaginary perspective, to see things in a kind of trompe-l'oeil of prospective space—to eliminate the imaginary, get to the bottom of illusion, make illusion so evident, so visible, so "present to the point of excess" that it ends up sustaining this series of myths (and obviously, the memory that feeds them).

Other possibly ritualistic acts, mainly those which relate to the commemoration of certain events (for example, Varela's educational reform), tend to emphasize the myths of the rule of law and the country of *culturosos*. The constant historical celebrations which are part of the Artiguista cult stress the independence of Uruguayans, their uniqueness, and a myth of equality which intermingles with the aforementioned myth of democracy as a result of consensus. I could mention many more rituals that reconsolidate each of these myths and contribute to the formation of the social imaginary.

The Creation of a Social Counterimaginary: The Crisis

The Uruguayan imaginary is expressed through myths and is closely related to the social memory it nourishes, but it is grounded in what is perceived to be "reality." Beginning in the mid-1950s, reality began to diverge markedly with respect to that imaginary while the latter tended to remain fixed. Face-to-face with the resulting contradictions, the reaction at the level of the imaginary was to deny that any changes had occurred. Little by little, the process of denial gave rise to a "counterimaginary."

The basic mechanism operated through the feeling that a Golden Age had been lost. The essence of the problem was how to recover it. This was the beginning of despair and of a growing discrepancy between reality and the desires (myths) that made possible the ordering of the symbolic universe, nourished collective memory constantly, constituted a history, and maintained intact the identity of Uruguayan society. Our reaction to despair was defensive, aimed not at "positive" myths but at conservative ones, and within the social imaginary a militant mythology gradually began to take shape in a frantic search for hope.

The myths enumerated earlier were maintained in toto. Averageness continued to be our goal; consensus persisted; identity crystallized and became a sort of lifeline. But now, consolidation of these myths implied the creation of a counterimaginary because now, the old myths were brought to bear on a separate countercultural vision. For some sectors, the myth of averageness as a prerequisite for security was transformed into a myth of the averageness that would bring back the happy Uruguay. The myth of consensus, of equality before the law, became so hyperreal that a two-pronged attempt was made to implement it at the expense of basic parts of those imaginaries—that is, a messianic tendency and the notion of salvation appeared in association with this myth. While messianic tendencies were not typical of the happy Uruguay (the dominant note there being a vision of an orderly, mediocre country that could be considered either Utopian or anti-Utopian), clearly what was sought now was the salvation that would bring back a lost age.

An inert society reacted with prudence and a good deal of concern. In their naif versions the basic myths turned conservative, discouraging rather than promoting reformism. This society of mediocre, selfish conformists engendered a myth of salvation of its own, albeit imbued with mediocrity. In the absence of new basic myths of an offensive (i.e., not defensive) nature, Utopian visions of change, very rational but not very explicit, and purposefully naif, proved unconvincing except to a group of visionaries. The dominant note was the conservative conformity of the mediocre masses, which, when driven to defend their private interests, agreed to a surrender on the terms imposed by their victorious adversaries. Mediocrity offered security to the middle classes in difficult circumstances but seriously eroded confidence in collective security. At the same time, that mediocrity made it difficult to advance beyond surrender.

The myth of the uniqueness that made us Uruguayan began to crack. Little by little it was displaced by a countercultural alternative centering on Latin American identity, the loss of Europeanness, and a growing distrust of the possibilities of our little country. The myth of a country of *culturosos* proved to be the most resistant. An editorial from this period entitled "La universidad es el país" ("Uruguay Is Its University")[33] perhaps epitomizes that myth. Obviously, Uruguay was not its university; but the myth persisted nevertheless, and its countercultural version implied hyperrealization of the country of *culturosos*. So important was the country of *culturosos* that the University and other educational institutions were considered more important than anything else, even a search for solutions to the political and economic problems that plagued us.

A series of naif myths and symbolic constructs were part of this countercultural process. While the happy Uruguay was one of Utopian averageness, the new Utopian vision sought its solutions in a socialist Uruguay. Whereas in the former a large elderly population held sway, in the latter the emphasis was on rejuvenation and youthfulness; new political groups with "anti" positions, especially those that opted for armed struggle, were frequently referred to as *los muchachos* ("the kids"). While the myth of consensus and equality before the law was threatened by corrupt practices, the counter-cultural phenomenon that appeared alongside it was a kind of reversal, a naif myth of purity to which those who sought a way out of despair also laid claim and which enabled them to take on wholeheartedly the task of restoring Uruguay to its past splendor. In other words, to speak of a social counter-imaginary is to speak not of a breakdown of the old imaginary but rather of the appearance of a parallel one representing an attempt to reconsolidate basic myths in difficult times. The breakdown would occur during the next stage.

The Imaginary of the Dictatorship

The process that culminated in the 1973 coup was a long one. In reality, Uruguay had only a quasi-constitutional government from 1968 on. But for the majority of Uruguayans at the time—Uruguay's subordinate (i.e., middle and working) classes—the handwriting on the wall was still unclear. The political elite knew that an institutional break would occur; the evidence was indisputable. On the other hand, among most of the population there was surprise and disbelief. No one believed that the basic myth of the secure, happy Uruguay of consensus was about to crumble because it no longer reflected reality (as myths have always crumbled, not because of disclosure but rather because of disillusionment). Hence the surprise; hard, disillusion-ing facts had to be faced before the breakdown of the old imaginary could be acknowledged. Not even those who had risen in rebellion with their counter-imaginary—ignoring the rules of the democratic game in order to secure democracy, creating new categories in order to establish our identity, declar-ing us Latinized rather than Europeanized, and taking on serious commit-ments beyond mediocrity—really believed it would happen. People acted as if a breakdown could not occur in the real world, as if that social imaginary were capable of dealing with alienation on its own. So autonomous had the imaginary become that it was not even perceived to be a social construct.

With the 1973 coup we were plunged into despair. By then, the old counterimaginary answers were no longer of any use. For many, a first solution was autism. Waiting and nostalgia were its principal components. Denial of the imaginary as embodied in the social imaginary was the second solution. Madness, leaving history behind, was a third alternative, although in this case the imaginary involved was of a very different kind. The preserva-tion of the social imaginary and its expression through our basic myths was becoming difficult. It was impossible to hold on to the myth of averageness as a prerequisite for security because averageness no longer provided any protection or security at all. The happy Uruguay slipped further and further into the past. Nor was there any longer a myth of consensus and democracy; its end result, the country of *culturosos,* had begun to crumble.

The goal of the autistic masses was an urgent restoration. For those who had introduced the social counterimaginary, several paths were opening up: those who still had their physical freedom could continue their activities in hiding; those who left the country would encounter the nostalgia of exile; for those who passed through the prisons, madness or the hyperrealistic reconsolidation of their ideological positions might offer a means of survival. For their part, those who took over the reins of government brought with them no ideas for new myths to replace the old ones; they sought to subjugate rather than to convince. Only at corporatist levels was a successful imaginary created. The handling of reality and the instruments used, although clearly antithetical to the forms of development applied until then, suggested no alternatives. Nevertheless, some forms of development led certain sectors of the subordinate working strata to introduce a naif myth of paternalism. A "paternalistic army for the people" protected the members of its officers' corporation and their allies, but its actions provided no alternative to the old prerequisite mediocrity. Only a tiny sector of the subordinate classes believed in it. Reformulation of the myth of security was now an urgent need. With the set of meanings traditionally corresponding to the public sphere having shifted, security had to be sought in the private sphere.

Efforts to create a third myth out of the old myth of uniqueness entailed the denial of *uruguayidad* in favor of a new concept known as *orientalidad,* or "orientalness." Although this attempt at manipulation used up important resources, it was a total failure. There was a basic contradiction behind the whole project. If its purpose was to "deabsolutize" the political in a community whose myths were of a political nature and whose imaginary was strongly tinged with politics, an opposing concept tended to create an equally political imaginary very difficult to introduce. The alternative would have been to focus on nonpolitical attributes; but no clear attempt was made, for example, to introduce an imaginary of the market and the consumer.

Especially for most of the middle sectors, the ordering of time came to a halt. Chronological time, or *chronos,* went right on; but subjective time, or *kairós,* was suspended. The idea was to wait things out, in private, nostalgically, and to hope for redemocratization. The social imaginary could no longer institutionalize the world in a positive way. Now it simply functioned independently of the society that had constructed it. Certain sectors of the elite that had been excluded from the coup attempted to recover and hold on to their positions; their actions were testimony to their ongoing belief in the survival of the old social imaginary. In no sense did they adopt messianic attitudes or preach salvation; they simply advocated waiting and nostalgia. Their hope was that the regime would eventually be done in by a combination of chance and fatigue.

What to imagine? How to make sense of a magma of social meanings when most updated versions of the old myths had changed and not even a persistent hyperrealism made it possible to forget the need for the imaginary? When all that was public was forced to seek refuge in the private sphere and the "good order" of the happy Uruguay had been subverted, what was available to replace that order? For most of the older generations who had lived in the happy Uruguay, autistic answers predominated; for a few others, life in hiding or escape were possibilities.

Meanwhile, other alternatives were opening up for the younger generations whose political socialization began at just this time. For those who had accepted the old myths and their referent, the social imaginary, these ran the gamut from hiding to the indifference of a private refuge. But for others, there was the possibility of constructing a new referent, a new meaning, because time and space had been reorganized.[34] Space had lost its continuity and become fragmented. There was private space, on the one hand, and, on the other, public space dominated by the vault of terror that would be introduced into the private realm—that is, the space for acts of resistance that might entail serious risks, and spaces in which to create alternative myths or to resignify the symbolic universe.

At the same time, to those attempting to create a new referent the distinction between chronological and subjective time no longer made sense. The social imaginary that had denied the passage of chronological time (and with it the changes that followed the crisis of 1955) appeared resignified. A postmodern period was at hand. While most of society still thought it was living in the "modern" and "premodern" world of the Uruguay of 1950, these new groups (still marginal) added a third level. Three diverse times could now be ordered in this same society. Diverse spaces were also appearing. The new magma of meanings thus created was not simply a countercultural response. The social imaginary was beginning to break down.

From then on, the question was whether this heralded a total breakdown of the predominant social imaginary which had introduced so much homogeneity into the lives of the subordinate classes in Uruguay and which interpreted their hopes. Grounded in collective memory and incorporated into an official history, already our basic myths were taking on foundational characteristics. The end of the dictatorship and the beginning of redemocratization were reframing the question. Would the basic myths that make up our social imaginary be preserved?

The Social Imaginary and Democratic Restoration

At present in Uruguay, the restoration of a democratic regime is a reality—a restoration obviously rich in imaginary aspects, although it is occurring under conditions in which the real referent has changed dramatically. The years of crisis have not passed in vain, nor have those of the dictatorship. With the reappearance of democracy, the new magma of social meanings that constitute the social imaginary has begun to undergo changes detectable at the level of myth. We no longer talk about the happy Uruguay, or about security; nor do we even aspire much to averageness, although we recall it fondly. Our basic myth has now become the *democratic Uruguay,* the Uruguay where consensus must prevail at all costs.

I have remarked elsewhere that an inverse Hobbesianism is currently at work in Uruguay.[35] We are no longer expected to sacrifice individual liberties for the sake of social and economic security; instead, we are urged to lay aside certain socioeconomic aspirations, precisely the ones that made Uruguay a secure and happy place, in order to give new content to our happiness. Happiness would be guaranteed not by economic and social assets but by assets of a political nature—namely, respect for the individual liberties consecrated by liberalism and coined in the bourgeois revolutions of the North Atlantic.

This myth is based on an expansion of neocontractualism.[36] However, virtually none of the actors who might construct neocontractualism seems eager to practice it seriously. To a large extent, neocontractualism implies a political interchange, a possible change of identities on the part of the negotiators of this new contract; and that has not occurred. The preappointed actors—both the ones who existed before the installation of the authoritarian regime and the ones who survived it—refuse to give up their old identities. They want their referents, their myths, their social imaginary to survive. Nevertheless, they have changed their style and their emphasis. The basic myth of democracy now seeks to prevail. The need for constant consensus (on a social as well as a political level) and the need to reduce—perhaps to remove from the horizon—the possibilities of war and domestic confrontation (whether social, economic, or political) have as their goal this new neocontractualism, which would serve as the foundation for a democracy based on fear. Instead of a potentially positive myth, we are faced with the possibility of a patently negative one. The "good order" in this case is not even a mediocre Utopia. It is a Utopia presided over by our fear of a return to circumstances in which the only available solution would again be autism or escape.

Fear is an essential part of every myth, since myth presupposes the transfiguration of fear. In the new Uruguay, we are involved in the construction of a new myth by means of mythologemes. Our objective is to present a metamorphosis of power—to build a real consensus, thus laying the foundations for a new myth of power. Since power currently derives from a "negotiated" solution in which the military remains a relevant political subject (and a ghost threatening to return), the mythologeme seeks to transfigure this situation using our fear of a return as its starting point. The new construct is less Utopian, less rational, and more mythical. Temporal references—a kind of nostalgia for a possible future—are always present, as are the kinds of appeals typical of "believers." When we call for a future now and for shouts of "Long live the future!"[37] what we are after is an atemporal dimension in reality. The process of mythopoeia now under way picks up on this same idea: "Reality is unacceptable; we want promises." But we want promises of a future to be realized now, recapturing all of our Golden Age. By resignifying symbologies and rituals, we seek consolidation of this budding myth aimed at transcendence.

The second great myth that has persisted is *uruguayidad,* but with new connotations. Our need to present ourselves as different is more pressing than ever. We have to be ourselves. Now when we talk about our *paisito,* our "dear little country," we both acknowledge its overwhelming problems almost unsolvable in the economic and social spheres—and express our will to make it exist; because without it, the possibilities for preserving our identity virtually disappear. That is, unless we succeed we will have no possibilities or referents for a social imaginary. Unless we succeed, our collective memory will be seriously threatened. It was not just nostalgic exiles who used the expression *paisito* to try to keep the clock stopped until their return. That expression is also used by people living in Uruguay. Here again, the will to persist manifests itself as a negative myth that takes on Utopian characteristics. We are no longer living in the days of the "model country"; these are the days of our very dear and badly wounded *paisito.*

The political will to consolidate these myths is still shaky. We are not living in the days of José Batlle y Ordóñez, with his project for a "model country." Our power elites endorse changes in our basic myths very reluctantly, and when they do, it is another way of seeking changes in our social imaginary. Of course, generally speaking, most of them do not share our approach to the facts. But in other terms and with other words, they refer to the same categories. The prevailing rationalism and a fascination with technocracy still constitute important restraints. And, of course, we are aware that myth can be dangerous because of its high degree of irrationality.

Our fears have to do with potential splits. The small groups of heretics, almost always young, which appeared under the dictatorship in the final phases of the transition toward democracy are not very much in evidence nowadays except in the cultural realm. The myth of the country of *culturosos* seems to be in decline. On the other hand, here and there disputes over the meaning of our culture have recently surfaced. And a major resignification is sought based on a single question: To what extent are we following the old guidelines of mediocrity—that is, the old guidelines of critical arrogance embodied by certain cultural generations—in seeking to formulate new proposals?[38] In the opinion of amateurs like myself, in some areas, such as music, this type of opposition has begun to take shape.[39] By and large, however, the new sectors seem to be excluded from the political sphere.

At present, reality finds us in a country with only one official university and an enrollment of almost fifty thousand; practically speaking, that institution has become a factory producing professionals, a storehouse for the unemployed, a cauldron of despair. Even if we tried, we could no longer write an editorial like the one I mentioned earlier by Carlos Quijano.[40] The problem is whether to incorporate these new dissident sectors. Collective memory is in danger of breaking down. On the other hand, our myths are not yet that explicit and do not appear to be in as much danger, at least on the surface. The social imaginary might well find itself split into an imaginary of the middle strata (i.e., those sectors that predominate without playing a leading role primarily because their values have permeated the entire society) and an imaginary of those subordinate sectors on the lower rungs of the social ladder for whom despair is not transformed automatically into hope by a shift toward democracy. Democracy is much sought after by those who have internalized middle-class values. For the lowest strata, on the other hand, that prospect may not prove as effective a rallying point as in the past. It is possible that such a split will occur; but ultimately, both imaginaries would be susceptible to manipulation by the power elites. Other cases in Latin America, among them that of neighboring Argentina, suggest as much.

But there are other dangers as well: that heretical attempts, apparently not too significant to date, may prove more significant in the future; that a new social imaginary may appear along generational rather than class lines; that new generations from whatever social class may forget the myth of the happy Uruguay of mediocrity—of Uruguay, the country of *culturosos*—and may also fail to find much meaning in the new (and as yet incompletely constructed) myth of democracy. Will it be possible to create a new hegemonic social imaginary for this Uruguayan society where so many changes have occurred but such an effort is made to hide them? At the moment, this is an open question.

March 1986

Notes

The original version of this paper, entitled "The Uruguayan Social Imaginary and the Dictatorship" and presented at the University of Maryland in March 1986 during a symposium organized by Saúl Sosnowski under the auspices of the Social Science Research Council, was published as chapter 1 of C. Perelli and J. Rial, *De mitos y memorias políticas* (Montevideo: Banda Oriental, 1986).

1 See Peter L. Berger and Thomas Luckmann, *The Social Construction of Reality: A Treatise in the Sociology of Knowledge* (London: Penguin, 1967).

2 My point of departure here is Cornelius Castoriadis's discussion in *L'institution imaginaire de la société* (Paris: Editions du Seuil, 1975).

3 See Oscar Landi, *Crisis y lenguajes políticos* (Buenos Aires: CEDES, 1981).

4 Castoriadis calls it *imaginaire effectif*, or "actual imaginary," distinguishing it from the *imaginaire dernier ou radical*, a "final or radical imaginary" that is presumed to be behind it (*L'institution imaginaire*, 177–88).

5 Berger and Luckmann (*The Social Construction of Reality*) indicate that the symbolic level (1) provides order for the subjective apprehension of biographical experience, (2) orders the diverse phases of biography (childhood, adulthood, etc.), (3) projects "correctness" upon individual subjective identity (identity is legitimated when placed within the context of the symbolic universe), and (4) orders history (fundamentally collective memory, the experience of the community which is transposed to a plane independent of the vicissitudes of individual existence). According to these authors, this symbolic level can be transformed into a sort of myth. Somehow, that myth fosters unity and makes possible objectivation, sedimentation, and accumulation of what is part of the symbolic universe. For a discussion of collective memory, see Maurice Halbwachs, *La mémoire collective* (Paris: POUF, 1950).

6 An example is offered by Roberto da Matta's excellent book *A casa e a rua: espaço, cidadania, mulher e morte no Brasil* (São Paulo: Brasiliense, 1985).

7 See Leszek Kolakowski, *The Presence of Myth*, trans. Adam Czerniewski (1972; Chicago: University of Chicago Press, 1989), 2–3.

8 See Georges Sorel, *Reflexions sur la violence* (Paris: Plon, 1950).

9 See François Laplantine's discussion in *Les trois voix de l'imaginaire: le messianisme, la possession et l'Utopie: étude psychiatrique* (Paris: Editions Universitaire, 1974), in which it is established that by *political* we are to understand the totality of human relations in their task of constructing the world, and that myth is the story constituted by the "bundling" (*enroulement*) of symbols. When Laplantine refers to poetic meaning, it is in the Greek sense of the poetic.

10 Ernst Cassirer, *The Myth of the State* (New Haven: Yale University Press, 1946); see also Manuel García Pelayo, *Mitos y símbolos políticos* (Madrid: Tauro, 1964). See

Georg Lukács, *The Destruction of Reason,* trans. Peter Polaner (1953; Atlantic Highlands, N.J.: Humanities Press, 1981).

11   As early as 1856, Müller stressed the strong relationship between myth and language. In polynomy, synonymy, and so on, the keys to the mythical world could be found. See Friedrich Max Müller, "Comparative Mythology," in his *Oxford Essays* (London: Parker and Sons, 1856).

12   Murray Edelman, *The Symbolic Use of Politics* (Urbana: University of Illinois Press, 1964).

13   Manuel García Pelayo, *Los mitos políticos* (Madrid: Alianza, 1981).

14   On Uruguay as a country of averages the source is still Carlos Real de Azúa, principally his *El impulso y su freno* (Montevideo: Banda Oriental, 1964) and "Política, poder y partidos en el Uruguay de hoy," in *Uruguay hoy* (Buenos Aires: Siglo XXI, 1971).

15   Sorel, *Reflexions sur la violence.*

16   On the size and social action of groups, see Georg Simmel, *Sociology,* ed. and trans. with intro. by Kurt H. Wolff (Glencoe, Ill.: Free Press, 1950).

17   A parallel example relating to so-called Frenchness can be found in Roger Darnton, *The Great Cat Massacre and Other Episodes in French Cultural History* (New York: Basic Books, 1984). On the Brazilian case, see Roberto da Matta, *Carnavais, malandros e hérois: para uma sociologia do dilema brasileiro* (Rio de Janeiro: Zahar, 1979).

18   The term *oriental,* historically synonymous with "Uruguayan," alludes to Uruguay's location on the eastern shore, or *banda oriental,* of the Uruguay River and its estuary, the River Plate. The full name of the modern state is La República Oriental del Uruguay [TRANS.].

19   A neologism commonly used in Uruguay to refer to a type of intellectual snobbery that acts and regards itself as more cultured than it really is [TRANS.].

20   For distinctions between ideologies in the "strong" and the "weak" sense, see Norberto Bobbio, *Saggi sulla scienza politica in Italia* (Bari: Laterza, 1969).

21   The term *Batllismo* applies to a fraction of the Colorado party, the ideology (in the "weak" sense) of that fraction, and by extension, also to the welfare state and the providentialist style of development created in Uruguay beginning in the 1920s. José Batlle y Ordóñez was the leader of that fraction of the Colorado party and the man who gave shape to that style of development. On this subject, see Real de Azúa, *El impulso y su freno;* Milton Vanger, *José Batlle y Ordóñez of Uruguay: The Creator of His Times* (Cambridge, Mass.: Harvard University Press, 1963); and Vanger, *The Model Country: José Batlle y Ordóñez of Uruguay* (Waltham, Mass.: Brandeis University Press, 1980); G. Lindähl, *Batlle, fundador de la democracia* (Montevideo: Arca, 1971); José P. Barrán and Benjamín Nahum, *Batlle, los estancieros y el Imperio Británico,* 6 vols. (Montevideo: Banda Oriental, 1979–85). Also J. Rial, *Partidos políticos, democracia y autoritarismo* (Montevideo: Banda Oriental, 1984); C. Perelli, *El batllismo* (Montevideo: CIESU DT 110/1985); Ana Frega et al., *La reforma del agro* (Montevideo: CLAEH, 1985); Gerardo Caetano, *El asedio conservador* (Montevideo: CLAEH, 1985).

22   John Bagnell Bury, *The Idea of Progress: An Inquiry into Its Origins and Growth* (New York: Macmillan, 1932; Dover, 1955).

23   "Sean los orientales tan ilustrados como valientes" (statement attributed to Artigas on the day the first public library was inaugurated in 1816).

24   Here I must mention the excellent article by Roberto Schwartz entitled "Las ideas fuera del lugar," in *Estudos* (São Paulo: CEBRAP, 1974).

25   The sentence was made popular by a politician from the Lista 14 fraction of the Colorado party, González Conzi, coauthor with Roberto Giudice of a well-known book entitled *Batlle y el batllismo*, 2d ed. (Montevideo: Medina, 1957).

26   For a discussion of other cases, see Wanderley Guilherme dos Santos, *Cidadania e justiça: a política social na ordem brasileira* (Rio de Janeiro: Campus, 1979).

27   The "black legend" regarding José Artigas, so-named by the inventors of its "blue" successor, presented our national hero as an anarchist and a bandit, a character hard to imagine as a hero. The "blue legend," which was constructed before the end of the nineteenth century and was at the height of its popularity in 1950, presented Artigas as the father of Uruguay's nationality, the founder of oriental identity (Uruguayan identity, according to others), the creator of institutions and democratic consensus, statesman, and so on. The "red legend," created from the 1950s on by leftist intellectuals, relates to Artigas as a social reformer concerned with the destinies of the subordinate classes. Finally, something we might call a "green legend" was created by the military regime, which stressed the role of Artigas as a commander of troops. In that version, Artigas became known as General José Gervasio Artigas.

28   The expression "model country" was used in 1909 by José Batlle y Ordóñez in a letter to one of his allies. In that letter, written in Paris, Batlle commented on how good it would be to create this model country. The manipulation of memory and power and the creation of a welfare state were on the minds of Batlle and his allies. While obviously they were not the creators of the imaginary, they did lay the foundations for the particular imaginary which culminated in the myth of averageness as a prerequisite for security and the attainment of a happy Uruguay.

29   "Uruguayos campeones de América y del mundo," beginning of a *retirada murguera* (a type of Carnival song), dating from 1932, which became very popular after 1950.

30   Argentina's Carnival disappeared because it didn't fulfill either of these purposes; it neither subverted reality for two days nor consolidated myth in a hyperreal form. Unfortunately, there are no historical or sociological studies of Uruguay's Carnival, or studies which analyze that celebration from the perspective of anthropology or social psychology.

31   Obdulio Varela, captain of the soccer team that won the world championship in 1950, can be considered a good example of the kind of man who lived in that happy Uruguay and belonged to the popular strata, the lower sectors of the subordinate classes. As such, he said, it had been very difficult to win the world championship; Uruguay's victory was largely a matter of chance; and if the winning game were to be replayed over and over, Uruguay would probably lose ninety-eight out of a hundred times. When Varela added, "Si le empatábamos a la realidad, le ganábamos a cualquiera" (roughly, his intended meaning was, "If we can do something that impossible, we can do anything" [TRANS.]), he expressed his desire and hope as a Uruguayan living in that country of averageness that Uruguay could rise above its averageness and become superior. As a reference to mythical and nonexistent indigenous ancestors capable of nourishing Uruguayan identity, the naif myth of *la garra charrúa*, or "the Charrúa claw," enabled us to trace that averageness back in time and thus to consider ourselves the best. In turn, it nourished the other naif myth that distinguished that happy country: "There's no place like Uruguay." (The myth of the Charrúa claw embodies the notion

that Uruguayans characteristically achieve their ends not through excellence but through "hanging on by their fingernails" against all odds—a trait they supposedly inherited from the Charrúa Indians [TRANS.].)

32   Hyperreality is the outer limit of prospective space, which is also the outer limit of the imaginary, the end of illusion. It is not realism but a kind of "surplus of reality" resulting from excessive detail. See Jean Baudrillard, *De la séduction* (Paris: Galilée, 1979).

33   Carlos Quijano, "La universidad es el país," *Marcha,* August 15, 1968, 5.

34   See Carina Perelli, "De la integración negativa a la herejía," and Juan Rial, "Los límites del terror controlado," in Perelli and Rial, *De mitos y memorias políticas.*

35   In relation to the notion of inverse Hobbesianism as applied to Uruguay, I am indebted to Alejandro Foxley, "Formas de la política después del autoritarismo," *Estudios CIEPLAN* 15:203–10. See also my "Concertación y gobernabilidad" (Montevideo: CIESU DT 124/1985).

36   Neocontractualism. I refer to the position of John Rawls in his *Theory of Justice* (Cambridge, Mass.: Belknap Press, 1971) and its derivations. On the theory of "political interchange" and "changes of identity," see Salvatore Veca, "Contratto sociale e identità," *Materiali Riali Filosofici* (Milan) 6:7–29; and Gian E. Rusconi, "Governare lo scambio politico," *Laboratorio Politico* (Turin) 2:70–82.

37   These expressions were used in July 1986 by President Julio María Sanguinetti and by Enrique Tarigo, vice president and secretary general of the Colorado party.

38   As examples, see Pablo Vierci, "El Uruguay verdadero," *Jaque* (Montevideo), May 23, 1986, and Vierci, "Reflexiones de un selenita," *Jaque,* June 5, 1986; and Sandino Núñez, article in *El Popular* (Montevideo) (January–April 1986).

39   See the polemic which took place in the pages of *Aquí, Jaque, La Democracia, El Popular,* and the "La Semana" section of *El Dia.* Also the polemic which appeared in *El Taller* during the first half of 1986. The following individuals (among others) participated in these polemics: J. Baltar, Jorge Bonaldi, Victor Cunha, R. Forlán, E. Rodríguez Barilari, Elder Silva, Gerardo Sotelo, and L. Trochón.

40   For new versions of "Uruguay is its University," see articles by Danilo Astori in *Brecha* (Montevideo) (May–June, 1986).

The Decline and Fall of Democracy in Uruguay: Lessons for the Future

Martin Weinstein

❂

Myths die hard. The image of Uruguay as the "Switzerland of South America" or, as the Uruguayans themselves used to say, "Como el Uruguay no hay" ("There's no place like Uruguay"), was based on a reality which had begun to fade badly by the mid-1950s.

During the first half of this century, Uruguay's small, homogeneous, and highly urbanized population lived under the joint benefits of a livestock economy tied to the British market and the sophisticated political institutions and welfare policies promoted by José Batlle y Ordóñez in the period before the Great Depression. The Batllista legacy was so powerful that Batlle's party, the Colorados, controlled the executive branch of government from 1903 until the 1958 elections, and even the Blanco governments from 1959 to 1967 were locked into the Batllista model. The system gave the average Uruguayan a middle-class life-style and access to an excellent education and health care infrastructure. The seemingly endless bounty made possible an extraordinarily democratic and complicated electoral system which prided itself on the ability of almost any group or faction to receive voice and representation, especially if they belonged to the two traditional parties. In sum, the Uruguayan system of the 1940s and 1950s was civil, participatory, distributive, and stable.

What changed all this? The short answer is economic decline signaled by the flagging of the populist experiment based on import-substitution economic growth and the failure of political elites to change policies and programs in the face of changing domestic and international realities.

The exhaustion of the import-substitution model by the mid-1950s brought on a steady deterioration in economic performance. The economic crisis had no single cause, but government policy certainly contributed to it.

The conversion of the large state monopolies known as *entes autónomos* from guardians of national sovereignty and motors of economic develop- ment, as envisaged by Batlle, into patronage machines of the Blanco and Colorado parties did not help productivity or decision-making. Montevideo virtually ignored the rural sector, the basis of almost all of Uruguay's export revenue. The land tax system, which might have promoted greater efficiency, was nonprogressive and was regarded as a means of raising revenue for the urban sector. Even though the Blancos favored the agricultural sector, they continued the populist policies of the Colorados when they finally gained control of the collegial executive from 1959 to 1967. This was not surprising, given the overwhelming importance of Montevideo and its middle-class population. The economically important export and industrial interests be- haved no better than the politicians. While the latter continued to seek votes and avoid hard decisions, the former sought to safeguard their positions and wealth through financial speculation and capital flight.[1]

Uruguay had lost its civility along with its economic well-being by the late 1960s; during this decade, its growth rate was the worst in the hemisphere except for Haiti's. Political sectarianism, masked until then by the infatuation of a homogeneous middle-class population with the game of politics, turned ugly as the economy worsened. Institutions that had managed to contain conflict in the past proved inadequate. The collegial executive was replaced in the 1967 Constitution by a more powerful single executive. Unrest in- creased at the University and in the secondary schools. The trade union movement became radicalized. The Left began to unify in opposition to the Blancos' and Colorados' hold on the electorate. The Tupamaro guerrilla movement emerged out of frustration and idealism. And, most important, the vast majority of Uruguayans clung to a security blanket of welfare-state populism that was dying while hardly anyone noticed.

The untimely death of President Oscar Gestido shortly after he took office in 1967 brought Jorge Pacheco Areco to the presidency. Whereas Gestido was a retired army general with a reputation for honesty and good admin- istrative skills, Pacheco, a newspaperman in the conservative wing of the Colorado party, was not well known in political circles. Within a week after taking office, the new president issued a decree outlawing the Socialist party and several small anarchist and leftist groups. The Socialist party's news- paper, *El Sol,* and the independent leftist newspaper *Época* were perma- nently closed. On June 13, 1968, the government invoked emergency pow- ers granted by the Constitution under the so-called Medidas Prontas de Seguridad (Prompt Security Measures). Except for a brief period in 1969, Pacheco governed under the Medidas Prontas for his remaining four years in office. Furthermore, Parliament twice acquiesced in the suspension of all civil liberties, once for twenty days following the assassination of U.S. police agent Daniel Mitrione by the Tupamaros in August 1970, and then for forty days following the kidnapping of British Ambassador Geoffrey Jackson in January 1971. All these repressive measures were justified in terms of the government's struggle against that guerrilla organization.

The Tupamaros were organized clandestinely in 1963 around a nucleus of disenchanted members of the Socialist party. The movement's leader, Raúl Sendic, was a thirty-six-year-old law student and party activist who had organized sugar workers in Uruguay's northeast. The guerrillas took several years to organize and arm themselves, finally declaring their existence to their fellow citizens in a 1967 statement which made their position and motives clear:

> For these reasons, we have placed ourselves outside the law. This is the only honest action when the law is not equal for all; when the law exists to defend the spurious interests of a minority in detriment to the majority; when the law works against the country's progress; when even those who have created it place themselves outside it, with impunity, whenever it is convenient for them.
>
> The hour of rebellion has definitively arrived for us. The hour of patience has ended. The hour of action and commitment has commenced here and now. The hour of education and enunciation of theory, propositions, and unfulfilled promises is finished.
>
> We should not be worthy Uruguayans, nor worthy Americans, nor worthy of ourselves if we did not heed the dictates of conscience that day after day call us to the struggle. Today no one can take the sacred right of rebellion away from us, and no one is going to stop us from dying, if necessary, in order to be of consequence.[2]

The Tupamaros first benefited from—and later were victimized by—the Uruguayan penchant for mythmaking. Extolling them for their efficiency, wit, and Robin Hood image, Uruguayans seemed proud that their guerrillas were the best in Latin America. However, after Mitrione's assassination this image deteriorated. With the onset of the military dictatorship, Uruguayan public opinion began to blame the Tupamaros for the loss of democracy—a view still held by many. In fact, the Tupamaros were never as adept (politically, ideologically, or tactically) as the public believed and cannot be "blamed" for the dictatorship. The record shows that civil liberties had been seriously eroded under Pacheco Areco, and torture had become an accepted police practice. One parliamentary investigation concluded that:

The application of tortures in different forms is a normal, frequent, and habitual occurrence and . . . among officials of recognized abilities, individuals have infiltrated who use their public positions to give free rein to their perverse instincts. It is also clear that the High Command lacks energy and courage, if it is not at times an accomplice, in transforming the prisons into places where the human being undergoes tortures incompatible with our democracy, our style of life and degree of civilization.[3]

The guerrillas must share responsibility for the escalating violence which increased the role—hence the political influence—of the Armed Forces in Uruguay; but they cannot be held accountable for the theories and practices that were employed by Uruguay's rulers from 1973 until 1984.

On September 9, 1971, after the spectacular escape of over a hundred Tupamaros from the Punta Carretas prison, President Pacheco put the army in charge of all antiguerrilla activity. The effect of this move was not immediate because the guerrillas called a truce in the months surrounding the November 1971 elections. This informal truce ended violently on April 14, when the Tupamaros assassinated several officials in various sectors of Montevideo and lost several of their own members in the ensuing skirmishes with police and army personnel. At President Bordaberry's immediate request, Parliament declared a state of internal war. In fact, this meant the suspension of all constitutionally guaranteed individual liberties and placed Uruguay under martial law.

In retrospect, the decision to refrain from their usual activities from October 1971 until April 1972 was a fatal error for the Tupamaros. Apparently wanting to broaden their base of support, the movement took a calculated risk and backed the Frente Amplio in the elections. But the Tupamaros never really believed that fundamental change would occur in Uruguay through the ballot box. Their very existence can be explained in part by their generation's frustration with electoral politics, the conservative nature of Uruguayan society, and the bleakness of their economic future. When the Tupamaros finally escalated their offensive in April, they faced a firmly entrenched administration backed by an increasingly well-equipped and adequately prepared military. Once they were handed a blank check to "get rid of the problem," the Armed Forces needed only three months to crush the guerrilla movement; by that time the latter had totally estranged itself from public opinion and was isolated from the liberal and leftist groups it had surfaced to support during the election.

The 1971 election was a watershed in Uruguayan politics. The incumbent,

President Jorge Pacheco Areco, sought reelection via a constitutional amendment to be "plebiscited" concurrently with the election. At the same time, Pacheco handpicked the Colorado party's regular candidate, Juan María Bordaberry, a member of a conservative ranching family. The Left, encouraged by the success of Chile's Popular Unity government, organized the Frente Amplio and received permanent party status under the aegis of the Christian Democratic party. Senator Wilson Ferreira Aldunate emerged as a major figure in the Blanco party, but his liberal positions on many issues did not sit well with the party's traditionally conservative sectors.

The election took place amidst increasing violence and polarization, but not from the Tupamaros, who had called a truce for the election. Physical attacks were made on General Líber Seregni, the nonaligned retired general who was the presidential candidate for the Frente Amplio. Newspapers warned that a vote for the Frente was a vote for the Russian bear. Two days before the election, conservative Blancos and Colorados participated in a large demonstration "in defense of democracy." To his credit, Senator Ferreira, who had emerged as the most liberal among the eight presidential candidates of the two traditional parties, asked his supporters to remain at home and not to participate in the demonstration.

The election itself proved to be one of the most controversial in Uruguay's history. A large turnout was ensured by the government's decision to enforce the obligatory voting clause in the Constitution. A late-spring heat wave did not help the long lines of voters already inconvenienced by procedural delays which necessitated keeping the polls open for an additional four hours. But the vote count itself quickly overshadowed the difficulties of the campaign.

Early returns revealed the expected pattern: a heavy Colorado plurality in Montevideo, with the customary Blanco advantage in the interior. The Frente received a solid 30 percent in Montevideo but did so poorly in the interior that its total national vote was a disappointing 18 percent. Attention quickly turned to the narrowing Colorado lead. With half the votes counted, the Colorado plurality fell below eleven thousand. Since late returns from the traditionally Blanco-dominated interior were still to be counted, Wilson Ferreira looked more and more like the winner. But surprisingly, after a mysterious halt in the vote count, the Colorado lead held and Juan María Bordaberry was declared the unofficial winner. Wilson turned out to be the most-voted-for candidate, with 26 percent of the vote to Bordaberry's 24 percent, but the Colorados outpolled the Blancos by some thirteen thousand votes, thus assuring a Bordaberry presidency under Uruguay's electoral laws.

In an earlier article I wrote that:

Wilson Ferreira Aldunate was prevented from winning the election by a determined Colorado president and the acquiescence of conservative Blancos who did not wish to see their own party's liberal presidential candidates elected, even if it meant that their party was defeated. There is strong evidence to support this view beyond the irregularities mentioned above. The amending ballot supporting Pacheco's reelection was deliberately almost identical to the regular Bordaberry ballot. Voting procedures enabled the citizen to put both the ballot for amendment and his regular election ballot in the same envelope. Given the large number of reform ballots cast (several hundred thousand), it is not difficult to believe that several thousand Pacheco ballots found their way into the regular Colorado tally. (One observer estimated that some thirty-five thousand extra ballots could have been credited to Bordaberry in this manner, over two and one-half times more than the winning margin.)[4]

The Bordaberry administration continued the policies of its predecessor. The Uruguayan government's priorities were reflected in its budget. Between 1968 and 1973 the education component of the budget fell from 24.3 to 16.6 percent while the military component increased from 13.9 to 26.2 percent. (The dictatorship's preoccupation with security would push army and police expenditures to over 40 percent of the central government budget.) In addition, Bordaberry proposed legislation to eliminate the University's autonomy and enhance the powers of the army and police. Nevertheless, the military grew impatient with civilian rule. It was now time for the Armed Forces to begin their final assault on the Uruguayan polity.

The military's most significant challenge to presidential authority occurred during the second week of February 1973, when the army and air force rebelled against President Bordaberry's selection of Antonio Francese as minister of defense. This skirmish quickly turned into a quasi coup. The military was demonstrating its intention to oversee national policy. Bordaberry managed to stay in office, but policy was henceforth to be supervised by a newly created National Security Council dominated by the military.

The military now pushed for the final approval and implementation of draconian national security regulations. Parliamentary reluctance to go along with such measures, along with President Bordaberry's loss of a legislative majority following the defection of several legislators, caused the military to issue several communiqués denouncing the nation's politicians for being soft on the war against subversion. When Parliament refused to revoke the immunity of Senator Enrique Erro, whom the military charged with complicity with the Tupamaros, and voted to investigate charges of torture leveled against the Armed Forces, the generals decided they had had enough.

Backed by the military, on June 27, 1973, President Bordaberry closed Parliament, prohibited the dissemination of any information attributing dictatorial motives to the government, and empowered the police and the Armed Forces to take whatever measures were necessary to ensure the continued functioning of public services. Thus the dictatorship was launched. Its record of arrests, torture, and murder combined with its actions against unions, the University, the press, and culture in general—all undertaken in the concentrated and intimate world that is Montevideo—soon established it as the most totalitarian on the continent.

The Uruguayan coup was a drawn-out affair, and thus far less dramatic than its Chilean counterpart. Perhaps the actions taken by Bordaberry and the military would have received more attention if Salvador Allende had not been overthrown on September 11 of the same year. The international preoccupation with events in Chile afforded the Uruguayan dictatorship the luxury of silence and anonymity, allowing it to act with impunity while creating a totalitarian regime in a nation with an even more democratic and civil tradition than Chile's.

The systematic but "constitutional" attack conducted by Pacheco and Bordaberry on the guerrillas, the press, the unions, and the University was extended and refined by the military. With no constitutional safeguards and nothing remotely resembling the rule of law, there remained only the brute force employed by the military in its paranoid quest for national security. As Rear Admiral Francisco Sanjurjo succinctly put it while defending the dictatorship's human rights record: "Before they criticize our Armed Forces so harshly, they ought to take a look at what happens to those plutocratic democracies that wave the flag of ideological pluralism and peaceful coexistence. . . . In spite of itself liberal democracy leads to communism."

But the military failed on all levels to carry out its mission. It did not destroy the Left, create a self-sustaining economy, or eliminate the bourgeois political system which it detested for having acted as midwife at the birth of the Left. The torture, murder, and culture of fear the dictatorship created has been amply documented—first, for obvious reasons, outside Uruguay, and more recently within. Since a number of essays included in this volume deal with diverse aspects of that subject, I will devote the remainder of this essay to a discussion of the lessons to be drawn from the destruction of democracy in Uruguay and the role and responsibilities of Uruguay's intellectuals vis-à-vis the future of democracy in their country.

The political culture of Uruguay stresses democracy and individual freedom, but it is not strong on national unity or the identification of individual or factional interests with those of the nation. The lack of a national vision capable of including everyone has haunted Uruguay since economic decline set in thirty years ago.

> Uruguay's Batllista experiment, as limited as it may have been, was an attempt to build a viable nation-state. The democratic nationalism which it propounded and the policies and institutions which it established gave the Uruguayan citizen a standard of living, a freedom of conscience, and quality of membership in the social nation that would be difficult to equal in many systems. The turning-away from that commitment in the 1930s put Uruguay on an ever more precarious course in which the Batllista legacy survived as a structure whose facade slowly crumbled as leadership groups tried to maintain their own position and their control of the state without the necessary commitment to the national community which effective action required.[5]

Whether it was the particularist-clientelist politics of the Blancos and Colorados, the isolated—if idealistic—action of the Tupamaros, or the speculation and capital flight initiated by the business community, no one really concerned themselves with the national interest. The situation was polarized, the actors were myopic, and the public was socially conservative. It remained for the military with their narrow but determined definition of *national interest* to take control of the situation. The military, so long an apolitical institution, decided to play a role we have grown accustomed to in Latin America—that of undertaker in the death of the social nation.

The 1971 election was a questionable exercise in democracy. The 1984 election took place with the leaders of two of the three parties prohibited from running, although their factions could participate. Given these circumstances, the 1989 elections will be a long-delayed test of Uruguayan democracy. The future legitimacy and stability of civilian government is still at stake.

A reform of the electoral system is long overdue. Uruguayans point with pride to their system of the double simultaneous ballot, which permits the votes of several candidates to accrue to the same party with the ballot counting for the candidate and his party at the same time. The candidate who receives the most votes from the party that receives the most votes gains the presidency. In effect, this turns the ballot into a concurrent primary and electoral decision. When combined with strict proportional representation in the Senate and Chamber of Deputies, the system has given a voice to small sectors of the two traditional parties and of the Frente. However, it also has meant that the president frequently does not have a majority in Parliament and that the parties are not programmatic in the European sense of the term. Complicating this picture is the fact that elections take place only once every five years for all national and local offices, thus freezing in place a frequently unstable but unchangeable balance of political forces.

When coupled with the easy factionalism permitted by the electoral laws, a small and homogeneous population concentrated in one principal city helps create an atmosphere of accessibility and proximity on which gossip thrives. There are no secrets in Montevideo, and politicians are seen close up, warts and all. While this has been conducive to sophisticated political games and sharp political humor, it also helps create the kind of familiarity that does indeed breed contempt. As the economic pie continues to shrink, this physical and emotional proximity exacerbates tensions.

It is in the above context that we must consider the meaning of anticommunism in Uruguay. Its impact has been especially felt in two areas: the labor movement and electoral politics. As the economic situation deteriorated, labor organized to protect its interests. Unions have a long and proud history in Uruguay, dating back to the turn of the century. In 1966 a new and more powerful trade union confederation, the National Workers' Convention (Convención Nacional de Trabajadores [CNT]), was organized under the leadership of the Communist party. As purchasing power declined drastically in the face of a record 135 percent inflation rate in 1967, public and private employees began to make direct demands on government for increases in real wages. The number of strikes and work stoppages skyrocketed. The government's response hardened with the use of troops to break a utility workers' strike in 1968 and the militarization of bank employees in 1969. Strikes and labor militancy made for rapidly deteriorating labor-management relations. Uruguay's industrialists came to view the destruction of the trade union movement as the dictatorship's most significant accomplishment, far more important than the dismantling of the Tupamaros, whom the industrialists saw as a nuisance but not the threat that the Communist-led unions represented to their interests.

In the 1984 election, Sanguinetti, while running a generally statesmanlike campaign, could not refrain from the occasional flourish of red-baiting:

Behind that person who acts so calmly [Seregni] there are groups whose strength is well known. We have seen that the flag with the hammer and sickle which has been hidden for twenty years has started to appear. And there is no doubt that they are now determined to try to assert—within the Broad Front—their predominance in the working sectors. They are stating this. This is not a personal issue; it is a political fact. There is a philosophical battle, a battle of principles, regarding these ideas. A front which has totalitarian currents, to the detriment of those which are not totalitarian, undoubtedly represents a danger and a threat to the institutional stability of a country.[6]

In the period since democratic restoration there has been little to suggest that this vision of ongoing communist influence in the union movement and participation in the Frente Amplio appeals to the average Uruguayan, let alone to the political Right and the military.

Intellectuals in Uruguay, as in most of Latin America, are by and large men and women of the Left. Most of them support one of many factions that make up the Frente Amplio. Unfortunately, this has meant that like its intellectual supporters, the Frente has not progressed beyond a vocabulary of opposition and negation to one of consensus building. The former may have been the natural vocabulary for the 1960s and early 1970s; it was the only conscionable vocabulary under the dictatorship. But a vocabulary and politics of opposition will not serve the Uruguay of the present or future well—if democracy is to survive.

Marcha lives on as *Brecha,* and that is as good as it is important. But it is not enough. Intellectuals must learn how to communicate with the government and the typical Uruguayan. Practical solutions must be offered, not mere rhetoric. Speaking truth to power is essential, but the harsh truths of Uruguay's economic situation are known to all. A creative political breakthrough is needed; and in this regard the intellectuals must be bold, not merely negative and sectarian. Uruguay is a broken country. That is the legacy of the dictatorship. It is a legacy that serves a fascist military well for the future.

A natural tension between class and nation exists in all social systems, especially capitalist ones. The strain between loyalty to nation and loyalty to class has been bridged historically by the "myth" of social mobility, which, while recognizing class differences, holds up the state as the impersonal regulator of the marketplace of opportunity for all citizens. But the exhaustion of the import-substitution model in Uruguay by the mid-1960s put an extra burden on the public sector. Enmeshed in a clientelist politics, the traditional parties increasingly used their control of state institutions to satisfy particularistic demands. Increasingly, the state became a provider rather than an arbiter. As Aldo Solari perceptively observed: "Rather than as a secular artifact destined to resolve social conflicts at the highest level, that state is conceived in a paternalistic manner, as the one who must keep the vigil in order to, in the last analysis, sustain everyone."[7]

Uruguayans are a dispirited people. They do not have a positive attitude about the future. Some might call this realism. But the intellectual and artistic community must engender a sense of the possible if Uruguayans are to build their lives and their country. They have as a basis a political culture which is democratic but has to overcome the sectarianism of the past and the impoverishment of the present. If nothing else, the military forced a cooling off in a conflict-ridden society. The cost was, of course, unjustifiable. Redemocratization should nevertheless take advantage of the "calming" produced by the dictatorship. Intellectuals along with everyone else must allow conflict to be resolved at the interinstitutional level; it must not be allowed to explode into the uncontrolled war of values of the early 1970s.

The system needs time if democracy is to survive. This is not an argument for conservatism or conformity. Any leftist movement in Uruguay—and most especially a revolutionary one—must come to grips with the socially and politically conservative nature of the society. Uruguayans now have an average age of forty. They are fiercely middle class in their values, if no longer in their incomes. They are nostalgic for the past and, for better or worse, lack the *viveza criolla,* or "local smarts," characteristic of their Argentine counterparts. The Frente Amplio may get 30 percent of the vote in Montevideo, but its dismal showing in the interior has condemned it twice to one-fifth of the total vote. Even if a discredited Colorado government and a Blanco party without Wilson lost to the Left in 1989—a highly likely outcome—it is difficult to believe that the Frente would come to power with more than 35 percent of the vote. Allende's Chile immediately comes to mind. Given the coalition nature of the Frente, one cannot be sanguine about its ability to govern in such a situation. The Left must change its confrontational image. The place to start is with its rhetoric. If in some ways the Sanguinetti government is a *continuista,* or "continuist," regime, the opposition is guilty of being a continuist opposition. Here the producers of culture have as much responsibility as the politicians. As Mario Benedetti so incisively observed:

> Both in those responsible for governing and in those entitled to oppose the government, a minimal dose of daring is needed. Without boldness (which is not the same as recklessness), there is no progress. I feel that at this very crucial stage, a little boldness is lacking both in the government and among the opposition. It's as if the dictatorship had knocked the wind out of all of us. In any case, we have to get it back. We have to dare to say no to the powers that be, both internal and external. But we also have to dare to say yes—sometimes from the top down, at other times from the bottom up. It is socially unhealthy to be slaves to formulas, no matter whose they are.

Additionally, in and from the Left, we should reconsider our language. It is less important to yell about unity than to act in unison. Above all, our united action must be reasoned, balanced, clear, and deeply felt; for otherwise, it isn't likely to hold together. For that too we need boldness, understanding of the other, a desire for truthfulness, a love of our country. These days I find myself less and less enamored of slogans, more and more eager for results. And it's the latter I miss.[8]

Meanwhile, efforts to bridge the rhetorical and policy gap between the Left and the government have fallen victim to the human rights legacy of the dictatorship. In September 1986, a government-backed proposal of amnesty for human rights violations committed by the military during the dictatorship was defeated in the opposition-dominated Parliament. Subsequently, a proposal by the Blancos, the principal opposition party to the Colorado government, also failed when both the Colorados (who thought it went too far) and the Frente Amplio (who thought it did not go far enough) refused to support it. The political stalemate got progressively worse, reaching its nadir on November 14 when for the first time in Uruguay's history, Parliament failed to pass the budget authorization for the following year. The Sanguinetti government threatened to call for early parliamentary elections (thus the presidency was not to be at stake) unless the budget and human rights stalemate could be overcome. By early December the budgetary impasse had been resolved amidst rumors that the Colorados and Blancos were close to agreement on an amnesty bill.

Shortly thereafter, the officers who commanded the Armed Forces during the dictatorship issued a declaration in which they recognized that "transgressions" had occurred while they were in power. Vice President Enrique Tarigo immediately proclaimed the statement to be a confession of human rights abuses by the military. The Sanguinetti government also hinted that Uruguay was still in a less-than-perfect transition period from dictatorship to full democracy. Such an admission—albeit oblique—was enough to give Wilson Ferreira Aldunate the excuse he needed to support an amnesty bill which he had vigorously opposed only months earlier; the Blanco leader claimed that his party was voting for the bill in order to ensure the stability of Uruguay's fragile democracy.

On December 22, 1986, by a vote of sixty to thirty-seven, the Uruguayan Chamber of Deputies passed an amnesty bill that was promptly signed by Sanguinetti. The legislation in effect prevents the prosecution of any human rights violations committed by military and police personnel from 1973 to 1985. In addition, the law terminated the thirty-eight cases already pending in the courts. However, the legislation was passed only after bitter debate in both houses of Parliament, fistfights between legislators, and violent street demonstrations. It took effect just an hour before Colonel José Nino Gavazzo was due to appear in court to testify in a case concerning the 1976 abduction of Uruguayan journalist Enrique Rodríguez Larreta in Argentina and his removal to a detention center in Montevideo. Gavazzo and the entire military institution had made it clear that they would not participate in any trials and would ignore or resist any subpoenas to do so. Such refusal would have created a full-blown constitutional crisis between the executive and the military authority in Uruguay.

The amnesty law is officially known as the Ley de Caducidad de la Pretensión Punitiva del Estado (Law Declaring an Expiration of the State's Punitive Authority). The issue of its passage became the dominant political question in 1987 when groups opposed to amnesty for the military began a campaign to collect signatures for a referendum to overturn the law. The government and politicians who supported the amnesty gave the pro-referendum forces little chance of success in collecting the requisite number of signatures. However, on December 17, 1987, the groups in favor of the referendum submitted some 634,000 signatures to the Electoral Court. With 557,000 valid signatures required in order for a referendum to be called (i.e., 25 percent of registered voters), it appeared that Uruguay would indeed have a plebiscite. The Electoral Court took most of 1988 to validate the signatures, promising a decision by September or October.

President Sanguinetti defended the Ley de Caducidad as follows: "What is more just? To consolidate the peace of the country where human rights are guaranteed today, or to seek retroactive values? I believe human rights trials would have been incompatible with peace and institutional stability" (*Los Angeles Times*, March 30, 1987). For his part, Foreign Minister Enrique Iglesias argued at the time that it was not an ethical question but a political one, involving the rights of the individual versus those of society. "No country can live permanently facing the past, in conflict with its army," he said. "Amnesty is an act of faith. We are betting the future on the army's historic tradition of non-interventionism and professionalism" (*Los Angeles Times*, March 30, 1987).

Finally, in late November and early December 1988, the Electoral Court validated 522,700 signatures and declared some 36,000 signatures in suspension.[9] The court then set up a three-day recertification period from December 17 to 19; during this time at least 23,000 of those individuals whose signatures had been suspended would have to appear in person and confirm that they had indeed signed the petition. Believing its task almost impossible, the National Commission for a Referendum debated whether to attempt to cross this hurdle or simply to refuse and denounce the entire process. They finally decided to try to get the necessary signatures recertified.

Through the use of computers and hundreds of volunteers, the tens of thousand of individuals cited by the court were contacted. Since many of them lived abroad or in the interior of the country, the pro-referendum forces had an especially hard task before them. At the end of the first two days set aside for recertification, some 21,000 individuals had appeared to verify their signatures. But the last day was reserved only for those individuals who were registered to vote in one department (state) in Uruguay and had signed for the plebiscite in another. Things looked gloomy and matters were complicated when a terrible electrical storm hit Montevideo on that fateful Monday morning. Additionally, on December 19 a summer work schedule went into effect in all government offices, giving people only until 2:00 P.M. to report. A request to extend the hours was rejected by the court by a vote of six to three. Yet almost miraculously, enough people showed up in the last two hours so that when it was all over, members of the Electoral Court announced that the referendum petition had carried by about 230 signatures more than the required 555,701.

Within a couple of days the government was conceding that the referendum would have to take place, but it was not happy about the idea. President Sanguinetti indicated that the country would enter a "long, risky and dramatic period of confrontation" if the Ley de Caducidad were annulled, but he expressed his confidence that the citizenry would "ratify the pacification contained in the amnesty law" (ANSA-Italian Press Service, December 22, 1988). Preliminary response from the military disparaged those who wanted to overturn the Ley de Caducidad and warned of military solidarity in the face of such action.

The depiction by the political Right of the pro-referendum effort as solely the work of the extreme Left—including the Tupamaros (the guerrilla movement of the late 1960s and early 1970s)—was an act of frustration and distortion. The Tupamaros are a marginal and legal political movement in today's Uruguay with an active membership of several hundred. The two-year struggle to collect over 600,000 signatures (in a country of 2.2 million registered voters) and have them validated in the face of a frightened government and an unrepentant military was the result of the hard work of thousands of Uruguayans of all political persuasions. The outpouring of emotion on the streets of Montevideo when the Electoral Court finally agreed that there were enough signatures was not a Tupamaro victory party. It was a victory for truth, decency, and courage. The fact that the citizens of Uruguay would vote on whether to amnesty the military for its past abuses was a significant human rights story in Latin America for 1989 and a unique chapter in the annals of civil military relations in the aftermath of dictatorship.

The plebiscite took place on April 16, 1989, and was preceded by intensive campaigning on both sides of the issue. The governing Colorado party counseled support of the Ley de Caducidad (yellow ballot), as did most of the Blanco leadership—the exceptions being Senator Carlos Julio Pereyra and his sector of the party, the Movimiento Nacional de Rocha. Those in favor of an abrogation of the law (green ballot) waged an energetic and effective media campaign based on the idea that no one should be above the law.

In the end the referendum was defeated by a margin of 57 to 43 percent. The green vote won in Montevideo by a clear-cut 55 to 45 percent, but given a massive 60-plus percent vote to uphold the law in the interior, the initiative failed. This geographically diverse outcome gave rise to a biting example of black humor: "The result of the referendum means that if there is a future dictatorship, the military will be able to torture in the interior but not in Montevideo." Nevertheless, the fact that more than 40 percent of the population said no to amnesty for the military—even in the face of government and Blanco pleading and bullying from the Armed Forces—is a statement about human rights and the feelings of a large segment of the population. Members of the government conceded privately that the choice presented to the voters was not a happy one and that discretion (peace) had taken priority over justice.

The Sanguinetti administration and the Colorado party have paid a high price for their victory in the referendum. Many voters feel (as does this observer) that there must be some airing of the crimes committed by the military—even if ultimately no one goes to jail—if Uruguay is going to continue to build its restored democracy on a firm foundation. Morality and ethics require that. But more important, so does the future legitimacy of a civilian government. To deny the past is to have one less barrier to the reentry of the military to direct government power. The Sanguinetti government's failure to account officially for human rights violations committed from 1973 to 1985 leaves it on shaky ground when it seeks support for its often painful economic policies. As I summed it up elsewhere:

> The amnesty law as a "solution" to the human rights legacy of the dictatorship is another example of less than courageous muddling through. The response may be viewed as a political necessity in the face of a still hardline military, but, once again, rather than coming to grips with a problem, Uruguay's leaders have chosen to ignore it or postpone its

resolution. I sincerely hope that the Sanguinetti government (and its successor) will demonstrate more courage as it faces the economic and social problems that must be overcome if Uruguay is to consolidate its recently restored democracy and enter the twenty-first century reclaiming its title, the "Switzerland of South America."[10]

Postscript

The November 1989 elections were a watershed. The first truly unfettered contest since the military coup in 1973 brought about remarkable changes. The elections gave the Blancos the presidency and the Frente Amplio control of the government of Montevideo, thus proving historic on several levels. Luis Alberto Lacalle is only the third Blanco president in this century, and the first of a purely presidential system. The Frente's clear victory in Montevideo, where half the country's people live, brought a socialist physician, Tabaré Vásquez, to the mayor's office. This has given the Left its first experience with executive power at any level in Uruguay, and they have started with the second most important elective office in the country![11]

Lacalle has pledged to reduce the fiscal deficit (now running at some 6 percent of the gross domestic product), streamline government bureaucracy, privatize or at least attract some private capital participation to the ailing state monopolies, and resolve the foreign debt problems. He also wants to encourage foreign investment and believes the unions must be regulated in order to help bring this about.

Many of these goals will put Lacalle's government in conflict with the leftist government in Montevideo, its municipal unions, and other unions—almost all of which are controlled by the Left, especially the Communists. Yet it is the Communists who will probably argue for the most cautious and statesmanlike position within the Frente. Running Montevideo is a huge challenge for the Left. If they can do it with some success, they will certainly be reelected in 1994 and have a realistic shot at the presidency if the Blancos falter. One should remember that elections for all offices in Uruguay take place simultaneously only once every five years.

The United States should be quite content with Lacalle's victory. Lacalle is a friend of the United States and a proponent of privatization and the free market. Uruguay's inclusion in the Brady Plan for debt reduction—or at least some formula for debt relief—is a cornerstone of his international financial policy. The U.S. government should not make Uruguay's foreign policy or set Uruguay's domestic agenda. It would be a serious mistake for Washington to put pressure on Lacalle to "do something about the Frente." Such a position would only strengthen the Armed Forces, whose more conservative senior officers are undoubtedly unhappy with the Left's electoral success in Montevideo. Lacalle has credibility with the generals and colonels and they support his program. He should be allowed to deal with their fears of the Left without aggravating the situation. An interventionist posture by the United States would not go unnoticed by the Left and would increase the possibility of confrontation between the central government and Montevideo, which would only serve to strengthen nondemocratic civilian and military elements.[12]

In March 1986 this essay ended with the following observation:

Uruguay is now very much a part of Latin America in many ways she wasn't—or thought she wasn't—in the past: underdeveloped, dependent, possessed of a politicized right-wing military, and drowning in debt. Democracy's survival will ultimately depend on political and intellectual skill in providing economic growth and social justice along with recently restored civil liberties. Unfortunately, there has also been a restoration of all the old habits that led Uruguay into its national tragedy. If the lessons of the past two decades are not learned and do not lead to new ideas and new ways of acting, then Uruguay's politicians and intellectuals may be doing nothing more than rearranging the deck chairs on the *Titanic*.

Over four years later, I am mildly encouraged by the changes that have occurred in Uruguayan politics as a result of the 1989 elections and the collapse of communism in Eastern Europe. Uruguay will not have an easy time restructuring its economy and finding a more secure place in the world system. But with imagination and tolerance from the Lacalle administration and from a surprisingly vigorous Left, the Uruguayan polity need not flounder in the sea of troubles that has plagued Latin America for the past generation.

March 1986/April 1989/October 1990

Notes

1   This paragraph is taken from my chapter "Uruguay: Military Rule and Economic Failure," in *Politics, Policies and Economic Development in Latin America*, ed. Robert Wesson (Stanford, Calif.: Stanford University Press, 1984).

2   "Carta abierta a la policía," printed in *Época*, December 7, 1967.

3   *Marcha* (Montevideo) June 5, 1970, 12–15. I have used Raymond Rosenthal's translation, cited in *State of Siege* (New York: Ballantine Books, 1973), 195. This volume is the screenplay and documentary appendix of Constantin Costa-Gavras's movie of the same name.

4   Martin Weinstein, *Uruguay: The Politics of Failure* (Westport, Conn.: Greenwood Press, 1975), 126.

5   Ibid., 135.

6   Foreign Broadcast Information Service, November 16, 1984, 14.

7   Aldo Solari, "Las estructuras sociales y su posible evolución," in his *Estudios sobre la sociedad uruguaya,* 2 vols. (Montevideo: Arca, 1964), 1:167.

8   *Brecha* (Montevideo), January 17, 1986, 30.

9   Adapted from my essay "Consolidating Democracy in Uruguay: The Sea Change of the 1989 Elections," Bildner Center for Western Hemisphere Studies, the Graduate School and University Center of the City University of New York, Working Paper Series no. 4 (January 1990), 2–3.

10   Martin Weinstein, *Uruguay: Democracy at the Crossroads* (Boulder, Colo.: Westview Press, 1988), 141–42.

11   Weinstein, "Consolidating Democracy," 11.

12   Ibid., 14.

II

Culture and Power

The Dictatorship and Its Aftermath:
The Hidden Wounds
Eduardo Galeano

✪

The Symbols

L ots of ashes have rained on the purple land. For the twelve years of the military dictatorship, the word *libertad* referred to nothing but a plaza and a prison. At that prison—the chief cage for political detainees—it was against the rules to draw pictures of pregnant women, couples, birds, butterflies, or stars; and without permission no prisoner could whistle, smile, sing, walk at a fast pace, or wave to another. But every Uruguayan was a prisoner except for jailers and exiles—three million of us, though only a few thousand seemed to be. One in every eighty Uruguayans had a hood tied on his head while the rest, doomed to isolation and solitary confinement even when spared the pain of torture, wore invisible hoods as well. Fear and silence were mandatory. Hostile to any and all living things, the dictatorship poured cement over the grass in the plazas and felled or whitewashed every tree within its reach.

The Model

With minor variations, a single model of surveillance and repression was applied during the seventies all over Latin America against the forces for social change. In the name of the Pan-American Doctrine of National Security, military forces functioned as occupying armies in their own countries—the armed wing of the International Monetary Fund and the system of privileges that agency embodies and sustains. With the guerrilla threat as a pretext, state terrorism set its gears in motion to cut real wages by half, dismantle the trade unions, and eliminate critical awareness. Through the wholesale use of terror and uncertainty, the military set out to create a society of deaf-mutes. On the computer at the headquarters of the Armed Forces Chiefs of Staff, all Uruguayan citizens were divided into three categories according to their "degree of dangerousness"; depending on how great a threat we were thought to pose to the military's plans for a kingdom of eunuchs, we were classified A, B, or C. It was impossible to get a job or keep one without the Certificate of Democratic Faith issued by that computer and dispensed by the police, experts in democracy trained in techniques of torture by U.S. professor Dan Mitrione. Even a birthday party required a police permit. Every home became a prison cell and every factory, office, and institution of higher learning a concentration camp.

The Assault

The dictatorship did away with our system of education, replacing it with a system of ignorance. By abruptly firing teachers and shutting down academic programs, it sought to domesticate students: to instill in them the barracks morality that treats sex as a prophylactic outlet or a conjugal duty and to enshrine the mummified culture that considers ownership of people and things to be a *natural right,* while the submission of women to men, children to parents, poor to rich, blacks to whites, and civilians to military is regarded as a *natural obligation.*

Orders were given to disconnect and deverbalize the country. All potential links of solidarity and creativity among Uruguayans became crimes; anything that might put us in touch with the rest of the world was labeled a conspiracy; any words that didn't lie were deemed subversive. Punishment was dealt the participant, the political or union activist, and whoever failed to denounce them as well. Since anything anyone said might be construed as damaging to the Armed Forces, the most innocent comment was liable to bring a three- to six-year imprisonment along with a beating that might prove fatal. Censorship even extended to publications from Brazil and Argentina; in the opinion of the generals, too much was revealed in the press from those neighboring dictatorships run by their colleagues. It was against the law to mention reality, past or present. A general obliteration of collective memory was decreed. After all, if José Artigas and José Pedro Varela were ever to break out of their bronze statues, they might provide dangerous clues to identity or a meeting ground for perplexed young people who wondered: *Where does Uruguay come from? Who am I? What am I part of?*

The Response

Yet somehow, Uruguayan culture found ways of surviving, inside and outside the country. The fierce persecution of those years turned out to be the greatest honor we had ever received. Uruguayan culture both survived and proved capable of a vital response to the machinery of death and silence. It thrived in those who stayed and those of us who had to leave: in words passed from hand to hand, from mouth to mouth, clandestine or contraband, hidden or disguised; in actors who spoke current truths through the verses of Greek theater and others who were obliged to roam the face of the earth as strolling players; in the songs of our exiled minstrels and those that resounded defiantly inside the country; in the scientists and artists who refused to sell their souls; in the brash *murgas* of our Carnival celebration and in papers and magazines that died and were reborn; in slogans scrawled on city walls and poems scribbled in dungeons on cigarette paper.

But if culture is a way of being and a style of communication, if culture is the set of symbols of our collective identity that we forge in everyday life, our resistance was even wider and deeper than my examples suggest. Obdulio Varela, a famous soccer player who knows Uruguay and Uruguayans very well, summed it up grimly in the final days of the dictatorship. "We've gotten so selfish," he said early in 1985. "We've forgotten how to put ourselves in the other guy's shoes. Democracy is going to be tough."

Yet somehow, Uruguayans responded with solidarity to the politics of disconnection. We found many ways of coming together and of sharing what little—what nothing—we had. These ways, which were a shining part of Uruguay's cultural resistance during the years of the dictatorship, were most numerous among the hardest-hit sectors of the working class. And here I refer not only to large street demonstrations but also to less dramatic undertakings such as soup kitchens, cooperative housing, and other works of courage and imagination, all of which prove once more that solidarity is inversely proportional to level of income. Or, as Martín Fierro puts it, that the fire that really warms comes from below.

The Damage

There is no such thing as statistics where the soul is concerned, no way to measure the depth of our cultural wound. We know that Uruguay exports shoes to the United States while we Uruguayans buy five times fewer shoes than we did twenty years ago; but we cannot know to what extent our innermost thoughts have been poisoned or to what extent our awareness, identity, and memory have been mutilated.

Some problems are obvious, of course—problems caused, or at least aggravated, by the dictatorship and the economic policies in whose name Uruguay was turned into a vast torture chamber. For example, there are books that could help us to know and understand ourselves better and that could contribute significantly to the recovery of Uruguayan culture. But if the price of even one of those books is equivalent to a full seventh or eighth of the salary earned by many Uruguayans, *price is just as severe a censor as the police used to be.* Editions of Uruguayan books are five or six times smaller than they once were; people have stopped reading not out of desire but out of necessity.

Another obvious problem is the difficulty of returning from exile. Nothing has been more damaging to Uruguay than the already serious sapping of human resources that intensified under the dictatorship. Some of us who went into exile because, as a certain police chief once said, we had *ideological ideas,* have been able to return. I say some of us, not all or even most of us. There are no jobs in Uruguay, and what jobs there are don't pay enough to live on. So how many of us can return? How many of the hundreds of thousands the system still forces to seek their daily bread elsewhere? *The system, sick with sterility, practices a strange kind of alchemy: it transforms what should be stepping-stones to progress into a national scourge.* The high cultural level of Uruguayan workers, which could and should foster development, works against the country inasmuch as it facilitates the exodus of the population. Now we have democracy, a civilian government instead of a military dictatorship, but the system is the same and the economic policy remains essentially unchanged.

Freedom of enterprise, enemy of human freedom, usurper of wealth, usurper of life: the cultural consequences of that economic policy are all too clear. Encouraging consumption, the conspicuous consumption which reached frenzied heights under the dictatorship, has netted us more than a stifling sixfold increase in the foreign debt; it has also discouraged creativity. Support for speculation strips us not just of material wealth but also of moral, and therefore cultural, values, because by denigrating productivity it confirms the age-old suspicion that anyone who works is an idiot. Additionally, the avalanche of foreign goods which is destroying national industry and decimating salaries, the readjustment of the economy to meet the demands of foreign markets, and the abandonment of domestic markets all imply, culturally speaking, that we hold ourselves in contempt. Uruguay spits at itself in the mirror and opts for the ideology of impotence.

"I'm sorry, but it's domestic," said a grocer who sold me some canned meat the day after I arrived back in Uruguay. After twelve years in exile, I must say I wasn't expecting that. Then, when I mentioned it to my friends, they blamed the "process." And I hadn't expected to hear the dictatorship referred to as a process either. *Our language was, and perhaps still is, sick with fear;* sadly, we are no longer in the habit of calling a spade a spade.

The Job Ahead

Our land of the free is wounded but alive. The military dictatorship that doomed it to twelve years of silence, lies, and mistrust has not succeeded in rotting out its soul. "They were wrong if they thought they could turn us into them," a friend told me at the end of the years of terror; and of that I am convinced.

But fear lives on in the guise of prudence. "Watch out. Be careful. This fragile democracy may come apart if it moves." In the eyes of the masters of an unjust system, a system perpetuated through fear, any creative impulse is a terrorist provocation. A responsible government is a static one; its duty is to leave large landholdings and the repressive apparatus intact, to forget the crimes of the dictatorship, and to pay promptly the interest on the foreign debt. The military left the country in ruins, and in ruins it remains. Meanwhile, old men water the flowers growing among the graves.

And the young? When the plan for collective castration was put into effect, they were its principal targets. The dictatorship tried to empty their minds along with the rest of them. The system that denies them jobs and forces them to leave operates against them—especially against them. Will they be as productive as they should be, as aggressive in word and deed against the system that denies them? Will they realize in time that the country cannot remain paralyzed if it is to remain democratic? Or will they disavow their youth and panic like ghosts when offered the oxygen of freedom? Will they surrender and resign themselves to a future of sterility and solitude that only ghosts could want for the country? Or will they work to transform it, albeit imperfectly, with a capacity for enthusiasm and sublime madness? Will Uruguay be a source of life or an elephant graveyard?

March 1986

Note

Also published in *Brecha* (Montevideo) March 7, 1986, 29. No reference was made there to its having been read during the symposium entitled "Repression, Exile, and Democracy: Uruguayan Culture."

Popular Music: Censorship and Repression

Leo Masliah

❂

I begin these comments on the censorship and repression of popular musicians under Uruguay's last military dictatorship by making it clear that they are in no way to be regarded as an exhaustive treatment of the subject, or even as a synthesis of the principal facts surrounding it. This essay is simply an exposition of certain information remaining in the memories of certain individuals who constituted a small part of the raw material upon which censorship was exercised during the years in question.

In the opinion of this author, the history of popular music under the dictatorship can be divided into two or three periods. The first represented an extension of the activities of popular musicians in the years immediately preceding the 1973 coup. In the case of musicians whose art characteristically involved direct and specific questioning of Uruguay's economic and political situation, this period was almost universally marked by exile, repression, or banning; they could neither sing, play, nor make new recordings, and broadcasting their previously recorded work was banned as well. But the bans in question were not issued simultaneously, nor were they equal in effect or scope.

The second period was marked by a resurgence of musical activity within the context of a new reality; life under the military dictatorship had ceased to be an accident and was regarded as normal—a normal annoyance, a normal cancer. By now all Uruguayans were aware of the mantle of green rot covering everything. No one could ignore it or be surprised by it. No one could sit around with arms crossed, lips pursed, and cheeks puffed out in protest, or lament the folly of those who planted or fertilized the rot with the virus Uruguayan society had harbored since the beginning of its century and a half of so-called independence. Musical activity during this second period was characterized both by the self-recognition that our songs encouraged, despite the rot that had polluted all 177,000 square kilometers of Uruguay's territory, and by the corresponding discovery that each of us could trample that rot within the modest space of about 150 square centimeters occupied by each foot.

Censorship was present throughout this entire period, but its nature varied and its application was characterized by a certain degree of incoherence; we cannot know for sure whether this was premeditated (though we think it was, we suspect it wasn't, etc.). It is entirely possible that the censors intended to play the same game with musicians and their audiences that guards at the Libertad prison played with the political prisoners. There is a parallel to be drawn between the latter's attempts to destroy their charges psychologically by creating and fostering certain vital expectations only to thwart them immediately thereafter, and the mixed messages sent repeatedly by the former: "I'll let you sing. No, I won't. Yes, I will. No, I'd better not. This concert is authorized. This one isn't. This one is. This one may be too, but let me think about it and tell you five minutes before it's scheduled to begin."

Finally, the last two years of the dictatorship may constitute a third period. During this time the music industry underwent certain small changes that were a consequence of its suddenly burgeoning interest in the local idiom known as *canto popular*. Now let's go back to the beginning. I'll repeat everything I just said; only this time around, I'll be more detailed and will add a few things that are somewhat independent of the others.

The history of censorship in Uruguay by no means begins with the 1973 coup. The first victim of censorship in Uruguay was none other than the Uruguayan people itself, as soon as the project known as the Oriental Republic of Uruguay became a reality. In fact, under the first Uruguayan constitution, no salaried servant or day laborer was allowed to vote. This is worth noting because although the situation has changed in this century, political power in Uruguay is still exercised by a privileged minority. The image of freedom traditionally associated with the erstwhile "Uruguay of the fat cows," or the "Switzerland of America," is only a partial view; it pertained only to certain social strata that were gradually stripped of their privileges over subsequent decades.

In the "Switzerland of America" it was considered so natural for certain social groups to be denied access to the country's prosperity that their notoriously marginal status sparked no social upheavals. In the same vein, it was very natural for a *payador*, or traveling musician, to have to request permission from the local authorities before he could sing; and it was those same authorities who decided when his performance could take place. By the 1940s it was also very natural, and not at all offensive to the refined sensibilities of a democratic Uruguay, that singer and *payador* Nolasco María Núñez should have been "exiled" from a number of towns in the interior because his words didn't sit well with the local police chiefs; that Carlos Molina should have been expelled from the city of Fray Bentos for the same reason; that the chief of police from a town called Batlle y Ordóñez in the department (state) of Lavalleja should have said, "As long as I'm chief of police around here, Carlos Molina will never sing again"; and that his counterpart from La Chilca should have remarked to Carlos Molina himself, "Singer, whore, what's the difference?"

Now let's go back to the more recent history of censorship, always keeping in mind that the ruckus raised by certain political groups over restrictions on their freedom of expression under the dictatorship and the calm silence of those same groups at other times in Uruguay's history, when the freedoms restricted weren't their own, are just two sides of the same coin. The June 1973 coup d'etat did in fact take place in Uruguay in 1973. But for a number of years before that political power had become more and more exclusively the prerogative of the president of the republic and his friends—so much so that already on March 26, 1971, in a speech delivered during the first large rally organized by the Frente Amplio, Doctor Crottogini (the Frente's vice presidential candidate) referred to the Pacheco government as a dictatorship. Restrictions on freedom of the press were numerous and ever present; we won't go into those. But returning to the field of popular music, we note that in 1972 (a year before the coup) singer Mercedes Sosa was expelled from Uruguay and forbidden to return; and that also in 1972, well-known singer Daniel Viglietti was arrested.

Viglietti's arrest was the beginning of a subtle political maneuver by means of which the government hoped to regain some of the popularity it had lost thanks to its growing collection of political prisoners, assassinated students, and methods of torture. A wave of rumors regarding alleged mistreatment accompanied Viglietti's arrest; it was claimed by some that his fingers had been broken, by others that his hands had been cut off, and so on. Several weeks later, the authorities brought Viglietti before TV cameras to show the viewing audience that his hands were still in one piece. Fortunately so was his mouth, and he managed to point out while answering the questions put to him that day that the treatment dealt him while in police custody was not necessarily the same treatment dealt other political detainees.

Following the coup, the military didn't seem to be in much of a hurry where censorship of popular music was concerned. Bans against musicians began very gradually and sometimes consisted merely of a phone call to radio stations and record shops stating that one singer's records could not be sold or broadcast, or that the radio station would have to take full responsibility for broadcasting songs by another. At other times the radio stations received written notices from the police; but the notices always emanated from some low-level official or department, never from the real ovens where such things were cooked up. That way there was soon a long list of banned musicians but no official public pronouncement concerning bans of any kind. Eager to preserve its image as a "civil military regime" in the eyes of international public opinion and Uruguay's less lucid citizens, the government approached censorship with a certain timidity, a reluctance to make it clear what was permitted and what was not as far as music was concerned. But that timidity didn't prevent, for example, the arrest in 1974 of the members of the group Camerata. Having been warned that their personal safety was in jeopardy, other performers of so-called protest songs chose to leave the country. In some cases this alone may have fostered an attitude of self-censorship; radio stations stopped broadcasting their music even though no corporal, sergeant, or police officer based nearby had communicated any orders to that effect. The only official public communiqué banning the broadcast and sale of records was issued in 1974 and referred to Los Olimareños, a duo extremely popular among the Uruguayan working classes. Then, in 1976, Braulio López, one of its members, was arrested and tortured in Argentina, after which he spent a year in prison.

The absence of official pronouncements regarding censorship and the military's reluctance to censor broadly and wholeheartedly stemmed from its desire to provide its actions with some semblance of legality. Coupled with a willingness to engage in brutal repression so as to root out all efforts at social, political, or trade union organizing deemed unfavorable to the dictatorship, it proved a very effective tool for the censors; it encouraged a degree of self-censorship which in many instances undoubtedly surpassed what might have been achieved by more direct means. A second superego was added to people's personalities. Rumors were rife—for example, accounts (erroneous or not) of people who had been taken off buses by secret agents in civilian dress and transferred to police stations or military barracks for making comments that were mildly critical of the regime.

The setting in which prior censorship of texts[1] was first applied was Carnival. As part of Uruguay's Carnival celebration, groups of humorists or parodists known as *murgas* circulate every day for a month among a large network of open-air stages located in different neighborhoods. Their repertoire is always based on events that have taken place during the previous year. In part because of content but above all because of the large size of the audiences addicted to this popular art form, the *murgas* were a prime target for the censors.

Prior censorship of *murga* texts became a veritable witch hunt through the dictionary, often extending way beyond the meaning of given words in their respective contexts. For example, one group that had worked up a comic sketch dealing with the period of Prohibition in the United States was forbidden to use the word *clandestine* to refer to the sale of alcoholic beverages, even though no double meaning was intended; that same group was forbidden to use the word *past* to describe the period preceding Prohibition. The word *pueblo,* which can mean either "people" or "town," could not be used even with the latter meaning. Captain Garfio, a character in a children's story, couldn't be referred to as "captain." Thus, the list of words transformed into antidictatorial references by means of some strange brand of witchcraft occupied a good part of the dictionary. And the Carnival lyricists might just as well have been students in a literary workshop taught by the police, who year after year reassigned them the difficult exercise of changing four or five words in each stanza of a text without changing the meter (because the music had already been rehearsed by the time they ruled on its feasibility or lack thereof) while at the same time attempting to preserve some meaning or—in cases involving a rare display of skill—the meaning originally intended. Police agents attended each performance, following along in the libretto word by word to make sure their corrections and suggestions for improvement had been duly incorporated. Any group found to be in error was duly admonished or suspended.

During the first Carnival seasons under the dictatorship, the groups known as Las Ranas, Araca la Cana, and La Soberana were definitively banned. Although some members of these groups were forbidden to appear again in public, others went on to form new groups, some of which walked a tightrope each year between saying and not saying what they wanted to, expressing and not expressing their opposition to the regime. But this was always the exception. The majority of the Carnival lyricists simply attached the filter of censorship to their pens and limited their subject matter to the most insignificant and ludicrous events of the year.

In the first years of the dictatorship, repression in the area of popular music didn't follow a geometrically coherent course. Perhaps its coherence derived from some other academic discipline. Two records by the group Patria Libre couldn't be issued as planned;[2] neither could a 1974 title by Los Olimareños. But while Aníbal Sampayo was a prisoner at Libertad, some of his records could still be found in record shops. In fact, the daughters of a number of military officers probably learned some of Sampayo's quasi-folkloric songs from their neighborhood guitar teachers (and practiced them at the top of their lungs at home) without anyone suspecting—not they, not their fathers, not even their teachers—that they were cultivating the art of a subversive and a political prisoner.

In 1975 Washington Carrasco's album *Antología de Canto Popular* came out. It contained little-known songs by well-known authors, all of whom had been banned in the aforementioned ways—Viglietti, Palacios, and Los Olimareños among others. Perhaps the fact that it was issued under a major label helped make that possible (the Patria Libre records had been cut by a smaller record company). Intentional or not, however, the confusion caused by this kind of arbitrariness fit in well with attempts to dismantle the political and cultural opposition in other areas. As regards the anthology in question, for example, one might have thought (or even remarked to friends), "Funny they let it come out; maybe Washington Carrasco has made a deal with the gorrillas." While in this case such a comment would undoubtedly have had very little to do with reality, the dictatorship did attempt on several occasions to win over a few "buffoons" in the music industry. And the years 1976 and 1977 saw the gradual proliferation of new places to perform popular music—albeit with lyrics that bore little resemblance to those of the protest songs of previous years. This apparent easing of censorship may have had to do with the same optimism that would underlie the military's decision to submit their fascist draft constitution to a plebiscite in 1980. Perhaps the same officers who believed that with the academic curriculum under their thumbs and all the authorized print and electronic media (except for a few radio stations) at their feet, they could generate a current of public opinion favorable to them also considered the increased availability of popular music to be, if not ideologically in tune with their interests, at least potentially neutral or inoffensive.

So it was that during those years—even as broadcasting of Joan Manuel Serrat's songs was prohibited in 1976 because of his participation in international festivals against the Uruguayan dictatorship; even as concert pianist Miguel Angel Estrella was refused permission to perform at the suggestion of the Argentine military, then tortured and imprisoned for two years in Uruguay; even as Osvaldo Pugliese's well-known tango band was detained at the airport and forced to return to Argentina in 1977 after all the seats for their concert had been sold—in a few *peñas* (clubs) and theaters there was a resurgence of a type of popular music which came to be referred to as *canto popular*. At first the *canto popular* movement was not subject to any prior censorship; the dictatorship was at the height of its power, and its confidence in people's capacity for self-censorship was very great. The decay of the system of education and the complicity of almost all the mass media seemed to provide sufficient cultural prophylaxis. And in any event, special envoys were dispatched to the clubs and theaters in search of anomalies or linguistic improprieties. Additionally, *canto popular* was a matter for small elites, and, in keeping with the principle that products should be judged according to their sales volume, it didn't warrant much attention.

In other settings, greater control was exercised over public performances. In downtown theaters, neighborhood sports clubs, and the common rooms of housing cooperatives (many of which were equipped with stages), the murky provision stating that any gathering of more than four people required a police permit was more strongly felt. There were many instances of failure to comply with this rule; a number of unauthorized performances took place, and sometimes the organizers subsequently received police citations demanding an explanation for this act of civic licentiousness. But in general, people did apply for permits—a process whose principal purpose was to deny participation to anyone figuring in the police files as having belonged to a leftist organization. At this level, membership in such an organization was of greater concern to the police than the content of songs, plays, and so on, although certainly the latter was far from a matter of total indifference.

Greeted with growing enthusiasm by audiences who saw it as an opportunity for self-reconciliation, little by little *canto popular* outgrew the limited settings of the *peñas* and small theaters. Soon concerts were held in provincial cities and in Montevideo, in sports clubs and other locales with seating for several thousand spectators and four or five policemen in disguise. But the burgeoning popularity of this musical trend, with its increasing numbers of fans and would-be performers, provoked concerns in some government circles. In addition to the musicians whose participation in these concerts had been announced and whose activities had been duly investigated, were there others whose names did not appear on the posters or in the publicity and whose past behavior might not be entirely to their liking? Beyond whatever their special envoys could discern in the piles of new song texts that were appearing, were there concepts that might be harmful to the health of the de facto regime? Might the funds collected during these concerts have as their final destination the hidden coffers of some leftist political party or other banned group (i.e., student organizations or trade unions)?

Accordingly, in 1979, *canto popular* was subjected to an ironclad system of prior censorship. Elements of the new system had been applied randomly in previous years, and always and without exception during Carnival season. Now, however, compliance became a prerequisite for any performance of this type except those which took place in theaters (perhaps because they involved smaller audiences). From 1981 on, prior censorship applied to concerts held in theaters as well. Anyone seeking a permit to hold a concert had to submit the following materials in triplicate:

—a letter addressed to the chief of police giving the name and date of the performance, the time it was scheduled to begin and end, the prices of tickets, and the name, address, age, marital status, and national identity card number of all participants;

—a form calling for seventeen categories of information, including all the details already supplied in the letter addressed to the chief of police (but received by heaven knows whom) plus the name of the person in charge of the performance, type of performance, type of publicity, cost of publicity, shop where the posters (if any) would be printed or method of production if handmade (detailing costs), name and other information pertaining to the master of ceremonies (if any), name of the company renting sound equipment, prices and details regarding financing of same, rental arrangements for the hall and number of tickets authorized by the municipal government, name of the person in charge of the refreshment stand (if any);

—the text of each song;

—a letter signed by the owner or manager of the hall stating that he was aware of plans for the concert, which was therefore not a fiction of the organizers' imagination.

Obviously, the application process was aimed more at creating difficulties than at providing oversight. It was required only for musical performances that fell under the heading of *canto popular*. Furthermore, while all the paperwork had to be submitted at least ten days before the scheduled date of the concert, the police's verdict might arrive five minutes before curtain time; that way, if permission to hold the concert was denied (as was often the case), the organizers would not be able to recover the money spent on publicity, transporting equipment, and rental of the hall. If the same concert was repeated on a date not anticipated and expressly mentioned in the letter to the chief of police, the entire application process had to be repeated from scratch. Furthermore, the three copies of each song text had to be presented even if the song had been approved for other concerts.

The censors were a bundle of surprises. They approved plans for some concerts in their entirety. They totally denied permission for others. In some cases, they approved certain acts and rejected others. Sometimes they rejected not performers but specific songs, even though these same songs might have been approved for other concerts. Judging by the behavior of the censors during the last two or three years of the dictatorship, by which time active opposition to the regime was widespread, the inventiveness of musicians had proved influential in police circles as well.

As a result, restrictions on concerts became more original and more imaginative. For example, instead of banning concerts by the duo of Eduardo Larbanois and Mario Carrero, only permission for Larbanois's participation was denied. Mario Carrero performed anyway, and the audience didn't demand reimbursement of half the price of their tickets. A similar case involved the Montresvideo Trio, one of whose members, Daniel Magnone, was banned. The other two sang without him, with a spotlight trained on an empty chair placed at their side. At some concerts they even played recordings made with Magnone's voice, since only his physical participation (not his voice) had been restricted; his records were sold freely and broadcast no less freely by the two or three radio stations interested in exercising their freedom. Another interesting tactic of the censors was to deny certain musicians permission to sing but not to play. Some musicians were systematically eliminated by the censors from lists of would-be performers—Eduardo Larbanois and Daniel Magnone, as already noted, and many others as well, including Carlos Benavides and Eduardo Darnauchans, both of whom were told that their banning was a consequence of their participation in an international youth festival held in East Berlin. As regards Benavides this might have been the case; however, Darnauchans had turned down the invitation to attend the festival. At the same time that they applied their long-range bans (which at this point did not include record sales or radio broadcasts), the censors engaged in a game of roulette, rewarding each of the rest of us with a denial or two whenever chance worked in our favor. In the later years of the dictatorship, some musicians used the fact that they had been censored as a juicy publicity ploy.

The following anecdote exemplifies the incoherent behavior of the censors, whose repressive tactics were often strikingly similar to those described by former prisoners at Libertad. Someone involved in plans for a *canto popular* concert went to the police to apply for the necessary permit. When the official who waited on that person examined the papers submitted, he politely observed that one of the seventeen pieces of information requested in the application form was missing. A few days later the applicant returned with the completed form and was waited on by a second official. Noting that the required note from the manager of the theater was not among the papers handed him, the latter proceeded to deliver a long-winded, angry, and overbearing sermon on the importance of complying strictly with all existing regulations. A few days later the applicant returned for a third time, now with all his papers in order. To his surprise, a third official accepted them without even checking to see whether anything was missing.

Another incoherent aspect of censorship was the discriminatory attitude exhibited by the censors toward Carnival texts, as opposed to those of *canto popular*. Whereas in Carnival texts the censors took the liberty of crossing out isolated words and recommending alternatives, in the *canto popular* texts they never did so; they either accepted or rejected each text as a whole. Perhaps an explanation for this lies in a particular kind of cultural stratification, characteristic of Uruguay and other Latin American countries, whereby only elements which derive in some sense from Western European models are deemed "truly respectable." Even within the area of popular music, a distinction is traditionally made between "cultured" or "learned" works, on the one hand, and, on the other, "intuitive" works—that is, works by people who are considered to lack culture by definition. In the eyes of the censors, the "learned" composer of popular music could be banned, imprisoned, and tortured; his work could be banned as well, but it was never to be treated with disrespect. However, the "intuitive" authors of Carnival texts were told to change this, that, and the other thing as if their work were comparable to that of an auto mechanic. Maybe it is, but if so, the same is true of the "learned" works the censors didn't dare touch.

Organizers of *canto popular* concerts outside Montevideo faced no major obstacles until around 1980. After that, censorship was even more severe in the interior than it was in Montevideo, and the police chiefs of a number of departments systematically denied all the requests presented to them. In the city of Colonia, habitual organizers of concerts were cited by the police and urged to make drastic changes in the way they spent their time. Paradoxically, for a number of years under the dictatorship an annual festival of *canto popular* was held in the city of Durazno under the auspices of the Ministry of Culture. In an attempt to add a few musicians to the regime's retinue of followers, certain soloists and groups were offered thousands of dollars in exchange for their participation. Some, like Washington Carrasco, had the decency to decline the offer. In 1979, another attempt was made to win us over in the context of a more general plan for the formation of so-called yellow (i.e., pro-military) unions. A few musicians sniffed around that one for a while, but in the end the plan failed.

Now a few words about how interpreters, composers, and organizers managed to survive censorship artistically. With some records issued around 1975, a decision was made to substitute the words *rights reserved* on the jacket for the traditional list of composers' names. But the following year, radio stations were ordered to announce the names of both composer and interpreter for everything they played. To be more precise, some radio stations were ordered to do so, because the more commercial ones never have been willing (and never will be) to sacrifice even a minute of their daily schedule that they could use for advertising. As one result of this, many listeners think the first movement of Mozart's Fortieth Symphony was written by Waldo de los Rios. Later on, other interpreters of texts by banned authors like Mario Benedetti listed themselves as authors of an "adapted" text without mentioning the author of the original. In some cases, songs were attributed to "anonymous authors"; that was how texts written by prisoners were first performed. For concerts held in neighborhood sports clubs, names were sometimes substituted for others on the application form if it was suspected that the artists scheduled to perform might be banned. In some cases this went unnoticed; in others, police citations resulted.

As to the texts themselves, some authors prepared special versions for the police, changing punctuation or the structure of certain lines so as to disguise the true meaning. Others preferred not to submit all the texts they intended to sing. Others did submit them all but hid "subversive" songs among a much larger number of sweet, innocent texts they had no intention of using. However, the censors paid less and less attention to the texts during the last couple of years of the dictatorship. By then, thanks to popular pressure and the existence of an organized opposition, enough verbal space had opened up so that singers no longer had to worry about choosing their words.

For this reason the poetic quality of canto popular began a downhill slide. But no; there was more to it than that. To some people, possibilities for employment in the area of canto popular became a potential source of the income long denied them because of the economic crisis. At the same time there were numerous attempts to capitalize as much as possible on the unique political climate that prevailed just before the elections. For example, it was really funny to see TV channels that had never shown the slightest interest in matters of cultural identity refer to Ruben Blades (in ads for one of his records) as "the most Latin American singer of them all." "Don't miss him," the ads ran. "Make a real commitment." Some opportunists made tapes privately at home and then tried to market them by claiming that the combative nature of the songs they contained made it impossible to sell them in record shops; prospective customers were referred to alternative places of sale.

Finally, we should keep in mind that the people the dictatorship employed as censors are still working for the police, their assignment for the moment being to keep an eye on other areas of activity in the society they are responsible for protecting. And one last comment, related to censorship but on a more subterranean level than the rest of our talk. Only good-for-nothings sing and play the guitar.[3]

March 1986

Notes

1   Prohibited by Article 29 of the Uruguayan Constitution, supposedly in effect at the time.
2   Only the producers of these records know if they were warned by the police not to issue them or if they themselves decided that this was an appropriate precautionary measure.
3   This final observation was distilled from popular wisdom by Carlos Molina, to whom I am indebted for much of the information contained in this essay. My thanks in this connection go as well to A. Percovich, R. Risso, E. Vidal, E. Riesco, and L. Hainintz, on the understanding that none of them had anything to do with my interpretations of their information.

On Suffering, Song, and White Horses
Mauricio Rosencof

✪

From mid-1973 to late 1985 Uruguay was officially a dictatorship. But by 1966 there were already political prisoners, and "extraofficially," the governments headed by Jorge Pacheco Areco and his successor, Juan María Bordaberry, were dictatorial in nature. Pacheco governed by decree, established a "death squad," closed newspapers, censored songs, and killed students. By 1972 Uruguayan prisons and barracks were filled to capacity. Torture, rape, and death were the order of the day even before the coup of February 9. This remained the state of affairs until March 1984.

It should be obvious that culture fared poorly under these conditions. With 40 percent of the national budget allocated to the police and the Armed Forces (a percentage that has not decreased by even 0.5 percent with the return of democracy), there was little money for public health (hospitals are still short of bandages) and still less for education. "When I hear the word *culture*," an expert in fascism once said, "I get out my gun." Among the 400,000 Uruguayans who were forced to emigrate were the country's most prominent writers—Mario Benedetti, Eduardo Galeano, Juan Carlos Onetti, and others. Technicians, teachers, and professionals swelled the ranks of the greatest exodus of intellectuals in Uruguayan history. Established writers who remained in Uruguay and new writers who emerged only to be censored and persecuted were able to publish very little.

But literature has a way of surviving, even behind bars. Uruguay holds the dubious record of having had the highest per capita ratio of political prisoners of any country in the world: during the years of the dictatorship, one out of every fifty-four Uruguayan citizens was detained. And it was precisely in the prisons that an extraordinary literary phenomenon occurred: professional writers (Miguel Angel Olivera, Jorge Torre, and Hiber Conteris among others) and others writing for the first time turned their suffering into song. The prisoners produced more fiction, poetry, and theater than was produced during the years of the dictatorship by all other Uruguayan writers together, both at home and in exile.

When that sizable body of prison literature is studied in its entirety (as I hope someday to do), it will undoubtedly prove to be of considerable testimonial value and will almost certainly reveal the existence of as yet undiscovered talents. Pending such a study, I will refer to my own experience, which is also that of thousands of comrades and compatriots who, under the most appalling conditions, sang a hymn to life.

> A coin of sunlight
> falls into my bank.
> It clinks on the walls,
> rouses the shadows.
> After endless years
> they'll only amount to a day.[1]

Some years ago, a newsreel told of the exploits of a French psychologist who had decided to see for herself what it was like to live alone at the bottom of a mine shaft for three weeks. The daring young scientist set up housekeeping with books and instruments, a tent, a sleeping bag. Three times a day, her potty was emptied and she was given food and water. At the entrance to the mine shaft, doctors, journalists, curious onlookers, and colleagues followed her fascinating adventure minute by minute. She knew that she would return to the surface after twenty days and that if things went badly, she could do so at any moment. She kept a journal about her experiment with solitude.

When I saw that newsreel, I wondered if it would be possible to write under such conditions; a poem, for example, or a play, or short stories. Could a person totally isolated and faced constantly with the need for survival occupy his mind for even a few moments in literary creation? Today, after having lived through something similar—except that instead of twenty voluntary days I spent over eleven years in forced isolation—I have an answer to that question based on experience. And though lacking the scientific background of my colleague in confinement, I too can offer some insight into the effects of extreme solitude and limited horizons on ordinary human beings, who, even in subhuman conditions, can turn suffering into song.

Beginning in September 1973, after nine consecutive months of torture, I was imprisoned in the dungeons of different barracks along with eight companions; we remained in that situation until April 1984. Cut off from the outside world and held in isolation cells, in all those years we never saw one another's faces. It was only during thirty-minute visits which took place monthly, and to which we were brought hooded and handcuffed, permanently surrounded by armed guards and dogs, that we saw the faces of our children from behind a double iron grill.

Our habitat was a space about three feet by six, with no furniture. We could take three short steps on a diagonal followed by a half turn, like rats in a cage, assuming that we were permitted to walk at all. We sometimes spent almost a year seated on little wooden benches, with our backs to the door and our faces to the wall. At other times we were forced to stand motionless, unable to sit or walk. A fellow prisoner spent four years like that. His feet bled.

> They blocked out the light,
> they censored the windows,
> silenced the human voice,
> everything was nothing.
> But they were there,
> outside.
> They stayed there.[2]

Generally, we were forbidden to have reading matter. Exceptionally, we were permitted one book a month, on limited aspects of Uruguayan history, always censored. We had no other means of distraction. Our lack of information was so great that we learned of the death of Salvador Allende three years after it occurred.

We found out about the Nicaraguan revolution thanks to the resourcefulness for which prisoners are justly famous; in one of his *Exemplary Novels,* Miguel de Cervantes described our seventeenth-century counterparts as "capable of schemes not to be found on the map." In this case, we had set up a "news service" in the bathroom—a kind of Associated Press which worked as follows: the guards would take us there once a day, hooded and shackled; they kept their eyes on us at all times, of course—even in the bathroom, which was the same one used by the troops. As toilet paper they used pieces of old newspaper that sometimes stuck to the sides of the basin, thus affording us glimpses of the day's events. It was on one of those filthy remnants that we learned about the overthrow of the Somoza dictatorship.

They also made a practice of denying us water. But sometimes we had a tin can for *aguas menores,*[3] as Sancho Panza used to say. This was doubly a relief. For one thing, we didn't have to wait for our single daily trip to the bathroom and spend hours thinking about nothing but urinating while our vital organs switched places and our bladders supplanted our brains. For another, we could recycle our urine, letting it stand until the salts sank to the bottom and the liquid came to room temperature. It was to be drunk at that moment and no other, because at that point it was bearable; in an hour it would be nauseating.

> There was no color
> none at all.
> The days colorless
> none at all
> and one time,
> I don't know
> maybe it wasn't
> but I saw it
> and it was.
> The empty rind
> blinked
> in a corner,
> was a color.
> Orange,
>   it seemed.[4]

As time passed, we forgot what colors were. Birds were but a vague recollection, and the sun a myth. Day and night were identical: an exasperating light bulb shone on us like a frenzied eye, even as we slept fitfully. At night they would awaken us every hour. Beatings were frequent; food was scarce; hope was slim.

Our lives hung by a thread. We had been informed that at any moment they might shoot us and claim that we had tried to escape. A few days after our imprisonment in the barracks, the director of the prison from which we had been taken declared, "Since we didn't kill them when they were captured, let's drive them mad." Two of the nine went crazy; a third died. As in Dante's *Inferno,* we who entered there were to relinquish all hope.

And yet, that gentle butterfly that fluttered its wings at the bottom of Pandora's box never abandoned us. So it was that there appeared—brief, unwritten, etched in memory—the first poems that transfigured our hostile, empty universe:

> I'm not sure I'll finish
>   the poem I'm writing you.
> One afternoon
>   the unpunctuated word

> will stay
>   suspended,
> its letters
>   nothing but cold ink.
> But you
>   will know my love
> even in the unwritten
>   verse.[5]

In the years to come, memory would be one of the mainstays of my existence. During my initial and final months in captivity at the men's penitentiary, and occasionally in the barracks, whenever it was deemed politically wise to "rehabilitate" us lest the death of one or more of us bring unwanted publicity, I was permitted writing materials and even a typewriter. But my usual practice was to commit my work to memory in the knowledge that sooner or later, chance or personal resourcefulness would work in my favor.

Since the soldiers knew I was a writer, they often asked me to compose love letters for their mistresses or acrostics for their children. These could be traded for a cigarette, a hard-boiled egg, or the stub of a pencil that I then used to scribble a poem or a fragment of a play on a piece of cigarette paper—to be hidden in a hem of the underwear I sent home every few weeks for laundering. Once my family failed to discover what I had hidden and my undershirt came back from the wash with inkstains on it. They "interrogated" me, convinced that I had smuggled out a subversive message; but it was only a love poem. Paradoxically, this forced reliance on memory ensured the survival of much of my work; once memorized, it was beyond the reach of my jailers.

Early one morning I heard rhythmic tapping on the other side of the wall. Someone wanted to communicate with me, another prisoner like myself, El Ñato. Seated on the floor, back-to-back with a wall between us, we reinvented Morse code. One tap for each letter of the alphabet was the key. For ten years, whenever our cells were adjoining (they moved us to different barracks every three or four months), we held a running conversation about political and literary matters, our plans, our lives, childhood memories, the weather, our ailments, the day's events: "Today they didn't give me my bread," or "I had to shit in my cell." One morning El Ñato mentioned that while he wasn't sure what day it was, he thought it was somewhere around his birthday. The next day, I sent him these verses in Morse code:

> And if this were
> my last poem,
> sad and subversive,
> threadbare but whole,
> only
>   one word
>   would I write:
>   *Compañero.*[6]

In my youth, I thought and read a great deal about the relationship of fantasy to reality. Rambling conversations at café tables about a philosophical matter so central to literature provided numerous incentives for further speculation. For example, when a play was described as "realistic" or when the critic wanted to be more "precise" and said "social realism," I wondered where the boundaries were—the lines separating reality from fiction that permitted an educated man (or at least a well-informed one) to affirm that this or that text fell within the limits of reality or transcended them. I never found such statements very convincing, and I was even less convinced by hard-and-fast classifications with their respective general laws.

Take, for example, the idea that a work of art has form and content. I think a work of art has to be seen as a whole, even if critics insist on dissecting it. In school I learned that the human body was divided into head, torso, and extremities. I believed that for a long time. Why did it take me so long to realize that the human body is a single entity? Why did it take me so long to realize that a masterpiece is a single body? And to realize that fantasy and reality don't represent a dichotomy but a unified whole, how long did that take?

Because in the last analysis it's impossible to write the biography of a human being without examining his dreams. If the history of José Artigas, the father of Uruguay's independence, were limited to an account of his battles and declarations, his literary image would be as cold as his metallic equestrian statue. For Artigas was defeated in battle, but the ideals for which he fought continue to inspire us over a century later. Thus, the essence of Artigas, the motor for his actions, must be sought in his dreams.

The same can be said for all of us. In the human brain—at least in mine—images take priority over ideas. For that reason, writers have to translate conventional symbols and general concepts into images. When a person thinks of his country, he doesn't see a flag or a coat of arms. Rather his nostalgia for his homeland calls forth memories of a path he walked as a child, the field where he played soccer, the stream where he used to fish.

You know what, my child,
dreams
have a strange way of moving.
Early in the morning
they slip
through the window
in smoky pirouettes.
They flap their wings,
thrive,
peck at crumbs
drink from the cisterns.
They're little cotton threads,
springtime vagabonds.
It's really wonderful
to go after them
on those clear days
when the wind's mischievous.
Don't you think so?
Let's go,
put on your little orange dress,
my child.
We've got to catch up with them.
The two of us
running,
hand in hand.[7]

Once when a journalist asked me what I thought freedom was, I remembered something my daughter had whispered shyly during a visit: "Daddy, when will we be able to go to the park together for some ice cream?" For me from then on, freedom was the image of a walk with my little girl, hand in hand among the trees, laughing and relishing a scoop of vanilla and one of chocolate. This image was so vivid that sometimes my teeth ached from the cold.

In daily life we scarcely notice, much less try to make sense of, the many situations in which real or actual contact with another person or an object is charged with intangible or imaginary elements. When a mother dresses her son and combs his hair before sending him to school, for example, she dresses and combs the hair of a physical child, but also of the man she hopes he will be or the infant she held in her arms.

> My face was
> in a cave,
> there was nothing but
> shadow and fear.
> Disembodied voices
> asked questions;
> I knew.
> But there was
> the gaze of a child,
> and the gaze of a friend,
> and something sorrowful,
> and the silence
> became human
> in my throat.[8]

My daughter, who was about five years old when I was arrested, used to send me drawings in prison. Those drawings contained trees that appeared to spring from the surface of the earth. She drew what she saw. But a couple of years later, in school, she learned about germination in that classic experiment involving a seed placed in a jar in wet cotton. The seed sprouted and put down roots. From then on, her drawings changed. She continued to make trees, but now they had roots. My daughter drew not only what she saw, but also what she imagined.

In his prologue to the Spanish edition of the extraordinary poems of Rabindranath Tagore, José Ortega y Gasset evokes Socrates preparing to die, hemlock in hand, as he says farewell to his disciples. "Why do you weep?" he asks them. "Death is not to be feared." And a disciple replies, "Master, you taught us that within each one of us there is a child, the child we were. That is who has to be convinced that he should not fear death."

Our common sense tells us that man cannot live by dreams alone—that at mealtime, bread is bread. And I agree. But I have known men (and I count myself among them) who without daily dreams would not have survived. It simply would not have been possible to live (remain alive) for over eleven years without seeing a human face, entombed in burial niches three feet by six, far from the sun and the trees, with nothing to do except watch spiders spin their webs meticulously in the corners, if we hadn't filled our tombs every day with dreams. Because every day, from God knows where, our children arrived to play with us and our wives and girlfriends to embrace us. How often I stretched out on the concrete floor when the guards weren't looking to take a sunbath on the beach! And you can't imagine what a nuisance it was to have so many bathers go by and cover me with sand. Annoyed at them, I would go for a cold drink. But then the problem was hiding the bottle, because my cell was searched daily even though it contained nothing but ghosts. If a soldier were to find a bottle there, he might interrogate me. "Where did you get the money to buy a Coca-Cola?" Hiding the objects acquired in my fantasies became quite a chore.

> My cell is a winepress
> filled with white grapes.
> I trample them endlessly
> the wine of the intoxicating
> sun distilling
> a hope.[9]

Sometimes, however, the line we crossed was that of sanity and we wandered into the swamps of madness. A fellow prisoner who, though unseen, was with me throughout my odyssey could sometimes be heard screaming: "Guard! Give me water! Take me to the bathroom! I can't stand it any more!" That *compañero* sank deeper and deeper into madness day by day, month by month, year by year. Like the rest of us, he was under permanent surveillance—that is, a soldier watched him day and night. Eventually, this provoked a psychotic reaction. Since he talked to himself, he thought a tape recorder had been hidden in his cell to record his words. The tape recorder that didn't exist began to hum. In his imagination it was controlled from the guards' room, and to harass him, the soldiers would turn up the volume so that the humming was a constant source of irritation. It kept him from sleeping, causing such sharp pain in his ears that sometimes he screamed in desperation. Somehow, he managed to acquire a little seashell that he could bite on to keep from screaming and breaking the silence of the grave, because screaming was forbidden and brought severe penalties. So I wonder about that tape recorder that wasn't real. Or was it? There are things that exist because we believe in them. And perhaps God is in that category. In the end, reality is everything.

> You're
> no
> kitten
> I tell him.
> You're a sandal,

a lifeless
thing.
He mulls it over.
And you?
he asks.[10]

One of our strategies for survival was to trap our ghosts, to get control of
them before they got control of us. Here I drew heavily on my expertise as a
writer, while others who weren't writers became writers; without knowing it,
they too trapped their ghosts by tying them to a novelistic, dramatic, or poetic
structure. So it was that an entire literature emerged from the dungeons. In a
play I wrote while in prison, *Antonio's Jacket*,[11] I transferred to an old spinster
some of my thoughts and feelings at the time.

In this play, two elderly sisters live in an old, ramshackle house, cut off
from the outside world which they fear. One of them, Magdalena, is visited
by her young lover, Antonio. Together Antonio and Magdalena stroll between pieces of furniture arranged to form a "footpath," as if they were in a
park surrounded by willows; they go sailing on a sofa, their boat.

The second woman, Consuelo, provokes a jealous quarrel with her sister.
And during that quarrel it is revealed that the two spinsters have invented
another being to keep the house safe from intruders. To make him credible
they have hung a man's jacket on the coatrack in the front hall. But Antonio
doesn't exist. Or does he? Magdalena declares that if there is a jacket, there
must be a man for that jacket. As is later revealed, she needs Antonio to share
with him the romance she had never shared with anyone—that is, her life
depends on a love affair that in "reality" never took place.

In the course of the play, when a delivery boy comes from the grocery store
with their order, it is further revealed that in fact the sisters are not two but
one: a single old woman, Consuelo, mad with loneliness, who has built
herself a world she can live in. Given her upbringing, she cannot even
imagine taking a lover. And so she invents both Antonio and another being,
the sister who is a projection of her repressed personality, so that the latter
can share with Antonio the romance Consuelo dares not even dream about.
When reality intrudes in the form of an impudent delivery boy, the dreams
that sustain her crumble. In her delirium, she imagines that Antonio and
Magdalena have run away together. The delivery boy leaves and Consuelo is
left alone, seemingly destroyed.

But once more she recovers through fantasy. The ghosts she has invented
reappear. Antonio comes on stage and takes the "other woman" (Magdalena)

by the hand, while Magdalena raises her skirts to climb into their boat. Antonio climbs onto the sofa with her and begins to row slowly, while his lover trails her fingers through the water, leaving a wake behind. In other words, Consuelo lives not by bread alone, by the contents of her grocery order. She lives also, and primarily, by her dreams, which to survive must be no less real than a can of sardines.

But there was yet another matter of great importance to us. Our objective was survival. To survive, we had to resist. And there is just one way to resist—with dignity. Even if a man is treated like a dog, he doesn't have to bark. That is why for the most part, the works I wrote in prison reaffirm basic human values.

Whenever I have compared notes with other prisoners, the first question to emerge has been, "How were we able to withstand torture?" A black friend gave me the key. "How could I do otherwise," he said, "when I thought of my brother Lumumba?" Others in the same situation have felt the presence of their fathers or of Ché. A Protestant minister told me he thought about God.

As for me, I had a readily available source of inspiration in the numerous relatives whose weekly letters my parents awaited anxiously—until 1940, when the postman began passing our house without stopping. It was only after World War II ended that my father learned of his mother's death. My paternal grandmother had been killed with an axe by the SS while refusing to turn over her two infant grandchildren. In my mother's family, nobody survived and a number died resisting. And so whenever it was my turn to be tortured, I thought about my daughter, but also about my relatives who fell in the Warsaw ghetto or fighting with the partisans in the forests of Poland, or who perished in the gas chambers and crematoria of Auschwitz.

> I feel
> in my bones
> the bones
> of those
> who once were.
> In me,
> they are
> skeletons,
> we are
> what I am,
> I am
> those who were
> yesterday.[12]

The point is that man carries within him a witness who observes and judges his deeds, his actions. For the Christian that witness is Jesus, and for the guerrilla, an exemplary revolutionary. Even a child at play senses the presence of a maternal witness who, though physically absent, keeps him mindful of the basis for all morality, the difference between good and evil. In other words, none of us, however alone we may be, is ever really alone. And in the most extreme situations, we are saved by our human condition, the cornerstone of which is not a particular ideology but rather a sense of solidarity: the strength of character which prevents us from transferring the weight of the crosses we bear to the shoulders of our brothers and sisters. That notion is common to Christians, Marxists, atheists, and Buddhists precisely because it lies at the heart of our shared humanity.

> I've built a castle in the air
> Why have you torn it down?
> Tower by tower I've rebuilt it;
> shaped it with volutes
> and the flags flew, like music.
> You can destroy it;
> I'll only start again.[13]

In prison we were denied the opportunity that is available to others every day. Ours was a defeat with no possibility of salvation. But no creature can bear a state of permanent frustration; faced with one, the brain struggles—however quixotically—if not to change reality, at least to reinterpret it. This is exemplified in the story of the optimistic and imaginative child who on Christmas morning runs to see what Santa Claus has brought and finds a pile of animal droppings next to his stocking. Nothing else. But the child runs happily to meet his parents shouting, "Mommy, Daddy, Santa Claus left me a white horse."

Strained to the limit by the conditions of my imprisonment, my brain decreed that victory and defeat were only illusions and that neither really existed. Because for one thing, our perceived victories are better viewed as mere stopping places on a longer road. Once attained, for example, civil liberties must be consolidated and then extended. How far? To infinity, in the sense that inquiries into the nature of social justice lead to more philosophical speculation, and ultimately to consideration of that thing called free will. In the same vein, our defeats are only temporary setbacks if we choose to struggle on toward a goal. So it is that I have often asked, Was Jesus a defeated man when Christian ideals continue to inspire us? And was Artigas, whose thought remains current to the present day?

From the perspective of my newly regained freedom, I remain convinced of the validity of what I understood then: defeat—and, of course, victory—are indeed illusions. For me, that is the message so poignantly conveyed in the reaction of the child who sees the white horse. We are only truly defeated when we, our children, or our children's children relinquish our most cherished ideals. If we hold on to them, our horses too can be white.

March 1986

Notes

1   "Una moneda de sol / penetra en mi alcancía. / Tintinea en las paredes, / despabila las sombras. / Al cabo de los años / sumarán un día." From Mauricio Rosencof, *Conversaciones con la alpargata* (Montevideo: Arca, 1985); also contains *Desde la ventana*. Poetic texts cited are from this work or from Rosencof, *Canciones para alegrar a una niña* (Montevideo: Ediciones Uno, 1985), and were translated by Louise B. Popkin and Julia H. Ackerman [TRANS.].

2   "Tapiaron la luz, / censuraron las ventanas, / la voz fue disuelta, / todo era nada. / Pero estaban ellos, / afuera. / Allí estaban."

3   A euphemism for urine, literally, "lesser waters" [TRANS.].

4   "No había color / no había. / Los días sin color / no había / y una vez, / no sé, / tal vez no fuera / pero lo ví / y fue. / Parpadeó / en un rincón / la cáscara vacía, / era un color. / Naranja, / parecía."

5   "Nunca sé si acabaré / el verso que te escribo. / Una tarde / quedará suspensa / la palabra / que no cierra el punto, / y serán sus letras / sólo tinta fría. / Pero tú / comprenderás mi amor / aún en el verso / que no diga."

6   "Y si este fuera / mi último poema, / raído pero entero, / tan sólo / una palabra / escribiría: / Compañero."

7   "Sabe una costa, hijita, / los sueños / tienen un andar extraño. / Por las madrugadas / se deslizan / en piruetas de humo / por las ventanas. / Aletean, / viven, / picotean migas, / beben en los aljibes. / Son hilitos de algodón, / vagabundos de primavera. / Es muy lindo / salirlos a buscar / en días claros / de viento travieso / ¿Verdad que sí? / Vamos, / póngase el vestidito naranja, / hijita. / Los tenemos que alcanzar. / Corriendo / los dos, / y de la mano."

8   "Tenía el rostro / en una cueva, / todo era sombra / y miedo. / Voces sin cuerpo / preguntaban; / sabía. / Pero había / una mirada niña / y otra compañera / y algo triste, / y el silencio / se hizo hombre / en la garganta."

9   "Mi celda es un lagar / con uvas blancas. / Las piso sin cesar / y el vino del sol / destila embriagador / una esperanza."

10   "Vos / no sos / gato / le digo. / Sos / alpargata, / algo / sin vida. / Medita. / ¿Y vos? / me dice."

11   Mauricio Rosencof, *El saco de Antonio* (Montevideo: Librosur, 1985); also contains *Los caballos* and *El combate del establo* [TRANS.].

12   "Siento / en mis huesos / los huesos / de aquellos / que fueron. / En mí / esqueletos / son, / somos / lo que soy, / soy / los que ayer / fueron."

13   "He construido un castillo en el aire. / ¿Por qué lo has derribado? / Lo he vuelto a hacer; / torre a torre he modelado con volutas / y las banderas flamearon, musicales. / Puedes voltearlo: / volveré a empezar."

The Repression of Uruguayan Culture: A Response to the People's Response to the Crisis

Ruben Yáñez

⟡

When the Pacheco government first applied the Medidas Prontas de Seguridad (Prompt Security Measures) in 1968, the Uruguayan Constitution was virtually reduced to one of its articles and democracy in Uruguay began to deteriorate. The process culminated on June 27, 1973, with the establishment of a fascist dictatorship which governed the country—within a framework of unprecedented repression—until March 1, 1985. This fascist regime coincided geographically and chronologically with others of a similar nature all over the Southern Cone (the region of Latin America which includes Brazil, Bolivia, Uruguay, Chile, and Argentina). Fashioned according to the formulas contained in the Doctrine of National Security, a cornerstone of U.S. imperialism, they were created as a means of preserving U.S. hegemony on that part of the continent. This is clear from U.S. documents of the period.

Such "fascist" dictatorships are very different from those usually found in Latin America. Traditionally, Latin American dictatorships have been instruments of continuity for feudal colonial exploitation during the stage of the multinationals; as such they have served to maintain society, its structure, and its institutions in an appropriately backward state. On the other hand, the fascist dictatorships were a repressive response to historical processes that were relatively advanced, as concerns both the unequal development of capitalism on the continent and the social and institutional consequences of that development, which have tended to strengthen and unify popular and national forces.

A fascist dictatorship differs from a traditional one in that traditional dictatorships characteristically attempt to maintain a historical backwardness deemed advantageous to both the empire of the day (be it Spanish,

French, English, Dutch, or North American) and a local oligarchy, which derives its own benefits from the arrangement and does the empire's bidding. On the other hand, a fascist dictatorship attempts to contain and turn back the historical process, lest national and popular hegemony displace the existing imperialistic and oligarchic hegemony. At the same time, the development of capitalism in its imperialist phase has been deforming in and of itself. By subordinating economic concerns and concerns about production to those of finance, it has transformed the relationship between imperial metropolis and neocolony and given to international finance capital (which has underwritten the empire's warmongering and international policing functions) a key role in the creation of fascist dictatorships in Latin America—or in the conversion of traditional dictatorships into fascist dictatorships, as has occurred in Paraguay and Central America.

The dictatorships established during the 1970s in Latin America fell within the broad strategy of U.S. imperialism at the end of the Second World War. In the ideological context of the cold war, and faced with a new set of international alignments (this time involving not just a socialist nation but a socialist option), the empire sought to tighten and consolidate its control over Latin America. By updating the Monroe Doctrine and adding new rhetoric about "ideological frontiers," the United States rose to its position as self-styled interpreter of Latin American reality. By framing its internal contradictions always in terms of a confrontation between communism and democracy or East and West, it provided itself with justification for both direct military intervention and more or less covert political manipulation.

Otherwise unable to win the ideological round despite its control over, and virtual monopoly of, the mass media (large subsidiary TV networks, radio stations, and the press), and in the absence of mass parties prepared to use violence in support of its hegemony, imperialism found the manpower it needed for this operation in the armed forces of Latin America. Beginning in the late 1940s with the signing of the Rio Pact (Interamerican Treaty of Reciprocal Assistance), the United States created what Latin Americans refer to as a "multinational corporation of armies"; in the name of imperialism, in country after country the army became an occupying force vis-à-vis its own people. In this process, which intensified once the triumph of the Cuban revolution paved the way for a new stage in the historical process, the Latin American armed forces were persuaded to redefine their philosophy and their roles. Henceforth, they would think not in terms of national sovereignty but of national security, understanding the latter to be the security of imperialist interests enmeshed with those of the small national oligarchies. The volume of crimes committed in defense of those interests over the last decade in Latin America is matched only by the barbaric genocide of the Conquest. That genocide was carried out in the name of God; nowadays—as Bolívar predicted in 1829, already anticipating the establishment of U.S. hegemony over the rest of America—genocide is carried out in the name of freedom.

Why, then, did the so-called civil military dictatorship—really fascist in nature—suddenly appear in Uruguay? Because the hegemony of the forces that defend its antinational and antipopular interests was threatened. Who posed a threat to their hegemony? The organized popular sectors: proletariat, middle sectors, trade union groups, small and medium-sized producers, businessmen, students, and so on. Beginning in the late 1950s, those groups gradually elaborated alternative proposals for dealing with the progressively more critical situation of the productive apparatus in a limited and unjust international market. Hoping to contain the spiral of foreign indebtedness that today has become such an impossible burden for the country and the continent, they countered the oligarchy's program of surrender of economic and financial control to the International Monetary Fund with a truly national program of their own. With the trade unions and growing sectors of public opinion solidly behind them, they formed a movement that eventually spawned the political entity known as the Frente Amplio. The strong showing of the Frente in the 1971 national elections did away with the traditional two-party system, which, though theoretically multiclass, had in practice been hegemonized over the preceding decades by the most regressive sectors in the country. It was this new political map of Uruguay with its vital outlook, repressed from the moment of its conception in the late 1960s, which the fascist coup of 1973 sought abruptly to obliterate.

The Role of Culture in This Process

Understanding the role of culture in all this requires some discussion of the historical development and context of Uruguayan cultural practice. As in the rest of Latin America, the development of culture in Uruguay implies contradiction, synthesis, mutual rejection, and conflict between what we can refer to broadly as autochthonous cultural elements and those of the European colonizers; but in Uruguay, this clash has taken a somewhat atypical form. In the first place, what we Uruguayans consider autochthonous is not really indigenous given the qualitative and quantitative weaknesses associated with indigenous life in our territory. Qualitatively speaking, in comparison with rich and complex indigenous cultures such as those of Peru, Central America, or Mexico, those of our indigenous groups were markedly elemental and historically backward. With no writing system and only crude artifacts of unfired clay and cut stone, they could hardly compare with the rich culture of the Spanish conquerors and colonizers, however backward the latter may themselves have been vis-à-vis the achievements of the metropolis. Quantitatively speaking, our indigenous groups were numerically sparse and had no permanent settlements. If we add to this the decimation of their ranks when the Artiguista army in which they fought was annihilated, and their extermination in 1832 by Uruguay's first constitutional president, Fructuoso Rivera, it seems obvious that as such, they had little to do with subsequent national development. This made Uruguay a country of immigrants, where autochthonous elements (or elements of popular origin) are the result of complex syntheses between the concrete human and cultural realities of both colonization and subsequent waves of immigration, all set in a new physical and human landscape.

Uruguay is thus unique as regards the components of its popular culture. Furthermore, our history has contributed to a Europeanized and scantly Latin American image of our own cultural practice. For that reason, the norms for that practice have derived primarily from European, and not Latin American, models. This is true of our referents, forms, and means of expression. As regards content, Uruguayan culture has oscillated between two antithetical ideals, which in the past were perceived either as corresponding to different moments in a single process or as contemporaneous and contradictory: on the one hand, the national, unique, peculiarly Uruguayan; on the other, the universal, general, abstract, and cosmopolitan. In either case, these two complementary categories were considered irreconcilably opposed, with the cosmopolitan frequently favored over the national and held to be more significant, more prestigious.

If we apply a democratic standard (with its dual components of freedom and extension), then the culture established in Artigas's day—and reinforced by José Pedro Varela's educational reform, with its social-scientific foundation and objective of empowerment for the exercise of democratic sovereignty—found its first great organic expression in the Generation of 1900. This occurred at the moment when possibilities for a modern Uruguay first took shape. With British imperialism as the country's link to the world market, with a new synthesis appearing at a new level to overcome the principal material and ideological contradictions of nineteenth-century feudalism, and without breaking its real ties of dependence, Uruguay took a qualitative step toward a modernity which, for those very reasons, was rooted firmly in ideology and only precariously in reality.

That generation was characterized by both Parnassian universalism and a concern for things Latin American and national. Rodó the Hellenist also held forth harshly on the U.S. invasion of Mexico; protesting U.S. involvement in the artificial creation of Panama in order to hegemonize the future canal, like José Martí he characterized Latin America as "our America." It is in that will to be Latin American—in that framework of incipient Latin American awareness, at once eager for identity, ignorant of our multiple realities, and rooted in the harsh Balkanization of the subcontinent—that we should view the rehabilitation of José Artigas as a national hero, the recovery of national unity around his great and reviled figure in Eduardo Acevedo's work of historical reconstruction and in the literary contributions of Juan Zorrilla de San Martín and Eduardo Acevedo Díaz. At the same time, our peculiar national blend of tradition and immigratory overlay was treated critically using the modern analytical tools of anarchism and socialism in the work of such playwrights as Florencio Sánchez and Ernesto Herrera, who laid the foundations for our national theater.

The national-reformist program elaborated by the Uruguayan bourgeoisie was marked by its authors' highly optimistic vision of the country's future. Equipped with the formal elements of the metropolis and many of its contents, the Generation of 1900 joined the bourgeoisie in their optimism, even as it turned a critical eye on Uruguayan reality and the great contradictions of America. Prosperous times justified such an attitude, which began to generate the self-delusion of a uniquely Uruguayan "essence." As the country exported sizable quantities of food, hides, and wool to a Europe in the throes of the First World War, the tensions of cultural practice involving Uruguayan reality eased considerably. But the first major crisis of capitalism, the stock market crash of 1929, raised the first major question concerning the national-reformist model and interrupted the democratic process with the establishment of the first dictatorship in 1933.

During the 1930s, definitions of Uruguayan culture entered a second phase. Though still lacking appropriately organic forms of expression, the outlines of that culture took shape around its defense of the Spanish Republic and its resistance to both rising fascism in Europe and the dictatorship at home. The Second World War, planned as a means of survival by international financial capital and the international market at a cost of over forty million lives, again brought prosperity to Uruguay. As an exporter of meat, hides, and wool to the peoples at war, the country found respite from national tensions and regained its democratic institutions. In the area of universal ideological themes, the war years brought certain gains for Uruguayan cultural practice as well—for example, a greater familiarity with the Soviet Union, until then the object of a virtual information blackout. At the same time, with attention focused on the great themes of the metropolis, it was sometimes thought that Uruguay lacked subject matter capable of generating meaningful culture of its own.

The early postwar period saw the beginning of the process that has marked Uruguayan life and culture to the present day. For Latin America, the postwar years brought the first signs of the empire's dramatic response to an altered balance of power. A socialist camp had now appeared, as had whole continents of colonies which, with the European metropolises weakened, prepared to undertake broad liberation struggles. Also in evidence on the horizon were the increasingly problematical deformities of a capitalist system which, in its imperialist phase, was subject to ever more frequent and deeper crises. Faced with this situation, the peoples of the world could be expected to go on attempting to sever their ties of dependence.

Basically, the postwar period meant four things for Latin America. In material terms, it meant the transformation of the world market so as to establish an international economic order progressively unfavorable to its interests; this would render obsolete all of Latin America's traditional systems of production. In ideological terms, it meant the inclusion of Latin America in the empire's cold war, McCarthyite, ideological frontiers campaign; this would enable the United States to interpret as clashes between democracy and international communism the objective internal contradictions of each Latin American country held captive by the crisis. In institutional terms, it meant the rehabilitation of the Monroe Doctrine and the creation of the Organization of American States as an instrument of political control. Once referred to by Latin Americans as the "Ministry of Colonies," that organization would henceforth regulate all international relationships on the subcontinent. Finally, in strategic terms, it meant the redefinition of Latin America as a security zone for the United States; within the framework of the Interamerican Treaty of Reciprocal Assistance, virtually all Latin American armed forces would be trained ideologically as defenders of U.S. security, and technically as specialists in domestic counterinsurgency.

At first, the ideology of the cold war caught on in broad sectors of Latin American and Uruguayan culture, not because these sectors identified with the objectives of imperialism but as a practical consequence of their apoliticism and presumed neutrality in the capitalist-socialist debate. But beginning in the late 1950s and early 1960s, two factors began to affect Uruguayan culture: on the one hand, the worsening of the internal crisis, which the dominant sectors sought to resolve even as they attempted to ensure their continued hegemony through still greater dependence on finance capital and international banking; on the other, the example in Latin America of the Cuban revolution and what it implied about taking a stand vis-à-vis the general situation on the subcontinent. And as an alternative to the program of the Uruguayan oligarchy, another national program began to take shape. Growing out of a deeply unified trade union movement, it rallied large sectors of the middle strata, intellectuals, students, and a wide array of social organizations as well.

This initiative gradually won the support of the broadest, most representative, and most prestigious sectors of culture, the University and scientific research. And a broad movement formed around a cultural and educational program aimed at substituting a more scientific image of the country and its possibilities for an increasingly discredited "official" image. By the early 1970s, virtually no manifestation of artistic or scientific culture of any significance remained outside that great popular movement. Uruguayan culture had spoken with a single voice that cut across party lines, and unified action on behalf of culture was a reality, notwithstanding the attacks of the fascists who would soon seize power.

Early Forms of Repression

From June 13, 1968, on, Uruguay lived under a state of exception. On that day the Medidas Prontas de Seguridad were imposed and the Uruguayan Constitution was reduced to the discretionary use of one of the clauses in its Article 168. In the economic sphere, this set the stage for the rapid plundering of the country, since representatives of international banking were put in charge of the key ministries. In the political sphere, it meant a campaign to discredit democracy, thus justifying the future fascist coup. The institutional and social destabilization undertaken by President Jorge Pacheco Areco (later to be the dictatorship's ambassador to the United States) and continued by President Juan María Bordaberry until the coup was marked by the following facts, among others:

—freedom of movement for fascist paramilitary and vigilante groups that assassinated citizens, bombed hundreds of private homes and political, trade union, and cultural institutions with high-powered explosives, and attacked scores of educational institutions, all for the sole purpose of creating chaos and "justifying" a crackdown;

—the administrative detention of citizens with no constitutional guarantees and the institutionalized practice of torture;

—assassinations of citizens by the repressive apparatus as acts of political provocation intended to generate an artificial climate of chaos;

—repeated clashes between the different branches of government in violation of the principle of separation of powers, with decrees issued by the executive branch in matters under parliamentary jurisdiction and reiterated presidential vetos of decisions by the legislature and the judiciary;

—repeated temporary or definitive shutdowns of the opposition press;

—nonpayment of funds authorized in the national budget for the University, in an attempt to starve that institution into submission;

—disregard for the constitutionally guaranteed autonomy of the secondary school system, which suffered interventions and even the suspension of its services;

—dismissal of the first several hundred teachers from the primary and secondary schools, and from higher education;

—official promulgation of a law regulating primary and secondary education, which undermined the best traditions of the school system and placed it under the direct control of the executive branch (public and professional opinion was overwhelmingly opposed to this law, which was enacted without the benefit of a parliamentary debate);

—declaration of a state of internal war, by means of which the task of governing the country was entrusted to the Armed Forces;

—initial attempts at censorship and the direct control of culture through measures such as a municipal decree prohibiting the adaptation of classic dramatic texts (this decree was a response to the critical thrust and great popular appeal of recent productions based on Lope's *Fuenteovejuna,* Cervantes' *Numancia,* and Sophocles' *Antigone*).

From 1968 to 1973, with widespread popular support, the most diverse and prestigious forms of Uruguayan culture definitively joined forces to struggle against the breakdown of democracy and in favor of the national solutions issued by the great People's Congress held in Uruguay in 1965.

The Institutionalization of Repression with the June 1973 Coup

Fascism in Uruguay operated very differently from fascism in Chile. Instead of mounting a homogeneous offensive against the people and attacking the entire spectrum of instruments evolved in the struggle for a national program, the Uruguayan fascists attacked progressively and selectively. Their immediate objectives were (1) to dismantle the trade unions, which had responded to the coup by occupying their workplaces and declaring a general strike; (2) the prohibition of all political activity and illegalization of its leftist expressions; (3) intervention of the entire system of education; and (4) the systematic repression of culture, its creators, and its organizations. In hopes of creating a climate favorable to their efforts, in late 1973 and early 1974 the dictatorship published two supplements (entitled "Documents I" and "Documents II") to the few newspapers which had not been shut down; in these, the University and cultural production were portrayed as allies of "subversion." The following are some results of the attack on culture which the dictatorship attempted in this way to justify.

—A sizable number of cultural figures and teachers were jailed and tortured.

—The fascists' hate for the University (expressed in numerous confrontations and rooted in that institution's national and popular orientation) increased with the results of the 1973 university elections, in which the dictatorship's representatives were defeated by almost 90 percent; this led the authorities to decree the military intervention of the University. The rector and the deans of the faculties were arrested, hundreds of the most qualified teachers and researchers were dismissed, institutes were forced to close for lack of teaching personnel, and many former university authorities were imprisoned. The academic level declined precipitously, and unprecedented corruption surrounded the appointment of new teachers. Intervention also brought the militarization of the University and the expulsion and imprisonment of hundreds of students; at the same time, limits were placed on admissions, blocking access to the University for thousands of secondary school graduates.

—On the primary and secondary levels, thousands of highly qualified teachers were fired as well. The curriculum was reformed on the basis of criteria succinctly characterized by reference to one item in the history program: while the Middle Ages was referred to as a "paradigm of civilization," other topics corresponding to subsequent periods (e.g., the Renaissance, modern science, the secularization of culture, the French Revolution) appeared under the heading "The Decline of Christian Civilization in the West." The practice of filling teaching positions by means of academic competitions was abolished, and positions in history, philosophy, and literature departments were declared "sensitive"—that is, set aside for political appointees. All contemporary Uruguayan authors and many foreign authors were eliminated from the curriculum. Parents were threatened with economic or criminal sanctions should their children be found guilty of "attacks on security."

—Incompetent members of the fascist groups were appointed to direct or teach in educational institutions.

—The entire collection of the journal La Paz, edited by the founder of

Uruguayan education, José Pedro Varela, was removed from the archives of the National Library because in one of its issues there was a reference to the existence of Marx.

—A decree was issued prohibiting the inscription of sentences uttered by Artigas in the mausoleum built by the dictatorship to house his ashes.

—The figure of Colonel Lorenzo Latorre, a military dictator from the last century, was rehabilitated, and attendance at public festivities held in his honor was made mandatory for all children and adolescents enrolled in school.

—A policy was instituted whereby anyone aspiring to a teaching or administrative position in the public or private schools had to have authorization from the Joint Chiefs of Staff; all citizens were classified into categories A, B, and C, according to their ideological views.

—The Uruguayan church came under repeated attack and numerous priests were arrested and tortured. The archbishop of Montevideo (along with Amnesty International, the United Nations, and even the U.S. Senate) was labeled "communist" by the dictatorship, and a number of Christian publications were shut down.

—Hundreds of thousands of books taken from public and private libraries and bookstores were destroyed. These included not just classic and modern works on Marxism but also books by antifascist Uruguayan and Latin American authors. Possession of a book of this nature was grounds for prosecution, torture, and imprisonment.

—Publishing houses like Pueblos Unidos and art galleries like Trilce were shut down, and the entire contents of their storerooms were destroyed.

—Tens of thousands of records were confiscated from record stores and radio stations and destroyed; these featured works by contemporary composers and performers, both Uruguayan and foreign.

—The archives of the Cinemateca del Tercer Mundo were dismantled and to a large extent destroyed; and the distributor for the Soviet film production company, Artkino Pictures, was shut down.

—The sale and circulation of works by a number of Uruguayan authors was prohibited. These included Francisco Espínola, Enrique Amorím, Mario Benedetti, Mauricio Rosencof, Eduardo Galeano, Juan Carlos Onetti, Idea Vilariño, Alfredo Gravina, and others.

—A number of popular singers were forbidden to perform in Uruguay, and their recorded works were banned both from the media and from record shops. Among them were Uruguayans Alfredo Zitarrosa, Daniel Viglietti, Los Olimareños, Numa Moraes, and Yamandú Palacios, as well as foreigners like Mercedes Sosa, Jorge Cafrune, and Joan Manuel Serrat.

—Uruguayan actors and directors, including Concepción Zorrilla, Villanueva Cosse, and Ruben Yáñez, could not work inside the country; neither could foreigners like Inda Ledesma.

—The theater company El Galpón, extremely active in Uruguayan theater and culture since 1949, was declared illegal. At the same time, many of its members were imprisoned and tortured, and all its assets were seized; these included two fully equipped theaters, its school, and the most complete archives then in existence of the previous thirty years of Uruguayan theater.

—Monuments were destroyed, among them *La niña y la paloma* (*Child with Dove*), by sculptor Armando González; this work, which had won the grand prize for sculpture in the 1951 Salón Nacional (the most important national competition), had come to be regarded as a symbol of peace.

—State cultural institutions such as the Comedia Nacional and the National Symphony suffered artistically and technically as a result of the ideological persecution of their members.

—Centers created for the purpose of fostering cultural relations between Uruguayans and other peoples were closed and their assets seized—for example, the Uruguayan-Soviet Cultural Institute and Bertolt Brecht House, which served as a cultural link to the German Democratic Republic.

In listing these assaults by fascism upon the best in Uruguayan education and culture, I have made no attempt to be exhaustive. The dictatorship did a lot of damage, and recovery will be an arduous process. At the same time, we can take comfort from the fact that not once in twelve years did Uruguayan culture provide an instrument for recruiting young people to the fascists' pseudoideology. Its essential elements remained intact, rooted as they were in the popular struggle that preceded the dictatorship and popular forms of resistance to it.

The Place of Culture in the Struggle against the Uruguayan Dictatorship

As occurred in all sectors of national life targeted for destruction by the dictatorship, Uruguayan culture was forced to choose between three modes of existence: prison, exile, and the public sphere inside the country, all similarly beset with difficulties. Generally speaking, the most prestigious cultural figures were removed from domestic public life, since they went to prison or into exile. Nevertheless, a few remained in the country and, while frequently obliged to carry on their activities in secret, provided a living link for the new generations which gained access to cultural practice during the years of the dictatorship. In the interest of brevity, I will limit my account of the battle waged by Uruguayan culture against fascism and on behalf of democracy to the following summary:

—The unity generated at the heart of cultural practice, in the years preceding the dictatorship and in the struggle on behalf of liberation, proved unbreakable; thus, the fascists' intentions notwithstanding, we can speak of a single culture in prison, on the outside, and in exile.

—The ongoing clearheadedness of Uruguayan culture with respect to its place in the historical process kept cultural workers from attempting openly to transcend the limits placed by the dictatorship on public freedoms (even to the extent that such action might have been tolerated in exchange for "good behavior"). Whether in prison, on the outside, or in exile, antifascist cultural practice was governed by the principle of historical incidence that Brecht defined in the following terms in his 1935 speech to the Congress of Anti-Fascist Writers: "Let us take pity on culture, but let us first take pity on humanity! Culture is safe only if men are safe. Let us not be dragged into claiming that men exist for culture and not culture for men! . . . Comrades, let us reflect upon the roots of the evil!"

This collective attitude toward cultural practice meant that prison was not just a place for vital human solidarity in response to the most immediate, violent, and permanent presence of repression. It also offered opportunities for cultural creation and study: the former with the most limited of resources for arts and crafts, poetry, or family correspondence; the latter by making of the memory of each *compañero* a substitute for a forbidden book. As a result (aside from the obvious costs of the dictatorship in terms of eventual psychological unbalance), to a great extent the political prisoners who came out of prison were even more intact as human beings and intellectuals than when they entered. This made them a symbol of life for those on the outside and was reflected in the massive celebration that accompanied their return to freedom.

—Public artistic practice became a gathering place for broad sectors of the Uruguayan people who could not meet in other social settings. In this way, it countered the dictatorship's attempts to increase individual isolation. At the same time, by inventing a language full of fresh contents and forms, it translated into public terms a long-standing covert dialogue between the creator and his audience about the key prospects for the historical struggle. Thus, a new semantic level appeared, complete with formal demands, that would be irreversibly incorporated into future artistic practice.

—Cultural workers in exile did not simply turn their backs on Uruguay and avail themselves of whatever freedom existed in their host countries for cultural activities unrelated to the struggle against the dictatorship. Instead, they worked in their foreign settings to denounce the denial of freedom to Uruguayans, developing practices aimed at heightening international awareness on behalf of democratic recovery.

Since I spent a major part of this period in exile as a member of El Galpón, it seems appropriate for me to end my essay with part of the report which that company presented to the First Conference of Exiled Theater Groups, held in Stockholm in 1983. In my view, this excerpt summarizes the principal objectives of Uruguayan culture in exile:

> Given its objectives, and with the respect due all national situations, El Galpón will not become a Mexican theater group. Topics specific to Mexican reality are the affair of the Mexican people and the organizations Mexicans create to deal with them. El Galpón is an instrument in exile of the Uruguayan people, with all the potential for rich cultural exchange which this implies and taking into account our common struggle against imperialism, but attentive as well to internationalist norms governing the struggle to reconquer and deepen democracy in Latin America. [Accordingly, our goals are as follows]:
>
> 1. to foster an exchange with Mexican culture and the different manifestations of Latin American culture, not in terms of an aseptic apoliticism but in the practice demanded by our agreed upon objectives;
>
> 2. to direct the results of our cultural practice as El Galpón toward the great current of solidarity with the Uruguayan people and other Latin American peoples struggling against fascism, as well as toward the processes of antifascist unity;
>
> 3. to contribute to the unity and prestige of Uruguayan culture in exile by means of common actions, and to be a factor in its dissemination;
>
> 4. to act in close collaboration with the mass organizations created by the Uruguayan people in its advance and in its struggle against fascism (the Convención Nacional de Trabajadores, the Federación de Estudiantes, Jornadas de la Cultura,[1] the International Solidarity Movement), and to contribute to the growing political unity of the Uruguayan people against the dictatorship, as expressed through concrete organizations;
>
> 5. to disseminate the highest values and richest traditions of Uruguayan culture now under attack by fascism—and especially, the most recent expressions of that culture within the country—to the extent that this is possible without compromising the safety of its creators;
>
> 6. to bring together members of the Uruguayan exile community, and particularly its young people, around topics pertinent to Uruguayan reality and culture, thus helping to create an attitude favorable to return;

7. to implement this theatrical and cultural policy in the understanding that the solidarity it awakens, and the opportunities for development offered us by Mexico and the rest of Latin America, do not derive basically from the intrinsic virtues of our artistic practice as El Galpón, but rather from the heroic struggle of the Uruguayan people against fascism;

8. to be vehicles for, and an expression of, the traditional solidarity of the Uruguayan people with other Latin American peoples struggling for democracy, self-determination, and the breaking of ties of dependence, as is presently the case in Nicaragua.

Once democracy was restored, return from exile was possible, and the freedom of the prisoners was a reality, fulfillment of these objectives enabled us to participate in a dynamic process of synthesis of the essential experiences of the three sectors into which the dictatorship divided Uruguayan culture spatially. There is no doubt that this synthesis has presented new problems. These are a matter not of contradiction but of our ability to respond to a new challenge: making Uruguayan culture a factor in the construction of a democracy which, by helping to eliminate the real sources of dependence that gave rise to fascism, will prevent that scourge from recurring in the future.

This challenge will involve extending culture to the masses on the broadest scale possible; deepening its popular and national meaning through the qualitative and quantitative conquest of a social space, thus reducing the influence of the products of cultural imperialism; and increasing our knowledge of, and exchanges with, Latin American culture, recognizing that in this connection and dialectically, exile was a positive experience as well as a tragedy. The dictatorship brought out both our uniqueness as Uruguayans and our identity as Latin Americans in economic, strategic, and political terms. It is up to us to take on this latter identity more fully in the cultural realm, without that implying either regionalist reductions or false contradictions with cultural expressions originating outside the continent.

March 1986

Note

1   A culture festival held annually in exile over a period of several years, beginning in 1977 [TRANS.].

The Power of Memory and the Memory of Power

Carina Perelli

❂

Collective Memory, the Basis of Identity

From time immemorial, humankind has concerned itself with memory, delving into it, attempting to understand and capture this weave, that texture or shading. Interest in the problem has not been purely academic. While theorizing on the subject can be traced from an early date to its culmination in the work of such authors as Alfred Schutz, Peter Berger and Thomas Luckmann, William James, and Henry Bergson (among others), the concern with memory, its control, its manipulation, and its preservation is present in all human groupings. For many peoples, to safeguard memory is to safeguard identity.[1] In the same vein, a primary concern of the political community in its struggle to impose a "good order" has always been to elaborate its own version of a particular historical event: to shape it, naturalize it, impose it as truth.[2] Thus, memory is the object of conflict. In fact, it is essentially a political weapon, even though its functions are not limited to that. What, then, are the functions that make memory part of the "infrastructure" of culture, of intersubjectively constructed "reality"? Why is it so important? What is there about it that in cases of occupation or extreme domination leads the dominant groups inexorably to attempt to eradicate the collective memory of their subjects?[3] Why is it that only the memory of the strong—of the "winners"—is recorded in what we refer to as history? Why does nobody talk about whatever it is that makes memory so essential?

Memory is both key and context, frame and contents, form and substance. Memory is sometimes *cronos*, but also *kairós*.[4] Memory is both silence and multiple versions. William James defined it correctly as a "chiaroscuro," with zones of light and darkness, with sharp, clear areas and blurred shapes.

Neither the sharpness, the shadows, nor the blurred outlines are gratuitous; neither are the light and darkness, the silence, and the conflicting accounts.

Collective memory frames our knowledge of the commonplace, defining the commonplace in contrast to the extraordinary. In reality, it sets the limits of the "possible" for a given society; thus, it is intertextuality. However, memory does not simply set limits. As an essential component of the "good order," it also establishes some of the contents of the possible, the probable, the desirable in that society, thus constituting the power mechanism of a particular historical moment.[5] It is in this sense that events are reinterpreted, situations are highlighted, personalities are given prominence, and versions are constructed.

Memory is also an interpretive key to a given reality. By delimiting the possible (constructing or reconstructing some of its central contents), memory functions, on the one hand, as a selector, and, on the other, as a qualifier, not just of past situations but of present or at least recent ones. These multiple functions of memory are, then, the ones that condense into it part of the "fringes of meaning."[6] For this reason, collective memory is one of the limits, perhaps one of the strongest, imposed on the abundance of possible social identities present in any human grouping. Memory "signifies" the past and the present—the present in the light of the past, the past in the light of the present, in constant interaction—as well as the position of the subject (whether individual or collective) in relation to past and present, itself and others, time and space. In short, what we know as "ego" and "alter," "I," "you," "we," and "they" would all be inconceivable without memory. And what makes memory especially political is the fact that "friend" can only be distinguished from "enemy"[7] within the coordinates of the memory of a human grouping.

Apart from that, the individual personal memory of each subject, and the memory of that microcosm which is constituted by small groups, find a frame of reference and a voice in collective memory. No personal biography is conceivable without a minimum of referents from collective memory, which in that case act as significative landmarks. Throughout the process whereby the identities of individual and collective subjects are constructed, then, there is a hierarchy of control at work whose importance should not be minimized. In that sense, memory can be regarded as the foundational myth which underlies the gathering together of identities, a myth continuously updated through both their constant re-creation and the possession or appropriation of past and future by present thought.[8] To use a now-classic definition, we can say that memory encompasses the three spheres that constitute the world we live in as we know it: the real, the symbolic, and the imaginary.[9]

Memory is based on lived experiences. But the echos of those experiences—
the distortions, the emotional shading that surrounds them, the ghosts, the
guilt feelings, the projections, the displacements—are memory as well.
Memory is therefore both real and imaginary. It is also symbolic in the
sense that "birth into language and the utilization of symbols effect a disjunc-
tion between a lived experience and the sign which replaces it."[10] That is,
symbols, the conveyors of meaning which condense and attest to lived
experience, are the crux of memory because memory is meaning—duration,
continuity, interruption as meaning; tradition and innovation as meaning;
belonging and strangeness as meaning. To manipulate memory, in other
words, is to manipulate meaning.

Memory and Power

Who controls memory controls power—the evocative power of Proust's
madeleine, but also the power to emphasize and to displace, to define and to
reconstitute referents as such; a power that shapes identity by defining its
models and resignifying times, spaces, and episodes; the power to obliterate
possible alternative versions of the past, present, and future; the power to
"sediment," or consolidate, distortion in the form of myth, ethos, and ritual.
To manipulate memory is to act upon a chiaroscuro: to resignify, naturalize,
conceal, illuminate, anathemize, exalt, forget.

We all manipulate memory on different levels. At the level of individual
biography, our emotions, our ghosts, our feelings of guilt, our frustrations all
give rise to distortion. In our interactions, we manipulate memory through
the presentation of self[11]—an entire program, a version per se. We manipulate it at the group level (consciously or unconsciously) in response to
interests, in defense of positions, as we struggle against the "other." We
manipulate it through the platforms of organizations, through propaganda, in
the struggle for hegemony. And we manipulate it at the level of a whole
society in that "construction of intersubjective reality" which serves to validate discourse, legitimate the participants, generate a "we."[12] But how can
memory be manipulated, managed, controlled? In what sphere—the real,
the symbolic, or the imaginary—can those actions be undertaken with some
hope of success?

Let us first examine that vast category known as "reality." Although Josef
Goebbels sustained that "a lie repeated a thousand times becomes a truth," it
seems difficult to radically alter the collective memory of a lived event, all the
more so if the event is a recent one. It is indeed possible to distort events that
occurred in what we might call the "past-past," or what we normally think of

as history.[13] It is also possible to lie about events that occur in distant places, beyond the immediate reality and knowledge of the subject.[14] On the other hand, lying about experiences which are still fresh and, above all, shared seems unlikely to be effective, unless the events considered are very peripheral to the lived experience of the subject.

If we think about Uruguay, and more specifically about the "present-past" of the dictatorship, we can see how difficult it would be to alter reality substantially in matters of importance to most of the collective subjects involved. For example, no one could claim, hoping for any degree of credibility among Uruguayans, that as a people we rose up in arms against the dictatorship. No one can oppose collective memory to that degree. There were no barricades in Uruguay; no actors took up the conventional weapons of war. In the sort of contest of "resistibility" that began soon after the return to democracy, those attempting to distort reality to their own advantage have only been able to do so to the extent that the distortion has some basis in reality. In other words, it is possible to increase the number of resisters in one's own group, diminish the ranks of other groups in the resistance, emphasize some facts, silence others, color certain events, or define them as more "resistant." But the credibility of such operations will depend on the response they elicit in the collective memory of the subjects. A construction that is radically different from reality is only possible with the acquiescence and collaboration of the members of a given society, or at least a sizable part of it. Thus to modify the real in the sense of manipulating memory is only possible if the manipulation is credible and, as a corollary, provided it does not violate society's keys to credibility.

If we now consider the manipulation of collective memory in relation to the social imaginary (and by social imaginary I mean that magma of meanings which operate as a referent in the symbolic sphere of a society), we must take certain factors into account. The imaginary is, perhaps, a society's ultimate key to interpretation and credibility. In a sense it is even stronger than reality itself, since it shapes the very concept of reality that prevails in a given society.[15] The imaginary is closely tied to collective memory, for which it provides a frame of reference and from which it derives some of its contents. It is the conjunction of imaginary and reminiscence that gives rise to the societal myths which, in turn, act upon reality. The social imaginary, however, requires mediation, which occurs through the symbolic sphere that functions in a particular society at a given historical moment. We can therefore ask whether the imaginary can be manipulated as such, or whether modifications of the imaginary occur naturally, either through "sedimentation" over long periods of time or over a shorter period, when sudden breaks occur in the sphere of reality.

In this connection, it can be argued that in Uruguay before the dictatorship, the prevailing societal myths were the products of a continuous history without sudden changes, one which, through the interrelationship of reality and imaginary, regarded itself as the result of a self-fulfilling "prophecy" or foundational myth. The 1973 coup and the dictatorship that followed would then have affected that imaginary, radically altering some of the foundational myths. Despite the almost total lack of research on the subject, it seems clear that there were substantial changes in some of the meanings that function as referents in the symbolic sphere; however, it is not possible to say whether those changes will be permanent. Thus, and simply by way of example, we can say that the myth of security, of "good order," that prevailed in Uruguay despite the numerous traumas provoked by changes in the economy, growing inequities, and the country's increasing ability to absorb tensions has gradually been replaced (perhaps from the late 1960s on) by an almost opposite myth of insecurity and instability, of a society "sitting on a powder keg." A Uruguay that claimed that "worse was really better," since things would only improve once the country had "hit bottom," now beats its breast, often with some of the best-known champions of that previous position acting as spokesmen—Mario Benedetti, for example, who declares that "worse is still worse."

The fact is that so radical a change in the imaginary appears to reflect a negative view of earlier myths, which nevertheless have not been totally relinquished.[16] On a symbolic level, this dissonance might be on the way to resolving itself in two directions. As believers in restoration, some hold that twelve years of dictatorship were simply a *década infame*, an accident in the life of the country, and that now "everything is just as it used to be."[17] For others, an important means of absorbing tensions is nostalgia; that is, a recollection of emotional and essentially subjective elements which acknowledges what we lived through but seeks refuge in the past-past and makes it the key to understanding the present. Both these processes occur in the symbolic sphere, where mediation between the imaginary and reality occurs.

Let us see, then, what modifications can be introduced into the symbolic universe[18] and what manipulations have, in fact, been attempted in the case of Uruguay. Obviously, to speak of the symbolic sphere is to speak of the formulation of collective representations. These representations are transmitted essentially through language, which mediates between lived experience and the memory of that experience. In that form they are as "real" as "reality" itself, despite the fact that their referent is the imaginary. The symbolic comprises a sociohistorical sphere which can be modified, manipulated, and controlled. At the same time, it is the constant actualization of myth by means of ritual, and the intersubjective generation of new myths—or new elements of old myths—through interaction, on the one hand, and discursive practice, on the other. The symbolic sphere, then, consists of shared, recognized, structured meanings, representations which we both partake of and refine. Therefore, its manipulation involves one or more of the processes known as *resignification, emphasis, displacement, projection,* and *silencing.*

The manipulation of a collective representation through *resignification* implies modification not of events themselves but of the "fringes of meaning" that surround them so that they will be interpreted in a different way. In the case of Uruguay, a number of such manipulations have occurred. First, as already observed, was the attempt to portray the period 1973–84 as a *década infame* and the dictatorship as a barbaric "accident," alien to the Uruguayan "we."[19] Another example of resignification occurred when certain of the actors characterized the defeat of a movement, or of the opposition as a whole, as a victory, alleging that triumph and defeat are one and the same since what really matters is the path taken.[20] Yet a third example of this type of manipulation occurred when the PIT-CNT took stock of the actions of its member unions during the 1973 general strike. While the sector led by the Communist party labeled the general strike "heroic," portraying it as the first step in the struggle of the Uruguayan people against the dictatorship and allowing for no discussion on this point, the Partido por la Victoria del Pueblo argued that the workers' movement had fallen short of its responsibility by ending the strike and giving in to the enemy instead of seeking actively to provoke a popular insurrection.[21] A fourth and final example of resignification can be found in the opposite camp, in the governing Colorado party. Faced with the undeniable fact that the return to democracy was negotiated (i.e., that it had been "granted" by the military and for some was therefore limited), the Colorados, chief negotiators of the Club Naval Accord, attempted to cast that situation in a favorable light by making it the virtual basis for their electoral campaign; their 1985 slogan was "Un Cambio en Paz" ("A Peaceful Change").

Closely related to resignification as a means of manipulating collective representations, the mechanism we call *emphasis* functions by highlighting certain events or aspects of events while leaving others in the shadows. Take, for example, the matter of responsibility for the collapse of democratic institutions in 1973. In a discourse in which emphasis is clearly placed on certain real events, unfailingly provoked by their enemies, while other events for which they themselves are responsible are shrouded in silence,[22] all sectors of the opposition (from the most conservative to the most revolutionary) lay the blame for what happened elsewhere. Curiously enough, of all the actors involved in the complicated political maneuvering that led up to the coup, only the military has not made use of that procedure. Obviously, emphasis is closely tied to another of these mechanisms, *silencing*. The silencing of certain facts is an attempt not just to deny reality but to make it vanish. Both mechanisms play with that chiaroscuro quality which James attributed to collective memory. In Uruguay, certain episodes involving the military have been manipulated through silencing. Even though so much of what happened during the dictatorship has come to light, the military still covers some of its actions (its conversations with the Tupamaros, for example) with an ominous mantle of presumed indifference.

Another common mechanism is *displacement,* in which an attempt is made to minimize the importance of certain events or players; in this sense, it is frequently used in conjunction with silencing and emphasis. For the period and place which concern us, one of the purest cases of displacement involves a shift in the way resistance was portrayed: from an "underground" struggle carried on by identifiable activists to a generalized, undifferentiated, and thus very global sort of process. That is, using this procedure the meaning of the attribute "resistance"—possibly of great relevance for the upcoming contest of political interests—was diluted, thus weakening the group or groups, generation or generations that really resisted the dictatorship more or less actively. This was a way of neutralizing potentially dangerous contenders in the "new-old" political and cultural community of a redemocratized Uruguay while allowing the rest of the population to satisfy some of its yearnings.

It is precisely as a satisfier of yearnings, expectations, repressed desires, fears, and guilt feelings that the mechanism known as *projection* functions. Projection manipulates the representations of collective memory by using the distortions and unconscious aspects of individual representations to benefit one or more actors who seek to reappropriate that memory for their own benefit.

Obviously, all these mechanisms function at some time, and the manipulation of collective memory as a whole involves all of them. It is difficult to find pure examples in which only one such mechanism is at work. In fact, what we call collective memory is probably just a condensation of the products of all these mechanisms applied to reality with a view to modifying or maintaining the social imaginary.

Who Controls the Past . . .

When the past is resignified so as to "explain" (and thus legitimate) the present, what is at stake is more than the here and now. To the extent that the resignification bears on the projects and possibilities of the actors in question, a dispute over the past is a struggle for control of the future. Although— as psychologists, linguists, and philosophers have pointed out—plays on words are never simply plays on words, in this context their inherently deceptive quality is enhanced so that potentially they are plays for power as well. Resignification of a term thus becomes a political problem. This is the case as regards numerous manipulations of the key concept "resistance" which accompanied the end of the dictatorship in Uruguay.

In our old-new democracy, *resistance* and related words (*resister, to resist,* etc.), as well as their antonyms (chiefly *collaboration, collaborator, collaborationist, to collaborate*), are used in two ways. The first limits use of the term *resistance* to a small nucleus of individuals who, individually or collectively, (a) undertook certain types of concrete actions, (b) of a clandestine nature, (c) against the dictatorship, thus (d) risking concrete sanctions. This definition does not take into account effectiveness of execution, the success of those actions, or the motivation of the actors in carrying them out. Here, in other words, a quality is attributed to an individual or group without regard for the results of the action or the process generated; the resultant "democratic opening" is neither a necessary nor a sufficient condition for affirming or denying the existence of actors belonging to the category "resisters." Instead, just the four conditions enumerated above delineate the global profile of a multiparty group shaped by its direct participation in and experience of both clandestine and everyday life under the dictatorship, a group whose common characteristics and aspirations are more pronounced than their differences. The fact of belonging to that group colors both their projects for the future (whether formulated or not) and their aspirations (whether explicit or not) to a share of power; it also determines which qualities they think they should possess and what means they consider legitimate for holding on to power.

The second way of using the word applies it more broadly to all situations that can be described by synonyms of *resistance*. Here, the term *resister* designates all those who, individually or collectively, (a) made it through the dictatorship, (b) were not won over to the other side, and (c) opposed the actions of the regime with the force of their inertia. *To resist* thus no longer refers to the realization of concrete, objective acts of a "positive" nature, but rather alludes to indeterminate, subjective circumstances of a "negative" nature, whose intentionality is, at best, difficult to assess. If we go by this definition, not being won over, disassociating oneself from the regime, surviving without "permitting" invasion of the *sancta sanctorum* of the self is the most salient feature of resistance. Additionally, possession of that attribute by a particular group cannot occur independently of the result of its action or the process it generates because the latter is what resignifies the past; the return to democracy is a necessary (and even sufficient) condition for claiming that there was a mass of resisters in Uruguay.

On a purely objective and academic level, resolving the conflict of meaning in favor of one or the other of these usages involves asking ourselves what the dictatorial regime really intended with its project of domination: to convince or to command obedience? If we accept the first hypothesis and assume that the regime intended to convince, then the majority of Uruguayans were resisters, and the antonym, *collaborationist,* is only applicable to the relatively small group of individuals who undertook positive and intentional actions in support of the regime. On the other hand, if we opt for the second hypothesis and assume that the regime intended to command obedience, then at some point—or throughout the whole process—all Uruguayans collaborated with the regime to the extent that they helped maintain it (and legitimate it, as Max Weber correctly taught) by submitting to its norms. Inasmuch as external compliance with the regime's definition of *normality* accompanied all forms of clandestine struggle in Uruguay, this is true even of those individuals or groups to which the narrower meaning of the term *resister* applies. In this second case, collaboration becomes a matter of degree rather than of kind, and we have to distinguish between collaborators and collaborationists.

However, the problem of definition is less academic than it is political. For in this case, choosing one definition of the term *resister* over the other would imply the following: (1) a play for power, or power games, since to choose one definition is to choose one strategy and one power group in the context of an elitist struggle in which the contenders (whether overtly or covertly) are the old leadership of the various political groups, often removed from the scene by imprisonment or exile, and the new subjects, born of "blackouts," rules and regulations, and the terrors of the "front line"; (2) games of pretense—complex masquerades staged by the players for and toward an audience, but also played by and with the audience in a two-way process whereby the latter is both the reason for the game and an actor in and accomplice to it; (3) balancing games on the part of society itself in its search for convincingly self-justifying versions of the events in question, for ways of absolving or condemning the faithful for their sin of apathy, and of confirming or denying the inherent rationality of nonaction in the days of the dictatorship (versions which would require heroes and villains as well as sacrificial lambs in order to be truly effective). The double absolution (of society by the political groups, and of the political groups by society) achieved by transferring the attribute "resister" in its diffuse form to most of the Uruguayan people, which thus becomes "heroic," would allow for honorable "completion" of a stage in our history, even at the risk of seeming to reinforce the myth of the military as an entity virtually alien to society. By rapidly establishing a common basis for validating discourse and a set of credentials that is shared by all the participants, this game would also help consolidate the entity "we" in opposition to a military "they."

To choose one definition over the other is to put the final touches on a single account—in other words, to write history. To write history is simply to reify a voice. "Putting on the final touches" elevates that voice to the category of Word and silences other voices by relegating them to the realm of the anecdotal: of the unarticulated, indeterminate, muffled *petite histoire*.

Memory/Memories: By Way of Conclusion

Having undertaken this excessively brief journey through the world of collective memory and its possible manipulations, can we now arrive at any conclusions? If we limit ourselves to Uruguayan reality—a reality marked by the partial breakdown of collective memory and by an attempt at restoration years later in which political interests have figured prominently—more questions are raised than there are answers at this time. For we Uruguayans did not experience a single reality. Besides the geographical distances imposed by exile, imprisonment, and "insile," there were temporal distances (time experienced subjectively, or as that of others); thus, dissimilar realities existed even for those whose lived experience was the same. Those differences are what underlie attempts to reconstruct our collective memory and manipulate it for political purposes. It is as if we were still proceeding on the old nostalgic assumptions that hold collective memory to be uniform and indivisible.

Apparently based on that assumption, the manipulations to which our collective memory has been subjected (and which I have tried to enumerate very briefly here) can only lead to winning or losing battles over status in the political realm. But our memories are multiple and varied, sometimes opposed, often contradictory. In that case—where a breakdown is prevented only by shaky bridges, by almost imperceptible threads that threaten to tear at each step—does it make sense to manipulate memory? For the immediate future, perhaps; it may be possible to gain ground, silence our adversaries, even run the show. But we Uruguayans have learned that silence is not the same as aquiescence. Attempting to impose hegemonic versions of collective memory where underlying reality does not allow for it is an exercise in futility—something like seeking to establish hegemony over a void. If the bonds that consolidate memories are not reinforced, and if they are not reconciled through an open and fraternal dialogue in which everyone listens to everyone else (exiles, prisoners, resisters, "the living"), then the breakdown of collective memory may yet occur. If it does, who can guarantee that the social imaginary will not break down as well?

March 1986

Notes

A first version of this paper, presented in Maryland, was published in *De mitos y memorias políticas: la represión, el miedo y después,* ed. C. Perelli and J. Rial (Montevideo: Banda Oriental, 1986).

1   This analogy between preserving identity and preserving memory is common among subjugated, conquered, oppressed peoples. Perhaps one of the most extreme examples is the Jewish people, which in the Diaspora and the persecution of the ghettoes often preferred sacrificing the lives of some members to "losing" its memory, assimilating. In fact, assimilation was often viewed as a loss of memory, which in turn was the most flagrant proof of loss of identity. Even today, for many nonreligious Jews of the Diaspora, being Jewish is not so much a question of ritual or faith as of tradition and cultural continuity.

2   In the famous Artigas case, Uruguayan historiography affords us a good example of a struggle to impose a hegemonic version of memory. Around the figure of José Artigas—considered Uruguay's national hero even though this idealization tends to overlook one of the fundamental characteristics of the Artiguista program—at least four versions or legends have evolved, each corresponding to the political interests of a particular sector. A first version, or what we might call the black legend, portrays Artigas as a smuggler, a bandit who broke laws and offended sensibilities, a dangerous evildoer who launched an attack against "order"—thus, the archetype of an anarchic caudillo. A second version, the blue legend, sees Artigas as the heroic father of our country but with an important characteristic: he is the creator of a democratic, pluralistic, redistributive Uruguay. A third version is the so-called red legend: in this case, Artigas is an illustrious social—if not a socialist—reformer. In a final version, which we might color green, the emphasis is on Artigas as an outstanding soldier, the patron of our national armies. At any given moment, one or another of these versions has prevailed over the others in keeping with the particular interests of those in power. On the question of "good order," see the works of Oscar Landi, in particular, his study "Sobre lenguajes, identidades y ciudadanías políticas," in *Estado y política en América Latina,* ed. Norberto Lechner (Mexico: Siglo XXI, 1981), 172–99; and his *El discurso sobre lo posible (la democracia y el realismo político* (Buenos Aires: CEDES, 1985).

3　By and large, the treatment of black slaves in the colonies of the New World exemplifies the eradication of the memory of subjugated peoples. The slaves were not
permitted to keep their language, their traditions, or their names. I note in this
connection that one of the first demands made by the Black Muslims in the United
States was that they be allowed to replace their surnames with an X (as in Malcolm X),
because they considered them to be the surnames of their oppressors.

4　The distinction between *cronos* and *kairós* is present in the work of Aristotle, especially in his "Categoriae."

5　Following Michel Foucault's example, Landi develops the concept of "power mechanism" in his "Sobre lenguajes."

6　The concept of "fringes of meaning" was introduced by William James in *Principles of
Psychology* (New York: Holt, 1890) and was especially utilized and refined by Alfred
Schutz. See the latter's *Collected Papers,* 3 vols. (The Hague: Nijhoff, 1964–67).

7　The distinction between "friend" and "enemy" as a fundamental criterion for defining
the political was created by Carl Schmitt in *The Concept of Politics* (1929; Rutgers,
N.J.: Rutgers University Press, 1976).

8　James, *Principles of Psychology.*

9　In the sense in which Cornelius Castoriadis uses these terms in *L'Institution Imaginaire
de la Société* (Paris: Editions du Seuil, 1975).

10　Anika Rifflet Lemaire, *Jacques Lacan* (Brussels: Charles Dessart, 1970), 112.

11　Erving Goffman, *The Presentation of Self in Everyday Life* (Garden City, N.Y.: Double-
day, 1959).

12　Peter Berger and Thomas Luckmann, *The Social Construction of Reality* (London:
Penguin, 1967).

13　A familiar example of a lie about events of the past-past that has endured involves the
Emperor Constantine's famous donation to the popes. Only recently, in modern
historical studies, has it been disproven; and it is still part of the memory of the
Catholic church.

14　Although real life affords numerous examples of lies which cannot be checked
because of geographical distance, I prefer to cite an invention of George Orwell's; in
his novel *1984,* a lie about a war between continents serves as a means of dominating
the population.

15　On this point and for the ensuing discussion of myths prevailing in Uruguay before the
dictatorship, see Juan Rial's essay in this volume.

16　See Leo Masliah's song "Regreso a la normalidad" on the cassette *Extraños en tu casa*
(Montevideo: La Batuta, LVC-031).

17　The term *década infame* ("infamous decade") was coined by the cooperative daily *La
Hora,* which has close ties to the Uruguayan Communist party. It never came into
general use despite determined efforts to impose it, which even included sponsorship
of a literary competition entitled "Uruguayans Tell about the Infamous Decade." A
well-known example of reinstatement ("As we were saying . . .")—in the real as well
as the symbolic sphere, with a strong appeal to the imaginary—involved our National
University, the only one in Uruguay: when the authorities imposed by the military
concluded their terms of office, all the deans and the rector of the pre-1973 University
were returned to their posts.

18　As examples of different tendencies in the sizable bibliography on the symbolic sphere
I cite the works of Ernst Cassirer, Lucien Goldmann, Georg Lukács, Alfred Schutz,

Teodoro Adorno, Max Horkheimer, Leszek Kolakowski, Lucio Colletti, and Galvano della Volpe.

19   A case of resignification corresponding to an opposite political tendency involves the distinction made by the military in the period prior to the coup between "seditious" and "subversives." The political community preferred to refer to the urban guerrilla movements using the highly charged term *sedition*, whose analysis would merit a study of its own. The term *subversive* was used less frequently, though clearly as a synonym, to refer to the same movements once the government prohibited the use of certain words such as *guerrilla* and *tupamaro*. During one phase of the "long coup" in Uruguay—on February 9, 1973, to be exact—the military began to refer to its own actions as "subversive," inasmuch as they involved the sanctioning of economic crimes and socioeconomic violence. On this point, see the testimony given by Rear Admiral Zorrilla, commander in chief of the Uruguayan Navy at the time, who recalls that moment on a cassette entitled *El golpe: antecedentes. Historia de un pueblo agobiado, Primera Parte* (Montevideo: Ed. Mundo Tercero, January, 1985).

20   Although less pure vestiges can be found on the rest of the Uruguayan Left, this view was expressed primarily by the Tupamaros in the months between the March 1985 amnesty and the end of the dictatorship. A clear example is Mauricio Rosencof's play, *Y nuestros caballos serán blancos* (Montevideo: Arca, 1985).

21   The communist position is set forth in a document entitled "Balance general del PIT-CNT," which was presented to the Third Congress of that organization in November 1985. (The PIT-CNT, which resulted from the fusion of the old Interunion Workers' Plenary and the National Workers' Convention, is the umbrella organization presently grouping all the unions that represent salaried workers in the public and private sector [TRANS.]. The PVP, which has its ideological roots in anarchism, currently advocates a mixture of anarchism, Marxism-Leninism, and Trotskyism.

22   See the aforementioned cassette, *El golpe: antecedentes.*

III

Literature and Repression

✷

Los Signos sobre la Mesa

Amanda Berenguer

✪

ante mis hermanos torturados

¿qué metáfora podría trasladar
              el trueno degollado de dolor
y poner los signos sobre la mesa?

digo rosetas en carne viva
        círculos rojo-brasa
        tazas de coagulación renovada
y me atraganto
en tanto se hacen crepitar los pezones
de esa mujer atada por depredadores
                    a una piedra de agonía

digo entonces el aliento el resuello primitivo
                    soplo de otra especie
                    cortejo de las llagas
y esa vagina forzada y deshecha
la mucosa vital entreabierta a la intemperie
y me rompo el cuello
            la palabra
            contra el umbral de cada violación

oigo un alarido abortado de pronto
            tapando las salidas
        la voz extrema informe expulsada del cuerpo
mientras las vísceras sangran entre los desgarros
                        del empalamiento
y me descoyunto el habla

The Signs on the Table
Amanda Berenguer

✧

be[for]e my tortured brothers and sisters

what metaphor could possibly convey
        the headless slaughtered thunderclap of pain
and lay the signs on the table?

i say searing raw rosettes
    rings of red-hot coals
    cupfuls of rekindled clotting
and i choke
as i hear her nipples crackle
that woman bound by marauders
        to her deathstone

then i say breathing primitive wheezing
        snorts of another species
        aftermath of wounds
and that ravished mangled vagina
the vital membranes exposed set ajar
and i break my neck
    my voice cracks
    on the threshold of each violation

i hear a cry suddenly aborted
    blocking the exits
    a shapeless last sound expelled from the body
while entrails bleed torn
    and impaled
and my speech comes unhinged

¿qué metáfora podrá enviar navíos
                a rescatar noticias ululantes?

los testículos los recios seminarios indefensos
se retuercen bajo la chispa de los electrodos
y crecen las uñas arrancadas
                        unidas por las cuerdas de los nervios
y retumban los huesos partidos mientras se apalea
                        o se estira el esqueleto
—el armazón que aguanta el empecinamiento—
y siento ese testigo acústico casi impersonal
            el chorro que viene desde la médula
la respiración—fiel hasta el fin—
                    recoge el dolor (estruendo secreto)
y lo arroja contra las paredes sordas y sucias

¿la palabra dónde
            la justa
para el vómito que se aspira
para el agua de la cloaca en los pulmones
la inmersión negra en el vaivén del oxígeno
cubierto de hongos y excrementos?

¿la palabra para el cuerpo montado
                    en el caballete de hierro
jinete cabalgando un cuchillo entre las piernas
y para esa hebra salvaje
el aullido que ata las entrañas con el aire?

la garganta reseca no es fuente de palabras

la escena queda despellejada
            es un rostro con las cuencas vacías
me rodean apenas imágenes mudas
                    sin cuerdas vocales

caigo vencida y balbuceo:
                    alguien lleva en la cara/
chorreando/pájaros decapitados/llora lágrimas/llora
sangre/madre/madre mía lame las entrañas/cubre el
corazón de negro espeso/he aquí el aleteo/el estertor/
la sombra sobre el fuego/he aquí la mirada/madre/
se me quiebran los ojos/la escritura

what metaphor can possibly send ships
                        to rescue mournful news?

the testicles robust defenseless seedbeds
writhe beneath the sparks from the electrodes
and extracted fingernails grow
                        still joined by the ropes we call nerves
to the rumble of broken bones
                        while the skeleton is flogged or stretched
—the frame that endures their doggedness—
and i hear that acoustic almost impersonal witness
                        gushing from deep inside the marrow
breath—true to the end—
                        gathers up the pain (that secret roar)
and hurls it at the deaf dirty walls

the word where is
                        the right one
for aspirated vomit
for sewer water in their lungs
black immersion in the ebb and flow of oxygen
full of rot and excrement?

or the word for that body astride
                                the iron sawhorse
that horseman riding a knife between his legs
and for that savage thread
the howl that binds his entrails to the air?

a parched throat is no source of words

now the scene is stripped bare
                        a face with empty eye sockets
only mute images surround me
                        vocal chords missing

falling vanquished i stammer:
                                someone/there is a face/
dripping/decapitated birds/weeping tears/weeping
blood/mother/ oh mother lick my entrails/drape my
heart in deep blackness/now the flutter of wings/the death rattle/
the shadow covering the fire/now the look in those eyes/mother/
my eyes shatter/words

en grabados minuciosos había mirado los cuerpos al sol estaqueados sobre litografías o envueltos en cueros frescos para que los anillos del viento los triturara

vi entre simétricas piedras diseñadas a tinta echar en las bocas cucharones de plomo derretido y miré las tenazas de trazo hundido y nítido arrancar pedazos bien dibujados de la lengua en las mesas expuestas del castillo de los Condes de Flandes

vi el potro de madera con ruedas dentadas que le mostraron a Galileo una noche de advertencia en Roma (el aparato estiraba las piernas y los brazos despacio sin apuro hasta hacer estallar los tendones y las articulaciones parecidos a troncos a frutos disecados a láminas de anatomía)

el joven Papa Urbano VIII a su vez mandó matar todos los pájaros del jardín del Vaticano porque le molestaban los cantos

yo observaba los detalles de las llamas como lagartos dorados como varas floridas rojiazules que consumieron a Juana de Arco

mientras doce servidores sostienen atado con cintas de seda al ruiseñor del emperador de la China

y miré los cuatro caballos negros sutilmente delineados que desmembraron de acuerdo a los cuatro puntos cardinales los cuerpos de los indios en las plazas de mi tierra sudamericana

> había mirado ilustraciones
> recorrí lugares
> > leí los textos
>
> > pero inventé vendas
> > > borré imágenes
> > > borré vías de acceso
> lo supe alguna vez y lo escondí
>
> lo sé ahora
> > muy cerca está ocurriendo
> entre los muros de esta ciudad
> entre estos muros
> > > hierve el pozo sufriente
> > > ahora mismo
> > > está hirviendo

on detailed engravings i had watched the bodies staked under the sun on lithographs or wrapped in fresh hides so the coils of the wind would crush them

i saw spoonfuls of molten lead thrown into their mouths amid symmetrical stones outlined in ink and i watched while tongs penned with deep clean strokes tore out well-drawn pieces of tongue in display cases at the castle of the Counts of Flanders

i saw the wooden rack with toothed wheels they showed Galileo one ominous night in Rome (that device would stretch the arms and legs slowly without haste until tendons snapped along with joints like tree trunks like dried fruit like anatomical drawings)

then there was young Pope Urban VIII who gave orders to kill all the birds in the Vatican gardens because their songs annoyed him

i was observing the details of the flames like golden lizards like bluish-red flowering branches that consumed Joan of Arc

while twelve servants hold the Chinese Emperor's nightingale by twelve silken strings

and i watched the four subtly drawn black horses dismember the bodies of Indians by dragging them in all four directions in the plazas of my South America

> i had seen pictures
> traveled the globe
> > read the texts

> > but i invented blindfolds
> > > scratched out images
> > > scratched out access roads
> at times i realized and denied it

> i realize now
> > it's happening so close by
> within the walls of this city
> within these walls
> > > the well of suffering boils over
> > > right now
> > > it's boiling over

la mañana es dulce
      es un soleado bizcocho azul
      que se reparten los niños
una mujer de amarillo luminoso
           sube al ómnibus
la luz verde del semáforo anuncia viento favorable
en una calle cercana
        ahora mismo
        a esta hora
en un pardo local sin salida hierve el pozo sufriente

una ferocidad doméstica rutinaria
        cuelga como una vejiga orlada de agujas
        o un panal negro que sudara aguijones
        o un infectado puercoespín de vidrio pegajoso

una máquina llena de pelos lacios
          parecida a una rata
arrastra una criatura por las alas
cayó encima premeditadamente
más que los perros de presa más que el buitre de cuello rojo
sobre el perseguido el inquirido el apaleado
      el destrozado el arrastrado por una soga
      desde la garganta desde el mismo sitio
por donde saldrían los signos y los nombres
         que nadie confesará
el aislado el arrojado a la sombra sin día sin noche
cuando la aguja llega a marcar una sola pregunta: ¿quién soy?
el caballo de quijada y dientes rotos
hundiendo las patas en arenas movedizas

la mirada del caballo subió los peldaños del estrado
la mirada iba más lejos que el recorrido del buitre
más lejos que los perros de costillares flacos

líneas hilos de la mirada cruzaron los triángulos
la proyección de la ignominia
y le subía un poder intacto
el valor de una yema que brota en mitad de la helada

the morning is sweet
            a sun-drenched blue cake
            shared by children
a woman in radiant yellow
                  gets on the bus
the green of the traffic light forecasts favorable winds
on a nearby street
            right now
            this very minute
in a dingy spot with no exit the well of suffering boils over

routine domestic savagery
                  hangs like a bladder edged with needles
                  or a black hornet's nest sweating stingers
                  or an infected porcupine of gooey glass

a machine thick with straight hair
                  resembling a rat
drags a living creature by the wings
pounced premeditatedly
more than a bulldog more than the red-necked vulture
on the stalked probed beaten prey
            torn apart dragged along by a rope
            at his throat at the very place
whence the signs might come and the names
                  that no one will confess
sequestered cast into shadows with no day or night
when the hands point to a single question: who am i?
the horse with broken teeth and jaw
sinking his hooves into quicksand

the horse's gaze approached the judge's bench
outstripping the vulture in his flight
outstripping the skinny-flanked dogs

lines threads of his gaze crossed the triangles
the projection of infamy
and there arose in him an untapped power
the spirit of a bud sprouting amid the frost

el perseguidor siente miedo y un estremecimiento
y se precipita sobre el otro
para apurar un temible ejercicio de disciplina
y el caballo recibe furiosas ráfagas de dominio

calza el dolor las espuelas
                       y a pedido de los jefes
se empieza a buscar una respuesta
                 el aborto de una respuesta
y los cables tiran desde el interior de los pulmones
y el caballo resiste el caballo aguanta ensangrentado
y ha dejado de ser caballo y ha dejado de ser persona

¿quién se atreve a apalabrar la extensión
de ese hilo de vida
               baba quemante
saliendo por las órbitas sin poder detenerse?

no es la muerte no
                no es la muerte
es más que la muerte
        es la hoja cortante velocísima y quieta
        es el estrépito en el filo de la dentadura
        es el temblor de las agallas
es el lugar en crudo
           donde todavía se sabe que hay latido
es el sitio indagado al descubierto
           donde el dolor reside y se enardece

lanzan látigos eléctricos
        golpes de fuego rígido
                y lo atizan

torax vientre cabeza miembros delimitan
un minucioso circo romano
donde la fiereza del dolor se come la memoria
y se mide la eternidad tragándose pedazos de sí mismo

"—éste no da más"
"—tírenlo al dique es carne para pescados"

the torturer is afraid shudders
flings himself on his prey
to wind up a fearsome exercise in discipline
and the horse is dealt furious gusts of domination

pain puts on its spurs
                        and on orders from the higher-ups
it's time to seek an answer
                a forced abortive answer
and the cables pull from inside his lungs
and the horse resists the horse holds out dripping blood
no longer a horse no longer a person

who dares put into words the length
of that thread of life
                        burning slime
oozing from his eye sockets uncontained?

it isn't death no
                it isn't death
it's more than death
        it's the cutting blade swift and still
        the clamor of teeth set on edge
        the frenzy of nerve
it's the tender raw flesh
    a faint throbbing at the quick
the spot probed openly
        where pain resides and is rekindled

they wield electric whips
        rigid fiery blows
                and they rouse him

thorax belly head limbs mark the boundaries
of a minutely precise roman circus
where the fierceness of pain devours memory
and eternity is measured in swallowed chunks of self

"this one has had it"
"throw him off the dock he's food for the fish"

el inquisidor con su lámpara de tubos quebrados
                    por donde sopla la nada
sostiene a la justicia viciada convulsa
                    como una drogadicta

pero ocurre a veces que el cuerpo no es sólo cebo
es también refugio entregado
    igual a un bien que se ejecuta

el cuerpo se aparta de sí mismo
          ve la salvación
          ve un satélite confuso que lo ciega
y se abandona despedazado
                    en un rincón de la persona

en seguida escurridiza orina de relevo
          o huevos con un coágulo verde
          o sonajeros llenos de piedra pomez
          sonajeros fuera de hora
                              encapuchados

atentos en la misma jaula
          avispones recurrentes
descuelgan la araña de espesa cabellera
y renuevan la tela de vidrio al rojo

a la oreja cortada asoma una tabla de salvataje
abandonados trozos aún latentes sobrenadan
"en la cuna del hambre"
                    emergen
"jazmines adolescentes" "con cinco dientes"
"con cinco azahares"
                    sobre el naufragio
"con cinco diminutas
ferocidades"
                    y se hunden
se oye vaciarse rojas pasionarias líquidas
                    por un agujero de cartílago
engranajes en celo se llenan de arena
                              y pedazos de hígado
los minutos se revuelcan entre alacranes
que succionan en el ombligo siempre oscuro

the inquisitor with his lamp
            nothingness howling through its broken chimney
upholds a tainted justice convulsed
                        like a woman addicted to drugs

but it sometimes happens that the body is more than bait
it's a surrendered hiding place as well
    like an asset attached

the body draws back from itself
            glimpses salvation
            glimpses a vague moon that blinds it
and abandons its mangled self
                            in a corner of its being

at once slippery urine changing shift
            eggs with green clots inside
            rattles full of pumice stone
            off-schedule rattles
                        hooded

watchful right inside the cage
            recurrent hornets
take down the thick-haired spider
repair the web of molten glass

near the severed ear a lifeline bobs
abandoned bits of flesh surface still palpitating
"in the cradle of hunger"
                        there emerge
"teenage jasmine flowers" "with five teeth"
"with five orange blossoms"
                        over the shipwreck
"with five tiny
ferocities"
            and they sink
there's a sound of liquid red passionflowers draining
                        through a hole of cartilage
rutting gears fill with sand
                and chunks of liver
the minutes wallow among scorpions
that suction the ever dark navel

y se cae
        y se espera manoteando en el vacío
como a la última sentencia

la palabra también se cae de sus andamios
        se descuartiza
y queda inválida en medio de las cosas que pasaron

ni la matriz vertiginosa
ni la imaginación entera desplegada
lograrían concebir
        el sufrimiento de otro
        el dolor ajeno

cada cuerpo da su propio testimonio:
una flor sangrienta que florece una sola vez
        en cada noche

en el parto como en los terremotos
el dolor era central en la columna del mundo
pero era un tulipán erguido
        un volcán de vida
        un memorable florecimiento

no hay memoria para el dolor

sólo restan semienterrados dientes
        mordazas
        objetos insomnes
chatarra hundida en un lodo obsesivo sanguinolento
que sube despacio
        o crece de golpe
desde el fondo del pecho
        tan caliente
que derrite gruesas ramazones de miedo sólido
incrustado en las costillas resistentes

y quedan cicatrices móviles
        interiores
        a oscuras
        corriendo de un lugar a otro
rápidos cienpiés en un sótano inundado

and there's a fall
    and a wait as for a death sentence
hands flailing in the void

the word tumbles from its scaffolding as well
        is drawn and quartered
remains an invalid in the midst of all that happened

neither the vertiginous womb
nor the entire imagination unfurled
could possibly conceive
           another's suffering
           someone else's pain

each body bears its own witness:
a gory flower that blooms but once
           each night

in childbirth as in earthquakes
pain was central to the backbone of the world
but it was a tulip standing tall
      a vital volcano
      a memorable flowering

pain has no memory

there remain only half-buried teeth
           gags
           sleepless objects
scrap metal sunken in an obsessive bloody mire
that rises slowly
        or grows all at once
from deep in the chest
          so fiery
that it melts thick boughs of solid fear
encrusted in the resistant ribs

and leaves movable scars
      internal
      in darkness
      scurrying to and fro
fleet-footed centipedes in a flooded cellar

me trago la saliva
la palabra me traiciona

acuso recibo de tu carta Dostoiewsky
"ante el dolor humano yo me humillo"
y quedo postrada
                    ante la puerta de la celda
                    ante mis hermanos torturados

                              invierno 1985

i swallow saliva
words betray me

i acknowledge receipt of your letter Dostoyevsky
"i bow down to all human suffering"
and lie prostrate
                    before the door of the prison cell
                    before my tortured brothers and sisters

                                        Winter 1985

From Silence to Eloquence: Critical Resistance or the Ambivalent Aspects of a Discourse in Crisis

Lisa Block de Behar

❂

> All living things are critics.—Kenneth Burke
>
> Seul aujourd'hui le critique exécute l'oeuvre
> (j'admets le jeu de mots).—Roland Barthes

In recent years my research has dealt with the reader's silence.[1] In the manner of Charles S. Peirce's unlimited semiosis, according to which all signs conceal other signs, I believe that silence concealed another silence which concerned me more and which, strictly speaking, was not literary or aesthetic. Closer to the silence of Wittgenstein's aphorism—albeit with its philosophical dimension trivialized by the repression we were suffering at the time—it was perhaps a personal version of his "what we cannot speak about, we must pass over in silence." That silence encompassed a silence imposed by the author and another silence imposed by the authorities; and those were not the only silences.

Now silence no longer interests me as much. Though still in relation to reading, the restoration of democracy has reoriented my work toward a different theoretical object: instead of the reader's silence, the critic's eloquence. The problem that arises is the following: If the interest (*inter esse*) of critical discourse is to *stand between*—between the author and the reader, between literature and history, between the past and the present—as an intermediary between media and in the media, what were the *(o)missions of criticism* during the dictatorship? As I have not yet completed my analysis of the historical alternatives in question, I will now summarize some of my theoretical premises.

So numerous are the problems implied by my proposed topic that the aforementioned chronological loophole hardly diminishes the inordinate complexities involved. The origins of those complexities should probably be sought in origin itself, antedating history, among myths and theories, at the beginning where curiosity first coincided with disobedience, and disobedience with knowledge, where knowledge and suffering were definitively identified and exile awaited the curious, expulsion and punishment the creator. Neither the earliest examples of this phenomenon nor its most recent recurrences offer much encouragement in our search. Science and creation, knowledge and imagination, objectivity and poetry are still regarded as the antithetical and suspicious expressions of an archetype which, for not very altruistic reasons, continues in use in republics far from ideal.

The Uruguayan case was one among many. The excesses of censorship, prison, and exile that have abounded in this century both anticipate and grotesquely confirm the repeated appeals of post–World War II philosophies. Clearly, totalitarian governments do not hesitate and aesthetic undertakings (with their concomitant theoretical inquiries) can hardly remain divorced from forms of action in the present or in history, even if they want to. For that reason, any option/opposition between "arms" and "letters" is as vain as it is superfluous: "It is well known that Don Quijote . . . decided the debate against letters and in favor of arms. Cervantes was a former soldier: his verdict is understandable."[2] For both Cervantes and Borges, battles, wars, and both debate and its parody are textualized. Without textualization there is neither literature nor history. For that reason, neither formalist exclusions, the escapisms of immanent analysis, the trustworthiness of codes, structuralist "intransitivity," nor those who purported to bypass methodologically the flow of historical events have escaped the rigors they attempted to deny with their theories. If there is nothing outside the text, and if all texts are problematical, there is no need to teach the need for *engagement,* which is necessary because it cannot be otherwise in a logosphere from which no world can be glimpsed beyond the text,[3] and in which the tensions between life and history, life and literature, literature and history have no value as antagonists save for their impossible independence. In this sense, literary discourse is no different from other types of discourse. They say—*mean* to say—twice over, as a matter of both will and power; in addition to the "pleasure of the text,"[4] the *power* of the text, or simply power.

But if throughout the ages, beginning and ending with eternity, *wanting to know and be (querer s[ab]er)* like the gods plunged man into different forms of an identical Fall, then *wanting to interpret* (the search for meaning, "la quête de la verité," the problem of origin) might be what is required for our return to the Garden of Eden. No hypothetical rebelliousness is needed to imagine that by "eating for the second time of the tree of knowledge, we may be able to regain Paradise."[5] Nor is this a question of a poet's extravagant desire. Without going any further, the very history of the term *paradise* contains the hope of a hermeneutic redemption. As a part of symbolic activity, the act of giving meaning, the interpretation of the text, knowledge and interpretation are forms of restitution.

Whether truth or linguistic fiction, *paradise* can be explained etymologically on the basis of an acronym formed by the initials of the four readings dictated by the Midrash.[6] Four levels of interpretation are prescribed there, from the most to the least accessible: the literal meaning, or *pshat;* the allusive meaning, or *remez;* the specific, or strictly exegetical meaning of the Midrash, *drash* (from *darosh,* "search," "questioning," "demand"); and the secret, esoteric, or mystical meaning, *sod.* The initials of those four terms form *pardés,* the word that designates the *garden* and from which *paradise* is probably derived, both etymologically and imaginatively. In Genesis one kind of curiosity precipitates the Fall; by means of exegesis another promises salvation. "Words about words," and the rest is silence. It is not theological hope which drives us (or "logological" hope, as Kenneth Burke prefers to say) but rather the methodological possibility of shifting one degree the task we have set ourselves—that of observing the steps in understanding, understanding understanding, seeking a sufficiently valid approach to textual interpretation by focusing on *critical reading* more than on literature itself (if, practically speaking, that distinction is still an apt one).

The "undeniable ontological priority" of the work gives rise to a type of discourse. The discreet act of private comprehension is exposed; the *interdiction* that is part of any reading[7] is reduced to a decree; and the reader's silence is lost in eloquence which appears in turn as the explicit object and the objective of a new form of comprehension. Thus begins the process of *critical precipitation,* a combination (in the chemical sense of the word) but above all an instance of textual harassment, a leaning over the abyss, the dual act of *reflection* whereby one's own image is repeated in the vision of an Other and gives rise to the infinite vertigo of interpretation.

For Ion, Plato's inspired and inspiring (*inspirado[r]*) character, both creator and interpreter are possessed by divinely propagated creative "enthusiasm." With equally convincing though less passionate arguments, in their most recent formulations the different contemporary literary theories defend that identification between author and interpreter. The character Pierre Menard embodies it paradigmatically, and Borges's imagination has given rise to multiple versions of an identification which not only literature and philosophy have personified. For their part, Socrates and the great Homeric bard had already dwelt on the two forms (theoretical and aesthetic) *interpretation* can take: the commentary, or critical interpretation; and the realization, or artistic interpretation. Once reestablished by mention of the *hermeneús,* we can never again abandon a duality seemingly validated by the vigorous ambiguity of *sense* (perception and meaning) implied by all comprehension: two senses at least, enlisted in a series that also encompasses the duality inherent in *theory* (inasmuch as that term originally referred to the aesthetic and visual as well as the conceptual, the intellectual, even if later usage limited its meaning to the realm of *reflection* and *speculation*).

The dialectic restoration of oppositions constitutes something more than an etymological caveat. The conciliation of polysemic contrarieties which this restoration involves is probably the source of one of the most interesting philosophical contributions of contemporary thought, specifically of those tendencies which do not shy away from *understanding by means of paradox.* If some years ago Umberto Eco considered all artistic form "if not a substitute for scientific knowledge, an *epistemological metaphor,*"[8] we would barely have to substitute one rhetorical figure for another in order to characterize twentieth-century forms of philosophical, scientific, and literary thought as an *epistemological paradox.* Without a doubt, it is specifically up to critical discourse to repair the semantic reductions of a useless simplification—that is, to "save the text" by calling attention to the potential words possess for a compatibility that does not obliterate difference.

Even worse, with the naturalness characteristic of what is taken for granted, a similar form of discrimination has opposed two literary functions which desire and call for collaboration (*se [re]quieren solidarias*); all credit should not be due the author, nor should all tribulations be reserved for the critic. For that reason, one can neither ascribe to nor totally disregard the (un)thinking of those who, like Sartre, claim that "the critic lives badly": "His wife does not appreciate him as she ought to, his children are ungrateful, and the end of the month, difficult."[9] Today, although the status of the critic has changed notably, "critical passion" nevertheless remains at a crossroads, expressed through a fluctuating discourse in a marginal space where one can no longer distinguish the diverse jurisdictions that schematically dichotomous thought has preferred to consider antagonistic. The mediation of writing leaves discourse midway between voice and silence. Neither one nor the other, it articulates a visual word that brings into play the reserves as well as the reservations, decidability, pronouncement, inherent in any reading. As both intermediary and the object of mediation, critical discourse leads a conflictive existence in a danger zone, overflowing the arbitrary linearity of its marginal space, piling up differences that should be neither radicalized nor annulled; because it is precisely in the continuity of those contradictions that the tensions inherent in the critic's situation are compressed. As I have already said, the interest of that discourse corresponds precisely to its *inter esse*—the *interest* of *standing between,* of forming and maintaining a relationship within a medium "on the edge." In attempting to cross the abyss, it momentarily bridges the gap between universes which are not opposed, but which are distinct.

From the outset, we anticipated the complexity of a proposal whose formulation necessarily involves the relationship between knowledge and creation. Our topic is further complicated by the analysis of certain opposing concepts. If these are considered irreconcilably antagonistic, it is up to criticism to tone down the antagonism, or better yet, to undertake a *critical analysis* of that antagonism and its relevance. Through the mediation of criticism, the opposition is diminished but does not disappear. Between truth/fiction, eloquence/silence, words/deeds, reading/writing (i.e., repetition/refutation), permanence/evanescence, collectivity (classroom, mass media)/isolation, the critic effectively *appropriates* meaning; just as the word says, this can legitimately involve either an acceptable interpretation or a usurpation. In that encounter he struggles, and not simply because of his specific function. His is the struggle pointed up by a postmodernist ethic that continues to create doubts and do away with certainties. If we can regard our era as originating in a crisis which altered our notions of truth, of origin, of identity, of a reality discredited by "the scant reality of the real," then the same crisis would necessarily have affected our notions of language, of representation, of image, of simulation (since "unmediated expression is a philosophical impossibility").[10] The challenge to, and discrediting of, traditional values diverted philosophical curiosity and sought in otherness—difference (and its variants, the *différance* of Jacques Derrida, the *differendo* of J. F. Lyotard), the marginal, dispersion, schism, and the fragmentary—the "disorder" which positivist optimism, with its confidence in the organization of models, the instrumentality of methods, the transparency of reason, and the efficacy of knowledge, had camouflaged.

Now, at the very center of the dualities which it questions, the critical event appears marked by the most visible transformations of contemporary society, where the mass media (mass several times over, since they both inform the masses and conform them) use their good offices to take control of the textual relationship; that is, they engage in officialized mediation, in a type of *intercession-interception* which both reveals and conceals. Myth affords an ancient account of that doubly contradictory function, or of the inevitable duplicities of a function carried out antagonistically. Thoth, the god who invented writing, and his Greek homologue Hermes, the messenger god, the interpreter of the gods, mediate craftily, communicating through both withholding and disclosure. Closer to multiplication than to substitution, representation repeats an ambivalent process. Presence makes its presence known *by means of* an absence, which, accordingly, is not absent.

In the media, the critic has established himself. His establishment is a modern phenomenon, discernible in the imposed and solid presence of specialized columns, bases for transmission that make mediation into a literary *site* and *siege* (*sitio*)—that is, a seat and a seizure of power. Nothing gets through/done except by way of that site/siege ("Nada pasa si no pasa por ese sitio"). Matthew Arnold defined literature as a critique of life. The advocates of deconstruction, in turn, are quick to treat art as a radical critique of representation.[11] If for Octavio Paz, critical inquiry is the very basis of thought, if a critical attitude is the basis for all literature[12] (or the faculty and process by means of which knowledge gains knowledge of itself), then the expansion of the media has made of criticism a mere occupation. The professionalization which has so trivialized the critic's task cannot be justified on the basis of cultural, literary, or philosophical considerations, but purely in terms of economic necessities. What began as a publishing strategy has become a conventional requirement, altering a literary relationship that had no reason to depend on the mediation of the media, their considerations of economic, political, or personal feasibility, their deals and bases for mere intrigue.

In the best of cases, that professional mediation provides a service. Nevertheless, we must recognize that in the peculiar circumstances of our recent, almost current, history, critical contributions have been part of the general *emergency,* and as such, have not been immune to the models of authoritarian surveillance which they neither questioned nor opposed. Critics have undoubtedly made a contribution; but in so doing, they consolidated a *resistance that was less combative than it was lasting.* The times especially favored that displacement of power, and a combination of factors present in our milieu would explain the intensity with which a continent-wide phenomenon manifested itself nationally: on the one hand, the void left by numerous intellectuals who, exiled by the threat of persecution at home and the promise of better opportunities abroad (two aspects of the same oppression), went in search of new horizons; on the other, the heightened contrast between the rhetorical exercises of critical discourse (even at its most precarious) and the grotesque deficiencies of an official discourse marked by the

nondialectical rigidity of authority/obedience, by the obstinacies of an ob-
tuse determination, by the jargon of the military barracks. Arbitrariness of
judgment and arbitrariness of power came together confusedly, at a time
when other voices could not be heard.

To recognize philosophically the need for the critical faculty is not to deny
the arbitrariness of the critic's *occupation;* and the military connotations of
that word are especially pertinent here. Universal interest in that critical
emergency has been accompanied in our milieu by a particular displacement. The public does not comment on films, stage productions, or literary
works; instead, the commentary comments. Perhaps that shift underlies the
imitation of authority (as a means of adapting to the official model), the
displacement of authority (from author to critic), and the authoritarian excesses that both those shifts involve—one of the most problematical aspects
of the dilemma under discussion. The enormous extension of the media has
aggravated a situation that is neither recent nor exclusive: "Oh! Journalism is
unreadable, and literature is not read." The wittiness of Oscar Wilde's observation should not deceive us as to the relevance of a shared concern.

Contiguous and parallel to the mass media and accepted without discussion, with complacent unconcern toward the natural or resigned tolerance of
the inevitable, the present postmodern period has accorded this critical
exercise—its metalinguistic fortune, this "enunciation raised to the second
power," its risky enjambments—an unusually generous space, excessive in
comparison with the reserves granted other forms of noncritical literary
discourse. Similarly, more recent theories (reception theory, the theory of
inter- or transtextuality, deconstruction) have focused on the literary participation of the reader, stressing the relevance of reception—a relevance
which as such does not exclude but does exceed that of the other components of a literary event: the author (and his biography within history) and the
work (with its basic elements, its structure, its relationship to a model). If the
anonymous reader amasses so much theoretical attention, with even more
reason the critic (that reader with a name and a reputation who makes
himself heard, who pontificates in an attempt to bridge gaps) is accorded the
greatest privileges. In this new instance, the dynamic attention of literary
theory ponders its own specific attributes, its literary functions, and its links
with related functions—that is, what it has in common with historical and
philosophical approaches. The critical occupation is extended by theoretical
and historical schools whose compatibility is no coincidence either.

"On a touché à la critique," said Paul de Man, lured by the mocking
sententiousness of Mallarmé's exclamation, "On a touché au vers." Thus he
began his reflections upon the crises of criticism, the changes and insurrec-

tions that have demolished the rules and conventions of traditional analysis over the last several decades. Though regarded as different and antithetical means of apprehending what we confusedly take to be reality, history and literature habitually share similar itineraries at the edge of a wilderness. Skirting a border which is blurred in critical discourse, they find themselves in a free zone that restores certain extraterritorial rights: neither truth nor fiction. Hence all the misgivings.

The controversy is an ancient and a captious one. Between the permanence of writing and the evanescence of reading, between silence and a voice, between saying and meaning to say and saying again, critical discourse minimizes differences by means of a writing-reading or a reading-writing which does not quite destroy the contradictions of a paradoxical task carried out as if it were not carried out. It is as if by denying itself, that task could give rise to the other task which it cites and displaces—another version of the *fort/da*[13] and of the coexistent alternatives presence/absence. Neither content with nor willing to renounce the vicissitudes of its spectral, fleeting apparition, this *preterition* of sorts also says that it doesn't say. Maurice Blanchot identifies it with "that snow which makes the countryside vibrate, white movement, impalpable and a little cold, which disappears in the warm shudder it provokes."[14] Effected in the fleeting present, historically the critic's interpretation pits itself against the ahistoricity of the work in a given time and place, in keeping with the cultural coordinates which determine comprehension through events. In that comprehension the writing read can no longer be distinguished from the reading written; and this confusion may capture the very nature of the phenomenon in question. "Who can tell the dancer from the dance?" This oft-cited Yeats verse points up the permanent enigma of interpretive duality.

Literary comprehension is historical. It is an event, and as such it occurs in a given time. Through reading, the text *accedes* several times to history—that is, it gains access (whether for entry or exit) and a concession. The critic makes a profession of comprehension. Hence, the historical responsibility of his discourse, the obligations of his secular mission: he violates the cloistered confines of the work, interrupts the silence of reading, preaches in his times. *In every age the text takes (its) place.* Comprehension becomes contingent upon circumstances when a reading-writing introduces or *presents* the text—that is, makes it present and thus subjects it to chance, assigns it to a period. Comprehension is nothing more than a *supposition* (likely or unlikely), a fact, and a conjecture. "Poems are antihistorical machines," said Octavio Paz.[15] But they run fortuitously, at a given time; and reading both comprehends and surprises them, in an untimely manner. Every day is different. The critic's reading of the text repeats it. But in Derridean fashion, each repetition passes over the text by updating it, produces an imitation that differentiates it.

Before the Constance school attempted to systematize the nature of reception, Oscar Wilde used to say, "It is [the] spectator and not life that art really mirrors." Hence, the everyday plausibility of commentary, but also the ephemeral agreement of all representation which besides being historical, "historicizes." We should have recourse to the veracity of that English statement. The reader's comprehension "realizes" the work, and this double witticism counts in the present. "For centuries and centuries, things have only happened in the present." This fixation of/with the present, the *Jetztzeit*[16] that obsessed Walter Benjamin, the here and now in which presence and representation are assimilated along with apparition and appearance, actuality and eventuality, is what makes nature dialectical—nothing more than the untimely result of contradictions and paradoxes. In its ever changing state it finds *permanence, maintaining* itself (French *maintenant*) now (French *maintenant*); and it is that maintenance in flight which engages the critic at every turn. Like the poet, the critic gambles, but that does not suffice. "Un coup de dés n'abolirà le hasard," because the text is still in play, and in each game what is at stake is its objective, its meaning.

The media assign the text to a historical period by means of regular terminal pronouncements carried out according to a customary rhythm, administering predictability and methodically ordering expectations. But this is not simply a matter of placing in proper order. Interpretation also implies an interpretive adjustment that normalizes the eccentricity of the work to fit the corresponding chronology. In each period what is perceived as unusual is *regularized* through the "naturalness" attributed to historical processes. In other words, each epoch socializes literary fantasy. "The nineteenth century as we know it is, for the most part, an invention of Balzac's," said Wilde. And the boldness of his statement goes beyond its familiar and doubly aphoristic speculation: "It is none the less true that life imitates Art far more than Art imitates life,"[17] because a literary version contests both historical and empirical knowledge.

Although critical interpretation is essentially different from the mechanical repetition analyzed by Walter Benjamin,[18] the analysis by stages which it imposes threatens to destroy the "aura" of the work. Through critical discourse, the singular eccentricity of the text (as observed in the silence of reading) is made the object of an institutionalization, academic or journalistic, which "normalizes" (in the sense in which Michel Foucault uses that term)[19] or, more simply, explicates it, makes the norm explicit. Divided into parts, structured methodologically, and ordered according to the good judgment of accepted opinion, the work is placed in a category which imagination organized by common sense labels probable. Through interpretation, the text both adapts to norms and helps to impose them; that is, critical normalization instructs and institutes, detains and decrees. A long-standing tradition of invoking Aristotle guarantees that critical judgment will tend toward moderation and that analysis will shift easily toward normalization. "It is necessary that" and "it should be" are frequent phrases in the *Poetics,* where even the improbable is foreseen and cataloged: "The Improbable one has to justify either by showing it to be in accordance with opinion, or by urging that at times it is not improbable; for there is a probability of things happening also against probability."[20]

As a result of that lapse from description into prescription, critical discourse can be expected to tend simultaneously in several directions: toward the work itself and its literary organization (elements, structure, genre), and toward society and its historical organization. The latter may involve study of the writer, the school, or the period, on the one hand, and, on the other, of the complex ideological implications which derive from the critic's perspective (i.e., the particular *present* which is the vantage point for his reading of the work). "We have only this *life* to live, in the midst of *this* war, of *this* revolution," is the *enunciation* customarily arrived at by the critic—and not the author, as Sartre would have had it—on the basis of what has been *enunciated* literarily. The critic *arrogates* to himself a social, political, ethical, rhetorical prerogative that broadens the notion of interpretive competence to encompass the proposing or imposing of canons. If normalization, the authority to impose canons, has been recognized as one of the prerogatives of critical action in the world, it is not surprising that determining meaning, defining "what is meant" (*el "querer decir"*), saying it, discovering textual truth and making it explicit continue to be part of a confrontation which is not purely literary and gives rise to a long history of death, prison, torture, and exile. All are aspects of the same interpretive arrogance, an arrogance in which a fusion takes place between the *will to say* (*querer decir*) and the *power to say* (*poder decir*)—or, as I stated at the outset, simply *power*. It would make considerable sense to treat the history of textual interpretation as a history of persecution or, conversely, of canonization; but we could not avoid rules that way either.

"Criticism is not a science, not even a 'human science,' and it is not a branch of philosophy."[21] Beyond or between those two domains, interpretation takes on an especially difficult task that involves one of the most frequently aired concerns of traditional and contemporary hermeneutics—

namely, the problem of textual truth, the legitimation of fiction, the possibility of a discourse that would make truth and fiction compatible. Whereas the "truth of masks" is the one that counts in a literary text, that same truth may be accepted or considered an error in a scientific text; in a critical text, it will be an error or, if one is inclined to be less indulgent, a hoax. To minimize certain controversies, but above all in keeping with the notion of infinite interpretive rewritings and the impossibility of reducing the text to a single meaning (since its meaning is to have several), deconstruction has evolved a principle that partially ends the dispute. It provides a way of resolving inevitable disagreements honorably by declaring all readers "aberrational."[22] According to this precept, interpretation is a *misreading*—albeit a necessary and creative one—since the text is worthwhile precisely by virtue of its mistaken creativity. It is literariness that transgresses against literality, contaminating the entire discourse with uncertain truth or certain fiction.

This, then, is how the crisis of the self-evident is dealt with: truth is presented either partially or in the guise of representation; and thus, through the text, the interpreter makes of verity a version,[23] a *crisis*—that is, a critical moment, a transition, a change in register. The alternative theories advanced by diverse schools and methods—sociological, psychoanalytical, linguistic, anthropological, structural, semiotic, hermeneutic, deconstructionist—make up the ideological spectrum of a century especially susceptible to "the crises" of *El Criticón*. It is with good reason, so as to avoid discredit, that the narrator of "Pierre Menard, Author of the *Quijote*" offers the reader a single quote from Cervantes that he literally reproduces twice on the same page. Except that the interpretation he introduces in each case is different, different by three centuries; and on the basis of that *difference*, the same quote is no longer the same. But the crisis does not end there, because the transcription refers precisely to truth and to history: "history, the mother of truth." Through repetition and difference, through meaning and reference, the text questions the very same truth to which it refers.

To set oneself the task of searching for truth is, if not an error, then surely an illusion: "Artistic truth is that truth whose contradiction is also true." Just as for Wilde, for the critic barely a half-truth is possible. Even so, that half-truth may be less partial than the "double truth" which is reduced by the sheer fact of its doubling. If figuration (and not propriety) is part of literary confabulation, if despite the appropriate and legal *proprietary* status of his rights the author is not the owner of truth either, then any critic who attributed *propriety* to his version would be a usurper. If he fails in this, he fails doubly.

March 1986

Notes

1 Lisa Block de Behar, *Una retórica del silencio: funciones del lector y los procedimientos de la lectura literaria* (Mexico: Siglo XXI, 1984).

2 Jorge Luis Borges, "Pierre Menard, autor del Quijote," trans. James E. Irby as "Pierre Menard, Author of the *Quixote*," in *Labyrinths: Selected Stories and Other Writings by Jorge Luis Borges,* ed. Donald A. Yates and James E. Irby (New York: New Directions, 1962), 42.

3 Jacques Derrida, *La Dissémination: 'hors livre'* (Paris: Editions du Seuil, 1972).

4 Roland Barthes, *Le plaisir du texte* (Paris: Editions du Seuil, 1973).

5 Heinrich von Kleist. Cited by Geoffrey Hartman in *Criticism in the Wilderness* (New Haven: Yale University Press, 1980), 21.

6 Michel Guggenheim, "Lecture juive de la Bible," in *La Bible au présent: actes du XXIIe colloque del intellectuels juifs de langue française,* ed. Jean Halpérin and Georges Levitte (Paris: Gallimard, 1982).

7 Block de Behar, *Una retórica del silencio,* 229.

8 Umberto Eco, *Opera Aperta: forma e indeterminazione nelle poetiche contemporanee* (Milan: Bompiani, 1976), 50.

9 Jean-Paul Sartre, *Qu'est-ce que la littérature?* (Paris: Gallimard, 1948), 36.

10 Paul de Man, *Blindness and Insight: Essays in the Rhetoric of Contemporary Criticism* (Minneapolis: University of Minnesota Press, 1983), 106.

11 Hartman, *Criticism in the Wilderness,* 112.

12 Octavio Paz, *Pasión Crítica* (Barcelona: Seix Barral, 1985).

13 Jacques Derrida, *L'oreille de l'autre: otobiographies, transferts, traductions: textes et débats avec Jacques Derrida,* ed. Claude Lévesque and Christie V. McDonald (Montreal: VLB, 1982), 96.

14 Maurice Blanchot, "¿Qué es la crítica?" *Sitio* (Buenos Aires) 4–5 (1985):75. I quote from the Spanish translation by Jorge Jinkis.

15 Paz, *Pasión Crítica,* 35.

16 A notion analyzed by Jürgen Habermas in *Philosophical-political Profiles,* trans. Frederick G. Lawrence (Cambridge, Mass.: MIT Press, 1983), 138–39.

17 Oscar Wilde, "The Decay of Lying," in his *Complete Works,* intro. by Vyvyan Holland (London: Collins, 1967), 970–92.

18 Walter Benjamin, "The Work of Art in the Age of Mechanical Reproduction," in his *Illuminations,* ed. with intro. by Hannah Arendt, trans. Harry Zohn (New York: Schocken, 1969), 217–51.

19 Michel Foucault, *Surveiller et punir: naissance de la prison* (Paris: Gallimard, 1975), 185.

20 Aristotle, "Poetics," 1461a–1461b, in *Introduction to Aristotle,* ed. Richard McKeon, Modern Library, vol. 248:665 (New York: Random House, 1947).

21 Harold Bloom, *The Breaking of the Vessels* (Chicago: University of Chicago Press, 1982), 25.

22 Harold Bloom, "Introduction: A Meditation upon Misreading," in his *A Map of Misreading* (New York: Oxford University Press, 1975).

23 L. B. de Behar, "Una hipótesis de lectura: la verdad suspendida entre la repetición y el silencio," *Jaque* (Montevideo), August 10, 1984.

On Spatial and Temporal Exile:
Expatriation and Prison Life
Hiber Conteris

✪

To those panelists who, like myself, have been asked to write on "The Shores of Exile," the word *shores*—in this context and aside from its poetic connotations—has a precise spatial and temporal meaning. In terms of space, "the shores of exile" are those places where most Uruguayans who had to leave the country ended up, or toward which they fled. In temporal terms, *shores* alludes to two key moments in the experience of exile, departure and return, the second of which, in my opinion, is extraordinarily rich in meaning.

I would like to refer to an experience which, though embodied especially in Mauricio Rosencof's moving essay, has, I think, been insufficiently represented here, thus somewhat obscuring an area, a region, a space the dictatorship created for many of us to live in: that of prison life, the years of our incarceration. If we want to understand the problems faced by returning exiles, we cannot overlook the simultaneous existence of an analogous set of problems: those affecting Uruguayans who never thought of prison in truly existential and historical terms as a real possibility for them; who for years were forced to endure the hardships of prison life; and who, suddenly finding themselves free again (often before they could have imagined it in their wildest dreams), have had to learn to make use of their freedom.

Of course, all this has been the object of considerable study by anthropologists, psychologists, physicians, and sociologists, in Uruguay as well as in other countries with a similar recent history (Argentina and Brazil). Most if not all former political prisoners have undergone detailed medical examinations and have been offered psychiatric treatment to help us deal with the problems of readaptation to life on the outside. But over and beyond those aspects of the released prisoner's experience, I am going to join the colleagues who have preceded me in focusing on what we narrowly refer to as "culture." What was prison "culture" like, and what problems does cultural return or cultural repatriation pose specifically for former political prisoners?

It is an established fact that the demographic—that is, the "social"—composition of a prison varies markedly, depending on whether its inmates are political or common prisoners. Who were the prisoners in the army barracks and at the prison known as Libertad? Who were the prisoners of the dictatorship? Largely, they were political leaders and trade union activists; overwhelmingly they were students. There were also professionals of very diverse backgrounds; and in smaller numbers—proportionate to their presence in Uruguayan society as a whole, thus significant nonetheless—intellectuals, writers, and artists.

How were these individuals reintegrated into society? How was this form of "repatriation"—in my view, no less problematical than that of exiles returning from abroad—accomplished? Before attempting to answer these questions, I note that the matter of reintegrating former prisoners took on increased importance at a particular juncture, with the passage of the 1985 Amnesty Law and the ensuing mass release of the many political detainees still being held at that time.

Given the peculiar workings of the system of military justice, the years of the dictatorship gradually saw the release of a substantial number of political prisoners; for those *compañeros* I imagine reintegration was a gradual, slow, and controlled process as well, because they were returning to virtually the same society that had incarcerated them in the first place, with all its mechanisms of oppression and repression intact. When the transition occurred—that is, when the military regime ended and the new democratic government came to power (I say "ended," not "fell," because the dictatorship didn't really fall and this seems especially significant today)—there was a very welcome mass exodus from prison. Yesterday, March 10, those of us who were amnestied celebrated the first anniversary of our release. As one of nine *compañeros* held hostage by the regime, Mauricio Rosencof got out a few days later, and the terms of his release were somewhat different. The same was true of a number of others, also considered special cases.

In any event, between March 10 and March 12 or 13, exactly a year ago today, a very large number of us regained our freedom suddenly, all at once; and obviously, whatever mechanisms and resources already existed for the reintegration of former political prisoners could no longer function in the same way. On the one hand, the numbers of released prisoners outstripped the available resources. On the other, conditions had changed; the problem now seemed different, less serious, less urgent. And nevertheless, it is precisely this moment that in my view has proven most complex in relation to the topic under discussion—namely, cultural repatriation.

Until a year ago, the relative difficulty or ease of reintegrating political prisoners into society varied according to the characteristics of the sector to which each belonged. Trade union solidarity worked wonderfully for workers and union activists. Upon release, most of the imprisoned union leaders immediately regained their positions of leadership as well as their jobs. This attests to the lucidity of the Uruguayan working class, which, understanding the situation, remained steadfast in its loyalty to, solidarity with, and support for its leaders, even after the dictatorship had relieved them of their responsibilities.

In the case of students, union solidarity was also a factor, of course. However, the dictatorship was especially hard on students—to the point of stripping them of all the rights they had acquired legitimately until the moment of their arrest. One much-discussed case at Libertad involved a very dedicated chemistry major who was about to get his degree when he was arrested. He got permission to take his final exams, and a special committee was formed to administer them at the prison; but when it came time for the last exam (the only thing standing between him and his degree), the regime decided that to let him take it would be tantamount to giving another weapon to the subversives. Since in the regime's estimation subversives had no rights, they could hardly be allowed to exercise their right to achieve professional status; so that student was prevented from taking his last exam and graduating. From then on (and this happened at a very early date, in 1972 or 1973), no formal study was permitted at Libertad. Several years later, the compañero who was kept from taking his last exam attempted suicide. While I cannot argue conclusively for a cause-and-effect relationship, I don't think that possibility can be ruled out when a failure of this kind is added to the normal frustrations, tedium, and stresses of prison life.

Aside from extreme cases such as this one, the reintegration of those students who were released while the military was still in power raises a number of issues: How did they return to their academic programs? How did they proceed with their career plans? How did they regain their professional competence? And in the case of professionals who had completed their training, what did it (and does it) mean to spend four, five, or ten years totally removed from the normal exercise of a profession, prevented from practicing because we weren't allowed to do so except when the prison authorities could claim some direct or indirect benefit as a result?

The regime did whatever it deemed necessary and possible in order to isolate professionally any prisoners considered especially dangerous in ideological terms. One well-known case was that of Dr. Hugo Sacchi, an eminent gynecologist who was called upon for assistance by the prison authorities each time their pigs had litters. At Libertad, the officials in charge identified the special interests of each prisoner so as to involve him in what they considered to be a totally opposite kind of activity. They played this game over and over, consistently and systematically. "So you were a teacher. You were an intellectual," they would say. Then, in keeping with their own values and priorities, they would assign that individual precisely the jobs that struck them as most humiliating. The prisoner in question didn't necessarily find them humiliating, but in terms of his ability and professional training they were as inappropriate as they could be.

After years and years, this kind of thing results in irreparable loss. When a professional, an intellectual, or a writer finds himself behind, out of sync with what has happened to culture nationally and internationally beyond the very limited confines of prison life, how can he regain his professional standing? How can he make up for lost time? How can a professional or intellectual prepare to begin practicing again, recover the skills he hasn't used for so long? Of course, there have been extraordinary cases not so much of recovery as of something we might call "maintenance"—an ability to survive under the most difficult circumstances. Mauricio Rosencof is one of them. The resourcefulness exhibited by prisoners is unique; the mechanisms and coping strategies with which they confront and overcome the handicaps created by prison life are inconceivable under normal circumstances. Even so, I think some obstacles are very difficult to overcome.

In this connection I want to mention one particular aspect of our recovery that undoubtedly warrants a longer, more detailed discussion than I have time for. Prison life gives rise to unique forms of culture. As prisoners, we made a life for ourselves, and while we were in prison we were convinced that our "microculture" could stand on its own—that it anticipated and provided for all our needs. This is precisely the kind of coping strategy that political prisoners depend upon for their survival.

Consider, for example, the role that books take on in prison life. I would describe their importance as qualitatively different from that which books possess intrinsically under normal circumstances—as vehicles for the transmission or exchange of culture. Books, all kinds of books—light fiction, a detective novel, any of those works we usually refer to as "escapist literature"—are a comfort and an invaluable, irreplaceable source of sustenance in the confines of a prison cell. All the more so if the book in question is worthy of serious study: a theoretical essay, say, or a stimulating commentary on some aspect of thought or cultural creation, art, history, or philosophy.

A book—reading a book—generates discussion, dialogue, or simply conversation. A book can become the topic for a *trille,* or "stroll"—that is, in jailhouse jargon, one of those brief once-a-day encounters, the walk (or recreation period) during which a prisoner can talk to somebody other than the cellmate with whom he spends twenty-three of the twenty-four hours in each day. Possession or use of a book also gives rise to another type of discussion, the *pelea,* or friendly "skirmish," during which prisoners vie for access, for the first possible chance to read it. A book in prison is generally a single copy—something which rarely occurs in normal life. You have to get to it, get your hands on it, read it, before it gets lost, before it begins to circulate outside your sector or your floor; otherwise, you won't be able to read it, at least while you're in prison.

For this reason, prisoners exchange what they call "news" as well—that is, commentaries or reports (often comparable to critical reviews) on the content and merits of a particular book. "Say, I've got such-and-such; I'll pass it on to you and you pass on what you've got" is typical of the way prisoners talk about books. This cultural "miniloan," as an anthropologist might describe it, becomes an absolutely indispensable strategy for survival. The prisoner begins to rediscover texts, authors, books, and topics he once considered unimportant and uninteresting, and which probably would still strike him as such on the outside, in a broader cultural context where more rigorous and careful choices are possible.

On the inside, in that peculiar form of microculture that flourishes inside prisons, a sports magazine, for example, can be considered required reading. For as long as it circulated freely at Libertad, the Argentine magazine *Claudia* provided us with distraction and information of the highest order. It was one of the few magazines our families were permitted to bring us; and it arrived in such great quantities that suspicions must have arisen regarding its true function, because one day it was no longer allowed in.

What does this prove? Only that needs are so great in prison and available resources so scarce that the political prisoner winds up making bogus—second- or third-class—material into first-class literature, ranking it in keeping with his circumstances and the options available to him. That is both good and bad. It is good in the sense that it constitutes one kind of survival strategy. The prisoner comes to value material intrinsically lacking in merit, badly written, because he finds it essential for the purposes of communication, consumption, and survival in prison; this is a way of resignifying from his perspective the "microculture" in which he finds himself immersed.

However, the negative side of that resignification and reordering of values in the context of prison life is that when the prisoner regains his freedom and begins to reenter the world at large, he also recovers his old values and priorities. And only then does he recognize that microculture for what it really is; only then does he realize he has been surviving on sawdust, wasting time on things that, objectively speaking, weren't worth it. How to get back that lost or wasted time? For each of us former prisoners the answer will probably be different, but clearly we have fallen out of step. And the disparity between our cultural life in prison and what happened to culture on the outside during those years has been particularly damaging to intellectuals, professionals, and artists.

One final observation regarding repatriation in a generic sense. In his essay in this volume, Jorge Ruffinelli stresses the importance of the literature written by Uruguayan exiles—its international repercussions—noting that by comparison, what was produced inside Uruguay during the same period was less influential, relatively lacking in resonance. That phenomenon was not peculiar to the dictatorship; it is simply a painful part of Uruguayan reality. Traditionally, Uruguay has been a terrible trampoline, lacking in elasticity and incapable of launching its writers' works abroad. This is clear to the many exiled Uruguayans who, notwithstanding the disadvantages of their situation, nevertheless found they had one great advantage, unquestionably important for any writer's professional advancement: exile proved to be a highly elastic trampoline. At the same time, thanks to the dictatorship, for writers who remained in Uruguay the trampoline was less elastic than ever.

Inasmuch as every historical experience has its pros and cons, I believe there is a lesson to be learned here, in cultural (and not just political) terms. Historically—and I don't mean to hypostasize the notion of history—the dictatorship served a purpose in the Uruguayan process; it was a necessary journey, a road we had to travel. While it existed, it focused attention on Uruguay. It showed us how we could and should live and, above all, that we could outlive the forces of repression that took over our country. And it showed us that with a sufficiently elastic trampoline, Uruguayan culture can make its presence known as a forceful and articulate voice in the concert of Latin American voices, and probably in the world.

March 1986

The Silences of Culture
José Pedro Díaz

✪

E arly in the transition from the dictatorship to this period of restoration of the rule of law, a group of people representative of diverse activities, concerns, and professions—journalists, writers, and politicians—were invited to participate in a series of public forums, the purpose of which was to document what had happened during those dark years. On that occasion it was suggested that I speak on the topic "Culture as Resistance," and though I made clear my unwillingness to use that title, it was announced anyway due to an error.

I rejected that title because it didn't reflect what I intended to say. Talking about culture as resistance is almost the same as talking about resistance in the area of culture, and the truth is that inside Uruguay during most of those years, I don't think we can refer to culture as a whole in terms of resistance. For several years, cultural life was greatly impoverished, almost clandestine. If we are to use the word *resistance* at all, we should use it in the sense of "endurance." Because it is true that culture held out, endured, wasn't totally annihilated, although it was greatly impoverished in the process; and there are extreme—in fact, remarkable—instances which underscore the critical importance of culture for some people on the verge of disintegration.

It is precisely because we humans don't live in isolation, because we are bound together by the strong, subtle matrix of culture, that humanity can endure and has endured so many difficult trials throughout its history. In that sense, culture is indeed resistant. It was because of culture that William Faulkner predicted man would prevail; and in hard times, culture is the bedrock that makes resistance possible. But often this happens in silence, and that is what I want to talk about now: that silence, the wounds inflicted by that silence, and their consequences.

First, some general comments about the conditions that governed our lives and affected all our activities under the dictatorship. All Uruguayan citizens were classified into three categories: A, B, and C. Only individuals in category A enjoyed full rights of citizenship—relatively speaking, of course. Individuals in category B could hold only some positions in the public sector, while those in category C couldn't hold any; the assumption was that they were, or might be, dissidents. Although the system of classification was aimed specifically at the public sector, several multinationals and domestic companies followed suit by hiring individuals sympathetic to the regime to head their personnel departments and by adopting the same hiring practices as the state. In any case, the barriers encountered by individuals in category C extended to other aspects of everyday life as well. For example, they could not serve on the administrative boards of buildings of which they were part owners, or on the board of directors of a soccer team or a charity; and they couldn't hold any elected position whatsoever. As I said, these citizens were presumed to be dissidents, even though that hadn't been proven. Even though in some cases they weren't.

While not all of us knew what category we had been placed in, we could infer that information by the degree of pressure and intimidation we experienced from the system. In general, we were made to feel that we were under surveillance. For example, if a panel discussion had been organized on a literary subject, the police might show up just as it was about to begin and announce that one member of the panel couldn't participate; that person would have to step down but the event would go on as scheduled, unless the organizer succeeded in convincing the officer in question that the sound equipment had broken down. That was how Jean Pradier managed to call off a tribute to Malraux, in which Carlos Real de Azúa, Lisa Block de Behar, he, and I were scheduled to participate at the Alliance Française, after the police advised him that I was forbidden to speak in public. The police would also appear at our places of work to ask us whether we still lived at the same address and whether our phone number was still the same—as if they had to ask. Not to mention the endless red tape involved in getting a passport.

All this created a strong sense that we might be interrogated at any moment; and unfortunately, we had excellent information about what interrogations were like, since we all had relatives or close friends who had been through them. We knew all about interrogations. We also knew that the precipitating factor could be absolutely insignificant, as simple as an expression of contempt for the regime. My friend Mario Arregui was arrested the night after something he said—one of his characteristically vulgar and categorical *puteadas*, or "expletives," to be sure—was overheard in a bus station.

While he was in custody he lost his teeth and was bitten on the thigh by the police dog that accompanied him to the toilet; additionally, his high blood pressure worsened and developed into cardiac insufficiency. As a result, after he was released for lack of evidence he needed a pacemaker. He died only a few years later, when his pacemaker malfunctioned. It all started because he was careless and someone overheard what he said.

Thus, the regime surrounded each of us with concentric circles of fear, and therefore of solitude, isolation, and, above all, silence. In my case, it was never clear when they began to consider me "guilty." Perhaps all they needed were certain friendships, along with a few articles I had written some time before and my correspondence, which they scrutinized openly (it would sometimes arrive with only part of the contents missing). What had they taken out of the envelope? How far would they go in demanding an explanation? What would the interrogation be like? What would they ask me?

During that period I often recalled a joke popular in France during the German Occupation and recounted, if I remember correctly, in the last volume of André Gide's *Journals*. A French hare is nibbling innocently at some roots near the border in Alsace when he sees a German hare come running toward him, panting and trembling. Once safely in France, the German hare flings himself to the ground, trying to catch his breath. "What's wrong?" the French hare asks him. "Why are you so upset?" "Haven't you heard?!" answers the German hare. "In Germany, they're after kangaroos!" "So what do you care? You're a hare!" "I know, but how can I prove it?" Yes, but how can I prove it? That was the question. Because there were people who failed to prove they weren't kangaroos, even though they were hares. And they were treated like kangaroos.

As I said, this generated concentric circles of fear and silence—a silence the military safeguarded by means both direct and indirect. One of the most important was, of course, the strictest system of censorship ever imposed in Uruguay, all the more effective for its lack of explicitness. Repression soon affected the press, both those sectors that tried to resist and were destroyed and the major dailies, where self-censorship became the norm. A few suspensions was all it took to reduce the Uruguayan press to a shadow of its former self. To tell the truth, not much more reduction was possible.

Then there were books. The first to disappear from bookstores were political texts, especially theoretical discussions about socialism of all varieties. Next were works by authors who had been deans or council members at the National University, as well as others considered antigovernment and known to engage in more or less "pinkish" activities (everything overtly Marxist or communist having been taken off the shelves the first day). Naturally, works by prominent authors such as Mario Benedetti, whose political activities were well known, were banned; so were works by writers like Francisco Espínola, who were simply known to have leftist leanings. At times, as in Juan Carlos Onetti's case, banning could even result from an error.

Censorship went much further than anyone could have anticipated thanks to the singular practice of not issuing specific bans. If a publisher or book-seller asked what titles were not to be published or sold, the usual answer was, "You know very well. Don't play dumb." As a result, self-censorship began to operate. This method can be astonishingly effective. In collabora-tion with a group of friends, I had begun to publish an inexpensive collection of good literature with no political content and a series of individual poems, each accompanied by a high-quality illustration and information about the poet and the artist. The tendency to self-censor was so great that we even had difficulty deciding whether to publish texts by Francisco Quevedo because they seemed to allude too directly to our own situation. And we ended up not publishing them. After all, how could we circulate a poem that begins:

> I saw the ramparts of my native land
> that once were strong now crumbled all away

and concludes:

> and not one thing I found of all I viewed
> reminded me of anything but death?[1]

Everything had, or seemed to have, a double meaning. Today, when I look back at what we published then, I find it almost impossible to understand our feelings. But I must confess that at the time we were afraid.

Furthermore, we all knew very well that if we hoped to avoid unpleasant surprises, everything we published had to be absolutely clear, unambiguous, and free of double meanings. At the time, a poet whose name escapes me published a book of poems written in a style best described as "hermetic." The book had a strange title, to say the least; it was called *Los gritos de mi galaxia* (*Cries from My Galaxy*), and its text was obscure. The police decided to investigate the author and demanded that she explain her poetry. I don't know how she did it, but she was promptly released. At the same time, many books were simply confiscated rather than investigated. Among these were the contents of Professor Parpagnoli's entire professional library, a splendid collection of books about cubism, on the assumption that they dealt with Cuba and the Cuban revolution. That kind of confusion has existed for years, if not for centuries. After all, wasn't Victor Hugo arrested for walking around in public with a book by Saint-Simon under his arm? As it turned out, the name on the jacket belonged not to the socialist but to the famous memorialist; however, people will make mistakes. That same heightened sensitivity to double meanings that perceived them where none was intended sometimes worked in our favor. Thus, the mere title of a book of poetry by a friend of ours, *Durar* (*Enduring*), evoked feelings of rebelliousness and struggle; and in the generally festive atmosphere that prevailed just before the 1980 plebiscite, a group of citizens announced their intention to vote against the generals' draft constitution by driving through downtown Montevideo in bright sunshine with their windshield wipers on.

Besides being censored, many books were destroyed. While under arrest in a military barracks, another friend watched a soldier who had been ordered to prepare for a midday barbecue use armfuls of books to keep the fire burning under the grill. And not only books were burned; the University's entire collection of the prestigious weekly *Marcha* was tossed into a bonfire in the patio from a second-floor gallery of the Faculty of Humanities and Sciences. Naturally, many libraries were destroyed. Whenever anyone was investigated, his library and papers were sure to be investigated as well. This led many dissidents to collaborate to a greater or lesser extent with the regime. Because we knew that our books, papers, and especially our correspondence might determine the nature and length of an eventual interrogation, many of us took the precaution of getting rid of certain items. Papers were burned or hidden away for safekeeping in the most unlikely places because here again, we shared the dilemma of the German hare. How to explain that you weren't a kangaroo if you had certain journals or books in your house, or letters from certain people?

Books were also confiscated by the postal service. I once had in my possession an odd notice from the post office to the would-be recipient of a package sent through the mail. The letterhead read Office of Forbidden Objects, and the notice stated that an object mailed to the addressee—in this case, a book—had been confiscated by that office. We never found out what book it was or who had sent it, although it was probably written by one of our friends. But the postal service didn't stop at the confiscation of books by Uruguayan writers, or political texts and works on political theory. It also became an impenetrable barrier for general cultural information, thus reinforcing the barrier erected by our increasing poverty and a rise in prices on the international market (factors that had already placed imported books beyond the reach of most Uruguayans). In 1980, with the plebiscite at hand and the first two weeklies already publishing (that is, at a time when repression had eased somewhat), a bookseller told me that government officials had seized his order of the Spanish translation of volume 7 of the *Histoire générale des civilizations* (*General History of Civilizations*), the one entitled *L'époque contemporain* (*The Contemporary Period*) and written by Maurice Crouzet. I then discovered that the same thing had happened to another bookseller, and that officials had also prevented the entry of Geoffrey Barraclough's *Introduction to Contemporary History*. In short, histories offering a general overview of our century had been banned; we were not to study the twentieth century. Since ancient history could also be dangerous, precautions were taken lest anything undesirable filter in from that area as well. For example, fifty copies of Plato's *Republic* were held pending investigation, and it was only two or three months later, after they were duly inspected who knows by whom, that their sale was finally authorized. This happened not just in one bookstore, but in several.

Editorial Arca, the publishing house to which I am connected and which I helped found in 1962 along with Angel Rama and his brother, Germán, was investigated and its premises broken into; the other managing partner, Alberto Oreggioni, was investigated too. This led to the confiscation of a good part of Arca's publishing list; books by Mario Benedetti, Onetti, Francisco Espínola—that is, by Arca's best-selling authors—were seized as a way of making it clear that they were not to be republished. I arrived after the books had been trucked away to find the storerooms empty, the street full of copies that had fallen out of the trucks, and the neighborhood children (who had never seen so many books lying around in the open) playing with them.

But while facts such as these provide the clearest and most objective measure of Uruguay's cultural isolation, of how information and the consumption of intellectual assets were restricted under the military regime, culture suffered even more in the area of education. In the first place, several thousand teachers were dismissed at all levels of the school system. The secondary schools, the schools for teacher training (i.e., the Instituto "Artigas" and the Institutos Normales), and the National University were the military's prime targets. Methods were extremely varied—from a simple phone call stating that a certain teacher would no longer be allowed to teach classes in a particular high school to indictments for ludicrous motives or, in higher education, the requirement that we sign a sworn affidavit written by the authorities in a very characteristic style and repudiating movements or political parties deemed "seditious." Refusing to sign that affidavit, or signing an alternative statement written in language more appropriate to a university professor, was grounds for investigation and eventually (as in my own case) for dismissal by reason of incompetence. In that way, communication between generations was disrupted. The only teachers not dismissed were those whose background and stated views contained not the slightest hint of dissent. The number of people in that category was minimal, and very few of them had participated in cultural activities of any relevance.

The end result of all this was an enormous and largely permanent loss, not just for education but for the entire country. As large numbers of university professors emigrated, we lost most of our highest-ranking and most brilliant faculty members in every academic discipline: engineers, physicians, agricultural engineers, historians, men of letters, architects, and so on, and so on, because once they reestablish themselves and raise their families elsewhere, very few find it possible to return. In other cases we suffered a double loss; a number of eminent Uruguayans died in exile after dedicating the most mature and productive years of their professional lives to enriching the cultures of sister nations rather than our own.

The competent teachers dismissed from our schools were generally replaced by individuals who lacked training and were appointed directly by the authorities. The healthy practice of filling available positions through academic competitions, or *concursos,* was abolished. This was all the more serious inasmuch as academic standards in Uruguay had traditionally been very high. As a matter of fact, just recently I spent some time reminiscing with Arturo Ardao, a friend who taught at foreign universities during his years in exile. When we talked about our experience on the faculty at the Instituto Alfredo Vázquez Acevedo in Montevideo, where the fifth and sixth years of secondary school are taught, we agreed that the level of instruction there was fully comparable to what we later encountered in undergraduate programs abroad.

As might be expected, the deterioration of the system of education was most noticeable in academic areas with a strong humanistic emphasis, such as history, literature, and philosophy. Particularly affected was a course entitled "Civics and Morality," which is required for three years as part of the high school curriculum and for which only expressly authorized textbooks could be used. In 1984, my dear friend Manuel Flores Mora published an analysis of these texts, along with an anthology of the nonsense with which they were supposed to indoctrinate our young people. Included in them was the statement that democracy "is the possibility of rising to power or achieving power directly as citizens." While potentially useful in democracies, the text goes on to say, political parties are not essential:

> We have the clear example of the Vatican, where there are no political parties, and which nevertheless is a real Democracy. . . . The case of the Vatican as a Republic can be explained this way: although His Holiness

the Pope does not receive the title of President, he rises [to power] through election by the College of Cardinals (the electoral body in this instance); this is also democratic because everyone has the opportunity of rising to power.[2]

The human condition is also examined in these texts:

Many deny that man has a spirit which exists independently of matter. Instead, they claim that man is pure matter, and thus we have the Evolutionists, who claim that human beings are the result of a process of evolution in the animal world and nothing else, and that man is the most highly developed animal, but he does not possess anything essentially different that sets him apart. For their part, Marxists hold that the spirit does not exist as such, that everything is matter, that matter is uncreated and eternal and there is only transformation of matter; that the human brain is matter and what it produces—thoughts—are material products.[3]

Having deprived the education system of its best-trained and most experienced teachers as well as its good books, and having further damaged it through the imposition of incompetent instructors who were obliged to teach the nonsense I have just transcribed, the regime went on to destroy any remaining potential for critical thought by transforming secondary and university-level institutions into little more than highly regimented kindergartens. At both levels, schools were supplied with a large number of monitors, generally police officers, whose mission was to ensure compliance with a new set of rules and regulations. Young men were forbidden to enter with sideburns extending below the tops of their earlobes; they couldn't wear beards, mustaches couldn't extend below the corners of the mouth, and hair had to be cut so that it didn't touch the shirt collar in the back. Young women were forbidden to wear pants; skirts had to reach well below the knees, and if asked to prove that they were of the required length, their wearers had to kneel before the monitors. Students were forbidden to talk in groups, and there was always the feeling that eavesdroppers were nearby. This surveillance and strict discipline were designed to separate and subjugate, to limit initiatives, to disrupt communication among the students and isolate them even in their places of study. The natural initiation to culture that takes place at cafés near high schools or the university, the lively conversations in school corridors, the ambitious projects that are educational even when not undertaken: all those things disappeared.

Another way of breaking cultural connections between generations was the obligatory silence surrounding the deaths of a number of our major cultural figures. On several occasions, even when they took place in Montevideo, we learned that important writers or artists had died only several days after the fact. Since the work of those figures could not be reviewed and discussed as it usually is on such occasions, no assessment could be made at the time of their real significance for Uruguayan culture. This in turn has deprived them of the role they should play vis-à-vis our cultural present.

There were many such deaths during the years of the dictatorship. One of our greatest prose writers, Francisco Espínola, died on the day of the coup; two years later, he was followed by the creator of *nativismo*,[4] poet Fernán Silva Valdés, and by poet and essayist Emilio Oribe. Then major Uruguayan critic Alberto Zum Felde died, followed almost immediately by his wife, poet and novelist Clara Silva. Roberto Ibáñez and Carlos Real de Azúa died, the former a poet and the latter an extraordinary essayist; so did Uruguay's most celebrated poetess, Juana de Ibarbourou. During the darkest days of the dictatorship we lost a master historian, Eugenio Petit Muñoz, followed soon after by his wife, writer Sofía Arzarelo. And toward the end of the dictatorship, when the weeklies were publishing again and we could mention our dead, we lost Jesualdo, followed shortly afterward by his mate, graphic artist María del Carmen Portela, by Domingo Bordoli, also a writer of fiction, and by poet, novelist, and playwright (but especially novelist) Denis Molina. Except for these last figures, of whom we were able to speak publicly, all of them died in secret. And some deaths were never even acknowledged officially—for example, that of Carlos Quijano's collaborator, educator and journalist Julio Castro, who was said to have "disappeared."

Outside the country, Carlos Quijano and Angel Rama died; so did engineer Oscar Maggiolo, our leading authority on hydraulics and rector of the National University before the coup. And those were only the best known of our exiles, people I knew well and whose integration into today's Uruguayan culture is a pressing need. Of course, we lost many more. It seems almost inevitable that simply remembering all this should still provoke feelings of guilt and impotence in each Uruguayan who lived through it, even though the fear which was our dominant feeling at the time has subsided.

❂

Having reviewed briefly the forms of silence that surrounded books and the system of education, let us turn now to the positive side of the equation. It should be obvious that the diverse cultural, artistic, and literary creations of every society make up an organized whole, a structured system, to the extent that each writer and artist occupies a given place within that whole in keeping with his or her ability or interest. While one of us writes reviews or critical articles and collaborates in journals or magazines, another organizes centers of discussion, professional organizations, or libraries, and a third simply writes stories or poems. Thus, a natural division of labor occurs and a system is constituted naturally. When the components of that system can no longer mesh with one another, what remains is the silence to which I refer.

And the fear. Because fear was our most persistent feeling during those years. It was very difficult to write, study, or even take notes when you could see a station wagon, painted the same blue as the police vehicles, driving slowly by your window and looking as if it were about to stop. Or if at 3:00 A.M., the time for police raids, you heard a car stop in front of your door or footsteps approaching. If you lived in an apartment building and you heard the sound of the elevator in the middle of the night, you couldn't help but be on guard until you were sure it had stopped at another floor or only one person had gotten off. We all were very much afraid, especially during the middle years, until 1980. But despite our fear we created; and some of our creations, though modest at first, have proved highly significant.

With the dismantling of traditional places for teaching and research, finding other places where those activities could continue became a matter of top priority. It was our mutilated cultural life itself that sought refuge in whatever nooks and crannies remained, or could be created, within that closed society. University professors who hadn't emigrated headed for a number of institutes that were set up as small centers for study and research. The many colleagues who found a place at those institutes (whether full or part time) were thus able to continue their work and sometimes to modify and reorient it, in keeping with the demands of the new situation.

In fact, most of the institutes—which offered virtually the only support available for serious study and research, and whose very existence attested to Uruguayan culture's will to survive, endure, and resist—were created precisely at this time. The only one that antedated the period of the dictatorship by many years was the Latin American Center for Human Economics (Centro Latinoamericano de Economía Humana [CLAEH]), founded in 1958. Although the Center for Pedagogical Experimentation and Research (Centro de Investigaciones y Experimentación Pedagógica [CIEP]) was created in 1972 before the coup, the political situation was already critical by then. The other three institutes all date from the years of the dictatorship itself: the Center for Information and Research on Uruguay (Centro de Informaciones y Estudios del Uruguay [CIESU]) and the Center for Economic Research (Centro de

Investigaciones Económicas [CINVE]) were both set up in 1975, and the Uruguayan Center for Interdisciplinary Development Studies (Centro Inter-disciplinario de Estudios sobre el Desarrollo-Uruguay [CIEDUR]) in 1977.

Funded by a number of international agencies and foundations, these centers were able to maintain their ideological independence. Almost imme-diately they became a source of significant studies, and by 1980 they were at the height of their activity. Besides contributing significantly to culture under the dictatorship and laying the groundwork for Uruguay's present cultural life, they played a key role in the return to democracy. The institutes provided encouragement and sustenance for the most persecuted forms of thought and inquiry—namely, those which related to social, historical, and economic problems. In all these fields they promoted new research, oriented new generations, and funded new studies. They created new paths as well as maintaining old ones. In them, a major group of seasoned scholars survived and a new generation learned to be equally thorough and intellectually demanding.

Some research conducted outside the institutes also produced significant and substantial results. Certain scholars preferred to work independently, and with support from foreign foundations they were able to continue impor-tant research begun years earlier; that was the case for historians Benjamin Nahum and José Pedro Barrán, to cite just one prominent example. However, Nahum and Barrán were far from the only ones who stubbornly persisted in their task. Many other fruits ripened that way, in secret—perhaps more than we know.

Outside university circles, there were other efforts on behalf of culture—for example, the book club my friends and I created in conjunction with a radio program of Ruben Castillo's. Through home distribution to our sub-scribers at a ridiculous price, we managed to keep up an important flow of publications and place high-quality literature back within reach of the read-ing public. Over a period of four years we published sixty-six titles; at an average of four thousand copies per edition, that makes a quarter of a million books. Using the same system, we published and marketed the aforemen-tioned collection of illustrated poems. The publishing house Banda Oriental later adopted our publishing and marketing practices for a series of their own.

By 1979 and 1980, other activities were possible. After relatively modest beginnings, restrictions on cultural life eased considerably. The change was apparent in other areas as well: 1980 was the year of the plebiscite in which Uruguayans voted down the military's project for a fascist constitution; in 1981, the daily *El Día* and the publishing house Acali organized a literary contest for best short story, novel, and poetry, and as many as three hundred manuscripts were submitted in the short story category; and in 1982, *El Dia* and the Spanish embassy organized a poetry contest. Also in 1981 came the reinstatement of the Florencios, prizes awarded by our theater critics in a number of categories (author, actor, director, etc.) in honor of playwright Florencio Sánchez. Finally, in 1984 Uruguay hosted the Primera Muestra International de Teatro, an international theater festival in which many foreign troupes participated. The wall of silence had begun to crumble.

Over a number of years much of the groundwork for this easing of restrictions had been laid by activities of another type. One complex, vital, and interesting area of activity was the song movement known as *canto popular*. The young singers—really modern-day bards—who participated in this movement created a type of popular poetry, set it to music, and performed it, generally accompanying themselves on the guitar, before larger and larger audiences whose response was increasingly enthusiastic. *Canto popular* concerts undoubtedly filled a silenced society's need for expression and also, perhaps even more significantly, its need to come together, to share feelings and hopes, to break out of its isolation and solitude. At those events spectators met again as citizens, as a people. Naturally, the lyrics were censored. Naturally, the singers were often banned and many concerts had to be canceled. But it was always possible that some as yet unknown singer would be tolerated, or that an approved song text would stir feelings of solidarity in the audience by offering a glimpse of something to those who could read between the lines. In fact, never before or since has so much been implied or read between the lines.

Canto popular was a fascinating phenomenon as well as a socially and politically significant one. As a social and political force, it operated simultaneously on two levels: on the broad level of public performances, and in small informal groups of young people, who gained both in solidarity and in awareness thanks to its resonance (often multiplied) and the generalized interest it stimulated. Because they felt safe when they gathered to study or talk with trusted friends in a familiar house, young people often sang together. Gradually they added to their repertoires songs known only through recordings made before the "process," songs banned by the authorities but copied from tape recorder to tape recorder because they expressed what those young people felt. Singing such songs in a warm atmosphere of solidarity was their way of shaking off the stifling authoritarianism they had to put up with day after day at school; that was why they preferred "songs with opinions," or what the author of *Martín Fierro* referred to as "cantar opinando." Then the songs of the Spanish Civil War began to circulate among those same young people (for example, Gabriel Celaya's poems sung by Paco Ibáñez), as well as songs by Daniel Viglietti, Alfredo Zitarrosa, and Joan Manuel Serrat, all of them banned. From 1978 on, while nothing that explicit could yet be heard in public performances, the slightest suggestion of a double meaning brought an immediate and enthusiastic response from the crowd.

Not all the music and lyrics in the *canto popular* movement were of the highest quality, nor was everything well sung. The need to "say something" or to share a moment of solidarity often mattered more than artistic excellence. Nevertheless, *canto popular* has made lasting contributions, and the complex undertakings those performances were—with a single individual serving as lyricist, composer, singer, instrumentalist, and frequently, actor as well—have given rise to rich and original forms of expression that are still evolving. During the dictatorship, all these things helped heal the wounds society had suffered and taught us to live more productively as a community.

Another creative and positive effort, though far less influential, was the neighborhood theater that flourished during the final years of the dictatorship in the common rooms of the housing cooperatives and in community centers scattered around Montevideo. Numerous small groups took part in that movement, usually performing brief plays set among the working class and dealing with the problems of everyday life. However, none of the efforts I have mentioned significantly diminished the damage done to culture by the dictatorship; Uruguayan cultural life deteriorated markedly during those years in spite of them all.

In that connection, let me describe what I think are some of the less visible consequences of that deterioration. At least for the moment, I find us to be less capable of solving problems than we used to be, less able to reach consensus and make the different decisions required by life in society from day to day. It's as if there were less intelligence in circulation. All the years of not being able to discuss things, exchange ideas, and engage in productive dialogue were not without effect. For too long we were forbidden to make decisions or even to have opinions. For too long we had to stand by and let things happen without intervening in any way. As a result, we find it difficult to take control now that we can. Many of us may not even know what it's like to feel truly responsible. When something goes wrong, we often respond automatically with the same formula we had to use for years, "It's not my fault!" Which means that it's someone else's business, even if we don't know whose and even if we had nothing to do with it in the first place. Anything that goes badly, even those things over which we do have some control, provokes that reaction—the best we have and the most carefully rehearsed, because for such a long time it was our only defense. But nowadays it isn't always true.

I am not referring here to decision-making at the top levels of government, where important barriers of an economic nature exist along with others. I am referring to lower-level, individual, and even personal decisions. Without wasting time on anecdotes, it's as if Uruguayan society were suffering from a kind of paralysis. Clearly we have pressing needs that are not being met. Certain situations created by the dictatorship cry out for immediate attention. Although they could (and should) be rectified without conflict between important groups or interests, they persist because we haven't been able to agree on what to do about them. Apparently we lack the capacity to face up to our problems and make the necessary decisions.

On other occasions, it's as if the pressure we lived under for so long had left us with a tic. In discussions we often say no even without thinking about it, as if saying no were the only possible act of self-affirmation. Surely, that too is a holdover from all the years when saying no was the single most important thing we could do. Apparently, all the pressure we endured reinforced certain reflexive reactions that resurface now, suddenly, at the most inopportune times.

However, such reactions may stem from another source as well. During the entire period, but especially over the past five years, Uruguay's cultural decline has been accompanied by a rapid economic decline. Here I refer to all those people who had to leave their houses and move into miserable tin and cardboard shacks on the edges of town. And to the shocking increase in the number of families who beg by day and rummage night after night through the garbage left on the sidewalks for pickup, in search of something to sell or to eat. And to all the forms of economic pain suffered by large sectors of society during the last years of the "process": the decline in real wages, partial or total unemployment, loss of health insurance, and finally, hunger. All that suggests a ready explanation for the very rigid and dogmatic positions sometimes characteristic of those broad sectors of the population— namely, that they have to do with basic needs. Of course, the economic decline wasn't universal. The luxurious homes in wealthy neighborhoods remain inhabited and well kept, and latest-model Mercedes and Renaults can be seen on the same streets as the garbage collectors' carts; but the shantytowns have grown in size and number, and in them the infant mortality rate keeps rising along with the crime rate.

Yet another obstacle to consensus and dialogue is totally different in nature. It is hard for us Uruguayans to come together again because each of us experienced the "process" differently—and not just because some of us were exiled, others were in prison, and others simply stayed in Uruguay. Even those of us who seemed to be in a similar situation experienced that situation in different ways, all the more so because of our isolation. The way things worked out during this period, we all had implicitly different contexts; therefore, we think differently even when we say the same things.

○

The situations I have discussed until now strike me as the most outstanding characteristics and the most pervasive consequences of the "process" for Uruguayan culture. Let me conclude by returning to something I mentioned in passing, which to me exemplifies one of the most powerful kinds of secret action culture can have—namely, serving as a living companion. In certain extreme situations, culture can be a form of solidarity surpassing words and deeds and deeper than circumstances because it puts us in touch with our roots, with that part of our humanity which is both individual and universal.

The story of Hiber Conteris, a friend who was treated very harshly by the dictatorship, illustrates what I mean with rare eloquence. Since he has told it in public, I can do so too. As I understand it, Conteris had broken with the subversive movement a couple of years before his arrest. However, that fact, undoubtedly important to him personally, couldn't be proven. I have no idea what he was accused of or on what grounds. I only know what he said. The treatment he received was very harsh. He confessed to all he could, signed his statements, and was sentenced. For a moment he thought that would be the end of the hell he had been through, a hell that defies description. But no. Even after his sentencing they kept him in a small dark cell, a dungeon he could leave only twice a day to go to the toilet, hooded and accompanied by a soldier who would beat him with the butt of his rifle as he crossed over to the other side of the barracks.

Thus the days began to pass: in darkness, hooded, punctuated by the two beatings that descended on him whenever his physical needs grew too urgent to be ignored. And after each beating all that remained was to await the next one, that day or the following morning. And each day was the same, day after day, and week after week: in darkness, unable to see, awaiting the beating that was sure to come, that was sure to be repeated. How many days? For how long? He had no way of knowing. He had no way of knowing how long he had been living that way either. And suddenly, he began to realize that he no longer knew who he was. The need to go to the bathroom, the hallucinations under his hood, the pain of repeated beatings, yesterday's and today's, began to occupy the place of his humanity. He was all that, not himself. He had told them everything he could, but they beat him anyway. Why?

But someone did something, and suddenly he remembers Dolon. Of course, Dolon. It was Dolon. Why does he know that? Dolon came from Troy. Dolon is the spy who told everything he knew when he was captured. And he used to tell that story. He had taught it. Dolon had been sent from Troy by Hector to check on the position of the Achaean troops, but he ran into others more skillful and powerful than he. One of them was Ulysses and the other Diomedes. They captured Dolon and made him tell everything he knew about the Trojans. Just the way he did. He had done the same thing. And after Dolon told them everything he knew, Ulysses and Diomedes rushed at him and killed him. And they attacked a detachment of Trojans and returned to the Achaean ships, bringing Dolon's remains as a trophy. That was what he used to teach. He remembers it. Dolon's story was just like his.

And through those images that could have been a model for his own story, he begins to remember who he is. He recognizes himself as the teacher who taught that story to his students. And he begins to take possession of the ancient Greek epic. And as he tries to recall that whole tenth canto of the *Iliad,* in the darkness of his hood and in place of his hallucinations vivid images emerge, anchored in verses sung for the first time over twenty-five centuries ago. A familiar world, the stories Conteris the teacher told his students a long time ago, the stories he can tell himself now. But he realizes that he forgets the stories as soon as he tells them. And to fix them in his memory, he begins to tell them again—only now in hendecasyllables, in hendecasyllabic quartets, scanning each verse and looking for rhymes. That way he can memorize them. And then he recites the quartets. That way he remembers the tenth canto, and he also remembers the lectures he used to give. Because now he knows who he is, who he used to be: Hiber Conteris, the teacher.

Then they transfer him to another place, another barracks; and there he has pencil and paper and can write down his quartets. There were lots of them, over a hundred (I seem to recall him saying 164). The next time they moved him, he lost his notes; but he was able to reconstruct them. And then one day he was released, so unexpectedly that there was no time for them to take his notes away. And he left prison with them, but not just with them. He also left with several other manuscripts: short stories, novels, and so on. Because when he discovered Dolon, he found himself, and after that, he knew who he was.

I can think of no better example of poetry sustaining a person a full two and a half millennia after it was written. Hiber Conteris found in Homer, in his knowledge of Homer's work, a way of finding himself during a time of utter defenselessness and despair—the greatest he had ever known. The images

Homer dreamed in ancient Greece were the handle a man of the twentieth century grabbed onto in order to survive as a human being.

I think that is an important lesson.

March 1986

Notes

1   "Miré los muros de la patria mia / si un tiempo fuertes, ya desmoronados . . . / Y no hallé en qué poner los ojos / que no fuese recuerdo de la muerte." Translated by David Gitlitz as part of his anthology of Quevedo's poetry entitled *Songs of Love and Death and in Between* (Lawrence, Kans.: Conrad Press, 1980), 95 [TRANS.].
2   Taken from *Jaque* (Montevideo), March 30, 1984.
3   Ibid.
4   A form of regionalism influenced by the vanguardist movements of the 1920s [TRANS.].

Fiction and Friction in the Imaginative Narrative Written inside Uruguay

Teresa Porzecanski

✪

During the thirty years immediately preceding the political events of 1973, Uruguayan literary history was dominated by a model, that of the Generation of '45,[1] which emerged primarily as a repudiation of earlier models. Since around the turn of the century—and notwithstanding important exceptions such as Francisco Espínola and Enrique Amorim—an outmoded lyricism oscillating between the varieties of local color known as *nativismo* and *criollismo* had predominated among Uruguayan writers of fiction. As their model appeared increasingly at odds with the kind of national self-searching called for by immediate circumstances, the task of proposing an alternative more in tune with the times fell to the brilliant polemicists of '45, who were mainly essayists and critics.

Their milieu was the brief literary review, newly popular in the papers and magazines of the period. This genre soon became the nucleus from which the Generation of '45 (also known as the Critical Generation) launched its deliberate and successful attack on the quietist attitude of their predecessors, an attitude far removed from national reality and traceable largely to the Batllista welfare state, which in turn was reaping the last economic benefits of the Second World War. The reassessment of earlier literature undertaken by the critics of '45, whose sociologistic criteria underscored the indifference of that literature (and thus its inappropriateness) to the slowly emerging economic crisis that peaked in the late 1950s, placed literary production for the first time squarely within a historicist framework. By treating it as a direct outgrowth of the escapist and generalizing mind-set peculiar to writers of a given period and situation, as a reflection of collective ways of thinking, their approach tended to devalue, by way of contrast, the introspective approach of psychologistic critics.[2]

The insistence of these critics on remaining aloof from individual creative processes, inasmuch as they considered literary production to be primarily a social phenomenon, was both a beginning and an end. A beginning because they finally attempted to rout out the verbose intuitionism of earlier critics, redirecting criticism toward the rationalist objectivity that should govern the study of literary production; and also because they lent historicity to literary events in Uruguay by treating them as a more or less mediated "reflection" of supraindividual categories. An end because by virtue of its prevalence, this approach wound up creating a demand that text and reality match closely, with the former regarded as a consensual description of the latter. With few exceptions, the works spawned by this approach formed a literature of realism and objectivization aimed at laying bare the pitfalls and contradictions inherent in reality and presumably hidden in the model put forth by the previous generation.

Describing and exploring the conflicts of gray, urban characters mired in a depersonalized bureaucracy: that was Juan Carlos Onetti's outstanding accomplishment. Devoid of illusions and worn down by an intensifying process of erosion, Onetti's protagonist was an authentic representative of the precarious paradise of material security and cultural flowering that Uruguay had been in the 1950s. With significant exceptions (notably the work of Armonía Somers and Felisberto Hernández), realist description of stereotypes, detailed to the point of exhaustion, predominated in the narrative of the Generation of '45.

Breaks

In the 1960s there appeared in Uruguayan fiction a tendency we can call the "imaginative narrative." While the works falling under that rubric exhibit dissimilar stylistic characteristics, they nevertheless have a common denominator—the central role assigned to fantasy.

Under the motto "Up with imagination!"[3] taken from the graffiti that accompanied the events of May 1968 in Europe, Angel Rama grouped Mercedes Rein, Gley Eyherabide, Cristina Peri Rossi, Jorge Onetti, Mario Levrero, and myself. Of our group he said, "These are not activist writers in the strict sense that they deal with political or social themes . . . but neither is it possible to consider them lacking in activism. The fact is that in their work forms are infused with [activism], as a result of which they blaze with agitation and ready insight into the new sensitivity."[4] In Rama's view, the new tendency first manifested itself as a fondness for experimentation, "an illusory exacerbation of real information, a fine-tuning of the art of transition that allows literary materials a more rapid give and take, a freedom to combine the ignoble, the vulgar, with the artistic, either in baroque forms, or with an apparently rough simplicity."[5]

In any case, for Rama, the emergence of a new group whose first works appeared during the 1960s signaled the eclipse of the Uruguayan Critical Generation and its literary model, which for three decades had dominated national culture. Thus he suggested the names Generation of '69 and Activist Generation for the creators of that narrative, "heavily dependent on the role of fantasy and imagination, qualities virtually buried beneath the urban realism and everyday grayness which . . . the Critical Generation cultivated during their thirty years of cultural dominion."[6] This substantive change also coincided with the new turn taken by Latin American literature around 1967, as evidenced by the popularity of Julio Cortázar, Carlos Fuentes, and Gabriel García Márquez. At the same time, it drew on national models considered marginal or little known during the preceding years—for example, the work of Armonía Somers, Felisberto Hernández, and L. S. Garini.

It is worth speculating about the reasons for this break, which occurred ten years before the establishment of the dictatorship. Why did these new writers find the style of the Generation of '45 so alien, even while they opposed even more strongly the literary model against which that generation had reacted? And what led those who chose neither exile nor silence to unite during the 1970s around the totally different vision that would become their hallmark? Throughout the years of the dictatorship inside Uruguay, as Mario Levrero and I were joined by Hector Galmés, Miguel Angel Campodónico, Tomás de Mattos, Tarik Carson, and Julio Ricci, as well as by Carlos Pellegrino (in certain of his works), an imaginative narrative gradually took shape. Nourished (as was only fitting) by a variety of styles and heterogeneous stances, but of a piece as regards the primordial role of fantasy, to a greater or lesser extent it challenged the notion that "objective reality," conventionally described, is central to literary production.

Imagination and Subversion

The need to communicate with readers who were under surveillance and therefore could only be reached through the demands made on them by the text might perhaps have offered a schematic explanation of this phenomenon, had the latter not made its appearance at least ten years before the military regime imposed its implicit system of censorship. But it was chiefly their preoccupation with the very materiality of language—inasmuch as some type of rhetoric is the repository of every ideology[7]—that cast these narrators in the role of subversive interpreters, seers and forecasters of a situation that had to be portrayed in allegorical terms if it was to be captured in all its stifling magnitude.

Neither pamphleteering, nostalgic nationalism, nor the superficial regionalism we call *costumbrismo*—not to speak of the conventional descriptions of realism and objectivization—allowed for deepening reflection on the inside of a culture of confinement. Accordingly, we set about multiplying to the point of exuberance registers potentially useful for interpreting a reality under siege (and not just by the military government). On the understanding that it could no longer be described or explained by conforming simplistically to the parameters of the model set forth by the Generation of '45, we set out to subvert this reality through distortion and metamorphosis, to apprehend it by starting from new and deeper levels. In our view, only fantasy could capture its essence, by opposing the *oficialista,* or "officialist," discourse which served the purposes of the military regime and which, though conventionally realist, emblematically eluded any semblance of truth.

It was in this sense that the imaginative narrative written inside Uruguay proposed to be an alternative. In its pure fiction, in its very artifice, it attempted both to counterbalance and to brutally oppose that other artifice decreed by the regime (and rooted in the regime's own values), so as to project a perfect image of what was then called "the new Uruguay."[8] As the military attempted to affirm that Uruguayan culture had suffered no significant fractures and that therefore, by definition, cultural matters were not their affair, our generation proposed to carefully dismantle the formal (and not just the thematic) inner workings of their ideological rhetoric. Our objective was precisely to create friction and thus to erode, little by little, the precarious apparatus of value substitution with which the dictatorship undertook the "restoration" of culture.

In other words, in the imaginative narrative, fiction and friction joined forces in a double challenge to the status quo by (1) opposing the model of the Generation of '45 and its realist descriptive discourse, and (2) opposing the alternative model rapidly developed by the new team of the so-called military process. While the writers of the Generation of '45 opted either for exile or for silence, narrative fiction under the dictatorship found original forms of expression that undercut conventional ways of thinking about the present.

Our group rejected the notion that national identity had anything to do with nostalgic evocations of the old Uruguay—a Uruguay irreversibly displaced by the contracture of political events. Nor did we seek any legitimacy or continuity in previous literary models. If it still mattered at all, we thought national identity should consist, precisely, of a renewed sense of opposition, split, fissure, which would deepen in direct proportion to the military's insistence on allowing only a single, homogeneous position. Through the mechanisms of an imagination gone wild and their narrative results, our group sought indirectly to throw into disarray the points of departure for "official" versions of events. By providing dramatic contrasts to the limited possibilities allowed to thought, we hoped to use fiction to destroy the categories traditionally accepted for understanding Uruguayan reality. And a narrative at the outer limits, the edge, the margins—marginal and marginalized by officialist criticism—was more suitable than the realist model for apprehending what was tragic and paradoxical in our situation.

Thus exercised, literary imagination intentionally distorted the foreseeable contours of characters and situations and systematically undertook—as has every revolutionary movement in the history of art—to destroy the fragile, carefully arrived-at understanding by means of which the world is described consensually. In our writing, characters overcome by their circumstances, blurring of limits, silhouettes obscured in the ambiguity of situations, fantasy that exacerbates reality and causes it to come apart, or a fantasized reality all signal a desire to depict as tremendously confused a historical moment in which the hidden takes on capital importance over and beyond the manifest.[9] The imaginative narrative, then, portrayed reality as something monstrous, profoundly "unreal," and as such, far removed from any simplistic view involving clear-cut contrasts between "good guys" and "bad guys." By so doing, it questioned not only the authoritarian regime as a whole but also—specifically—its categories for thought and interpretation, its discourse, and the values implicit in that discourse.

By altering the mechanisms of description, our writing favored a language of versatility, of accumulation and excess, potentially open to multiple hermeneutic levels in the sense in which Umberto Eco uses the term *open work*. Breaking out of the closed field of a single permitted interpretation, it undertook, in an endless string of allusions, to double the assumptions underlying the attempt to construct an axiology of regularity and order. In this sense, fiction can be a highly valuable form of resistance, of convulsion from inside a culture of confinement, and our "excesses" were a form of opposition to the containment and prudence on which officialist literary criticism thrived. Hence, the annoyance we characteristically provoked in officialist circles.

It can be argued, in other words, that the collapse of democracy in Uruguay affected not just the political realm but, first and foremost, a value system which for years had been the bedrock of Uruguayan life. And that collapse began to manifest itself in two fundamental and not necessarily related aspects of our writing: (1) its content, which explicitly emphasized the distortion of reality; and (2) its form, which destructured conventional discourse in a variety of ways, including use of the absurd, of an extreme and redundant logic, and of anarchical levels of meaning, the purpose of which was to create a sense of disorder.

Officialist and Semiofficialist Models

Organized into groups, the officialist and semiofficialist critics promptly took it upon themselves to fill the vacancies created through dismissals and exile. Once comfortably ensconced in the pages of certain dailies, they proceeded to serve as vehicles for an ambiguous philosophy of restoration, while on the whole ignoring the appearance of this fiction that was so much more innovative in scope. Acceptable narrative was to be visibly understandable and readily understood by a vaguely defined, hypothetical average reader, whose attributes they never specified. But a majority of press reviews made it clear that what they sought was an audience of cautious, "prudent" readers, directly representative of the impoverished concept of culture with which the "process" attempted to prove that in Uruguay nothing important had occurred. Regularity, predictability, conventionalism, and repetition were the values they embraced in search of a literature that would offend no one and question very little, a literature formally uninteresting and thematically traditional. In that connection there was renewed scrutiny of the supposed parameters of an overworked concept—namely, national identity in the new Uruguay. A number of contests in the mass media uncovered the so-called hidden talents that officialist culture resolutely sought, in order to fill the spaces left by the untouchables. As a result, a parallel *costumbrista* trend emerged in the form of journalistic chronicles or vignettes.

Increasingly sterile and apt to take no chances, for the most part criticism under the dictatorship was limited to long-winded studies of the prose or metrics of classical works far removed from and irrelevant to the situation at hand; at least until 1982, these literally filled the spaces in the press. The best-seller status of foreign books was another favorite subject for critical comment. Still a third was the obsessive (and daily) search for the "great Uruguayan novelist," or the "best novel," or the "best short story," among the works of authors who figured briefly in the annals of *costumbrismo* while aspiring to the status of latter-day Onettis. Many of these same works nevertheless dashed the hopes raised by the critics when their quality failed to withstand scrutiny. In other words, in my opinion, there was an almost total void during and after the dictatorship where Uruguayan literary talents were concerned. The dictatorship brought no explosion of good literature; neither did exile, for that matter. Nor did either of these circumstances, in and of itself, bring a demand for excellence in narrative writing. Nor did the generation emerging at the time exhibit all the merits which officialist criticism, in keeping with its own objectives, claimed to find in it.

When the new literary production of that "new Uruguay" was inventoried by the officialist critics, what resulted was a long list of practitioners working in the mass media. Naturally, that list encompassed the writers who had emerged under their tutelage, so as to make it clear that their exclusion of others had not compromised creativity. In the always brief attempts at writing to which I refer, mechanisms of inclusion and exclusion were at work, and the mass media were used for the purpose of self-promotion. For this reason, the forms of discourse characteristic of this writing barely rubbed against the rhetoric of official discourse; certainly they never challenged it in any significant way. Thus, an officialist criticism that claimed to know what it did not became little more than a group strategy for imposing—in one way or another—names and works that were made to appear artificially as the country's culture while having nothing to do with real Uruguayan literature.

Generally speaking, then, Uruguayan fiction under the military was neither relevant nor vanguardist in its stance, preferring instead to remain on a very discreet secondary level. The dictatorship fell primarily because its spectacularly failed economic policies came increasingly under attack from the political and trade union circles that gained ground during the waning days of a more and more discredited government. A minor exception might nevertheless be the imaginative narrative, whose goal was not a lyric vision of distant paradises or infernos but rather the allegorical unveiling of immediate ones. Naturally, the friction between this narrative and officialist criticism led to a certain cultural tension, which toward the end of the period began to chip away at the stagnation, encouraging a reexamination of priorities. In a manner at first devious and later direct, fantasy eroded the ridiculous solemnity of the "culture of the process"—albeit always tangentially.

Some Results

In 1979 an anthology appeared under the title *Diez relatos y un epílogo* (*Ten Stories and an Epilogue*).[10] Surprisingly, most of the works reproduced in that volume fall within the category I have referred to as imaginative narrative. Significantly, it was Armonía Somers who wrote the epilogue, which was an inquiry into the experiences underlying the stories. Was this an ahistorical trend or, on the contrary, one deeply rooted in the historicity of its circumstances?[11]

Somer's analysis implies more than a connection between the anthologized works and her own fiction, which even in earlier decades had been considered marginal in relation to prevalent models; it also uncovers some highly revealing common traits. Disintegration of the personality, problems with self-recognition, a sense of being spied upon, a need to flee, the experience of fear, and the sense of being a spectator at a performance are the leitmotivs of most of these stories, whose overt contents are lodged squarely in the center of fantasy. A feeling of asphyxia, an asphyxia not necessarily contained literally in the plot line—in "what happens"—but rather in the way events are portrayed, can be discerned in all the writers of this group. There is also a piercing sense of being lost, of having been left to their own fate, which strikes them not as dramatic but as terribly predictable. Thus, these stories are veritably shot through with historicity. Political and social circumstances, which inform everyday life permanently and naturally, reveal their presence in a variety of ways. As Rómulo Cosse stated, "We can consider as 'reflections' both realist forms, in the strict sense of the word, and those which for whatever reason, ostensibly have no counterpart in the real world. . . . However mediated, there will always be a reflection, just as there is always a referent, no matter how remote."[12]

It is in this sense that the imaginative narrative written inside Uruguay under the dictatorship successfully captured the tensions of its time. Its form in particular was a source of the friction central to our efforts to erode authoritarianism. Rama anticipated as much when he observed that the imminent new literary generation began by "rejecting the forms, *and therefore the philosophy,* which inspired accepted literature."[13] For us, that is, form and content converged in a single literary phenomenon, with each implying the other. In attempting to unsettle the reader and encourage critical questioning, in offering him a variety of codes, in stirring him out of his lethargy, our writing was a convulsive means of apprehending reality. As such, it made a significant contribution to the struggle against authoritarianism and the fascistization of Uruguayan society.

March 1986

Notes

1   A comment by E. Rodríguez Monegal is to the point here (*Literatura uruguaya del medio siglo* [Montevideo: Alfa, 1966], 33): "One need not be addicted to the genera-

tional method to apply it in this instance. Analysis of our national reality very clearly reveals the emergence of a group around 1945. Unquestionably influential almost from the outset, it remains so to the present day—notwithstanding pressure from a new group over at least the past five or six years."

2　The rationalistic objectivity sought by positivist philosophy led to the treatment of social phenomena as "things" that could be studied as objects; that is Durkheim's position in *The Rules of Sociological Method* (1938).

3　I refer to *La generación crítica (1939–1969)* (Montevideo: Arca, 1972).

4　Ibid., 101.

5　Ibid.

6　Ibid., 222.

7　Here I refer to Michel Foucault's treatment of the historicity of discourse as a moment representative of circumstances, whose values become relative and remain beyond any criteria of truth. See his *L'Archéologie du savoir* (Paris: Gallimard, 1969).

8　Official propaganda in the mass media held the "new Uruguay" to be the country to which the "military process" was giving rise.

9　"Borderline" writing is the term employed by Julia Kristeva to refer to literary expressiveness in an extreme situation. See her *Pouvoirs de l'horreur: essai sur l'abjection* (Paris: Editions du Seuil, 1980).

10　Armonía Somers, ed., *Diez relatos y un epílogo* (Montevideo: Editorial Fundación de Cultura Universitaria, 1979). Included are stories by C. Pellegrino, E. Estrázulas, R. Loza Aguerrebere, T. Carson, T. de Mattos, H. Galmés, M. A. Campodónico, M. Fornaro, M. Levrero, and T. Porzecanski; epilogue by Armonía Somers.

11　Ibid., 115 (paraphrase).

12　Rómulo Cosse, *Crítica latinoamericana: (propuestas y ejercicios): Horacio Quiroga, Ricardo Güiraldes, Rosario Castellanos, Fray Matías de Córdova,* Universidad Veracruzana, Instituto de Investigaciones Humanísticas, Cuadernos del Centro, no. 14 (Jalapa, Mexico, 1982), 14.

13　Rama, *La generación crítica,* 328 (italics added [TRANS.]).

IV

The Shores of Exile

Postdictatorship, Democracy, and Culture in the Uruguay of the Eighties
Hugo Achugar

❂

This essay was written in two parts and at two different times. The first part, "Between Two Shores: Necessary Bridges," was written in January–February 1986 at a moment when Uruguayan society and culture were still engaged in a heady reencounter with democracy after over a decade of dictatorship. The second part, "Uruguay on the 'Raft of the *Medusa*,'" was written in late 1988—by which time the exhilaration of the period immediately following the dictatorship had dwindled and given way to our present disheartened bewilderment. I have kept the text of the first part practically intact, not just out of faithfulness to the spirit of the March 1986 symposium at the University of Maryland and to what was said at that gathering but because when both parts are read together, they give a clearer idea of what today's Uruguay is like and of the speed with which basic changes are occurring there. At the same time, I note that while the first part focuses, albeit not exclusively, on literary criticism and on the relationships between returning exiles and Uruguayans who remained in the country, the second, written once the repatriation stage was over, is intended as a global assessment of Uruguayan culture.

Between Two Shores: Necessary Bridges

For Paco because he held on

Both in exile and after repatriation, working as a critic has involved cardinal gains and losses. Many of us gained new countries and cultural realities—in my case, the endearing and enigmatic Venezuela. And whereas once we were homesick for Uruguay, now we are homesick for the people and places we grew attached to while in exile. Although much else might be said about criticism in exile and in this repatriated present, I will focus here on three issues: (1) the experience of marginality or foreignness, (2) the conditions of production surrounding critical discourse in exile and after repatriation, and (3) the future responsibility of the critic in Uruguay.[1] At the same time, while this essay deals specifically with criticism and the role of the critic, it also reflects my ongoing concern with the situation of culture in general. In that sense, many of my thoughts about criticism are equally applicable to Uruguayan cultural production in its entirety.

❂

"Beings between two waters, on the shores of yesterday and tomorrow: that's what they made us into," said José Emilio Pacheco in "Transparencia de los enigmas" ("The Transparency of Enigmas").[2] In the late sixties, the Mexican poet's observation (or his image) referred to the peculiar situation of people who, convinced of the need for a social revolution, nevertheless held on to the legacies of a bourgeois or *petit* bourgeois upbringing, thus remaining "on the shores"—that is, uninvolved, marginal. Almost twenty years later, those verses could refer to us exiled and repatriated Uruguayans, and perhaps to the released prisoners as well. We too are beings between two waters, on the shores of yesterday and tomorrow. This notion of marginality relates in turn to a fundamental part of the experience of several thousand Uruguayans over the past decade: "foreignness." We have been "foreigners" in a real as well as a figurative sense, whether in exile or as we return, with the sordid years of the dictatorship behind us.

The notions of marginality, foreignness, and "being between two waters" have spatial connotations. They allude to a sense of not being there, of being out of place, of not belonging. But they also allude to something which characterizes all of Uruguay, not just the returning exiles: the marginality or separateness of a society torn apart by the dictatorship, a wounded society laboriously searching for wholeness.

In some sense, our return was proof of the obvious: "You can't go home again," as Thomas Wolfe once put it. The kind of voluntarism which claims otherwise has not grasped what is happening in Uruguay today. The mythical Uruguay was real in its potentiality. As a concrete reality, it is a place of conflictive contacts. The snapshot is blurred. We find that the Uruguay we have returned to is neither that of the prisoners nor that of the other Uruguayans who stayed. There is not just one Uruguay; there are several.

Notwithstanding their desire to be rational and to avoid idealization, the discourse employed by some exiles in their eagerness to return depicted a marvelous paradise temporarily invaded by the forces of evil. Especially at first, life went on in the realm of the temporary, the transitory; exile was but a stage in history, a process that would end. Historically, this was an expression of faith in our eventual triumph; but it was also a refusal to wholly accept our situation. In others, for example, the Ruben Yáñez of January 1984, the discourse of return was an expression not of homesickness but of mission and activist commitment: "[Our goal is] to return. To return not because we want to, but because when the situation changes they'll let us return. . . . [And though] we would want to return even if the situation stayed the same, . . . [we propose] to change the situation so as to make our return possible."[3]

Back home, or at least under the illusion that we had really come home after the retreat (definitive or temporary?) of the military, we found everything and everyone changed, beginning with those of us who had left. We repatriates were regaining our country and losing it at the same time. If temporariness was the hallmark of part of our exile, what we faced as we returned was also labile, insecure, transitory. We are still in the process of repatriating, since repatriation is not an all-or-nothing proposition. Repatriation is not a single, noisy gesture or a one-time, definitive act, but a gaping wound which may or may not heal.

The building of bridges that David Cámpora and Ernesto González Bermejo have written about in *Las manos en el fuego* (*Hands in the Fire*)—bridges between those who left, those who stayed, and those who were imprisoned—is an urgent and necessary task, in which a goodly number of Uruguayans are already engaged. It is a daily assignment that will take years to complete, and it will end when the youngest among us has but a faint recollection of all this. It will end, finally, when all of us—those who stayed, repatriates, released prisoners, and those Uruguayans who have not yet returned—can work together as a team. It will end when we can look back with Cámpora to "building a bridge between the two of us, *chernesto*, the necessary bridges."[4]

○

The time and space of exile and return are among the conditions of production surrounding Uruguayan critical discourse in recent years. Exile affected critical and narrative discourse in different ways. Although in contact with a specialized professional community and a supportive foreign community, critics (both scholars and journalists) were separated during exile from their closest national counterparts. This separation, which presumes a change in the identity and nature of the recipient of the critical discourse, may have had greater consequences for newspaper critics than for academics. In exile, the interpretive or recipient communities we addressed were different; above all, dialogically they demanded very specific types of discourse. On the one hand, there was the specialized scholarship, stripped of ideology and uncontaminated by social reality, which is characteristic of the Groves of Academe—a marginal space, as Edward Said put it, "premised on its own harmless social obsolescence."[5] On the other hand, there was an academicism which, though equally specialized, viewed its action as part of a political and ideological program.

Several options were available to critics, both those with a specific ideological practice and those who wished to work in cultural journalism as well as, or in place of, the academy. There was the often tempting possibility of participating in local projects—that is, some of the many projects under discussion in one's country of residence—or in the Uruguayan exile community's more general project of resistance to the dictatorship. Some critics, especially those of us who lived in Latin America (I know less about what happened in Europe), attempted to do both; for many of us, that was a way of avoiding total marginality and foreignness. Some of us saw the experience of the Spanish exiles in Mexico as a way of overcoming foreignness. However, either option implied certain obligations for critics—not so much at a theoretical level (although some traces might also have been detectable there) as in relation to subject matter. Thus, studying Uruguayan culture or literature, and writing press reviews of what Uruguayans were doing inside and outside the country, enabled us (may occasionally have enabled us) to denounce the atrocities of the dictatorship, directly or indirectly.

Some studies—for example, those of Alvaro Barros-Lémez, Mario Benedetti, Mabel Moraña, Jorge Ruffinelli, Rafael Varela, and Hugo Verani—dealt directly or indirectly with the Uruguay of the seventies. Theirs were not the only ones. Equally significant were the contributions of the Uruguayans exiled in Sweden and those of Norah Giraldi, Rosa Olivera-Williams, Nicasio Perera, Gabriel Saad, and others who placed Uruguay and Uruguayan literature in the forefront of academic discussion. That this occurred was not merely a question of political activism or a political decision; nor did the exiled critics (or those simply residing abroad) limit themselves exclusively to Uruguayan topics. The works of Angel Rama, Rocío Antúnez, Javier García Méndez, Martha Canfield, Roberto Echavarren Welker, Leonardo Rosiello, Jorge Ruffinelli, Horacio G. Verzi, and Ida Vitale (among many others) all testify to the breadth and scope of our efforts.

At the same time, theoretical discussion was affected by the fact of exile. Even more, the extended discussion about text versus context served at certain times to define positions or, as it were, to "part the waters." Defense of literary specificity and adherence to textualist theories, which in one way or another—in keeping with poststructuralist or psychostructuralist models—rejected all attempts at the historical interpretation of literary phenomena, were often means of seeking refuge in the rarified atmosphere of the Groves of Academe and thus, in effect, of attempting to set dubious limits on the struggle against the dictatorship. As Terry Eagleton pointed out in *The Function of Criticism,* in a sense critical practices are social and political practices as well. In fact, the critical options exercised by certain Uruguayans during the dictatorship were fundamentally "deideologizing"; as such, they helped preserve the status quo inside and outside the country.[6]

❂

For returning exiles, the conditions of production surrounding critical discourse have entailed rejoining the Uruguayan community, especially entering the national debate about culture—our own debate, different in its theoretical and critical emphasis from similar debates taking place in the rest of Latin America, Europe, or the United States. In some cases, the differences are products of our isolation during the years of the dictatorship. In others, they simply involve options offered by our own cultural process. For example, the dichotomy between nationalism and universalism has long been present in Uruguay. José Enrique Rodó, Julio Herrera y Reissig, Pedro Figari, Alberto Zum Felde, Carlos Real de Azúa, and Angel Rama have all held forth on this topic, as have many others, in both novel and unchanging ways. Some persistent features of this debate have been reaffirmed over the years of the dictatorship, while others lie dormant. Above all, there is a tremendously conservative quality and a fear of so-called novelties—a fear now reactivated by the presence of "the outsiders." For the repatriate, the theoretical part of the debate is complicated not so much by the experience of renewed and often conflictive contact with a cultural reality that has been traumatized in recent years as by psychological resistance to change and emotional attachment to the past. And as if that were not enough, there is the harsh reality of competition in the job market. The team efforts so crucial to the construction of a future Uruguay are undermined by quarrels which generally have more to do with prejudice or disputes over a limited number of jobs than with true theoretical or political differences.

The returning exiles and the fellow Uruguayans who greet them eye one another with distrust. After an initial period of mutual celebration, doubt and suspicion set in. What we call *reencuentro,* or "coming back together," is largely a bureaucratic invention—little more than the name of a quasi-governmental commission created to deal with the problems of repatriation.

We are not the people we were; the others are not the people we left behind; and Uruguay is different as well. Obvious as it is, this truth is hard to remember in daily life.

Whether in the academy or in the press, when it comes time to produce a critical discourse, critical assessments and descriptions are not always understood on an ideological level, and often the discourse becomes personalized. An obvious example is the discussion that surrounded Angel Rama and Emir Rodríguez Monegal, both explicitly in the press and on a very powerful subterranean level. Some participants confused compassion for a dying man with forgiveness or, in a surprising display of solidarity, preferred to keep their differences to themselves. Others identified (misidentified) critical positions using ideological yardsticks more suitable for police chiefs of the Left and the Right. For those who stayed in Uruguay, reassessment of the unquestionably important contributions of the Generation of '45, and of those critics who preceded and followed, remains anchored in a theoretical and cultural reality somewhat frozen in the fifties and sixties. On the other hand, the exiled critics learned to relativize and globalize; and as we returned, the discrepancy was obvious. This temporal fixation is another of the major problems presently confronting Uruguayan criticism. Some nostalgic repatriates have tried vainly to return to Uruguay as it was before the 1973 coup, and some of those who stayed have also attempted a pre-1973 restoration; in their eyes, everything that existed before the coup was good and sacrosanct. This has often been the case at the University, with questionable results. Once again, temporal fixation kept us from realizing that time had passed and the world had changed.

The debate is under way, and repatriation is a dialectic process, involving those who stayed as well as those who have returned. Repatriation is a task for both the returning exiles and those who greet them. In that connection, it should be understood that return is a matter of belonging. We are not returning because the outside world is any worse than Uruguay or because, as the saying goes, "There's no place like Uruguay." In many cases, we now have new countries and cultures as well. Venezuela, for example, is just as legitimate a place to identify with as Uruguay—all the more so because we got to know it despite the traditionally scornful attitude of the *rioplatense,* or southerner, toward the tropics and the Caribbean. Those of us who left learned that we were not the center of the world and that our values might not be absolute. We return bringing our experiences with us, prepared to learn and to share, not to dictate. We look forward to frank and productive discussions. We are eager to build the necessary bridges. Learning and changing are always painful processes, and that is what we are all engaged in.

❂

What matters is the Uruguay of the future. By now, the term *modernization* is almost a cliché—as common in official discourse as it is on the Left. The problem, of course, is how, for what purpose, and for whose benefit modernization should occur. And specifically as regards Uruguay, how to modernize our own critical discourse in terms of concrete social projects. One option always open to us is to create technocrats with no social or political awareness. A not much better option is to promote social and political awareness with no technical training. Both options should be avoided, for in both cases the future would be dependence. Dependence is not simply a matter of technology. Especially in the realm of critical discourse, it is the abandonment of personal or national efforts for the sake of authoritarian solutions, whether the empire's or those of the latest intellectual guru. Only collective discussion, bridges jointly built, can modernize Uruguayan critical discourse. It is up to all of us to look everywhere; when certain privileged solutions silence others, the winners are always the same.

Knowing that there is criticism in Paris and at Yale, or in Bologna or at Stanford, or at Oxford or in Constance is a good thing. Overlooking the fact that there is also criticism in Cuba, in Venezuela, or in Peru may be suicidal or ill-intentioned. The reverse, of course, is another form of cultural suicide. The future of Uruguayan culture depends on our moving beyond the isolation of the years of the dictatorship. Helping to end that isolation can be part of our contribution, as returning exiles, to the necessarily collective building of bridges that Uruguayan society so badly needs.

Uruguayan Culture on the "Raft of the *Medusa*"

Two, almost three, years have passed since I wrote the first part of this essay.[7] My returns are no longer those of a returning exile, although I am still "commuting" back and forth between the United States and Uruguay. What follows is largely self-explanatory but warrants a brief observation: it is closer to cultural opinion than to an academic essay. The latter will be possible a few years from now, when this moment has also passed.

Postmodernity, Postdictatorship, and the End of the Century

As it turns out, that whole matter of the second postwar period, the cold war, the Cuban revolution and the Vietnam War, the sixties, the age of rock, TV, and video, the "boom," satellites and the adventure into space, dependence and late capitalism, the multinationals and shopping centers, the Third World and computers, the self-centered or apathetic seventies and the godless eighties with their limited democracies and real socialism, was, among many other things, postmodernity. So, here we are in the Postmodern Age.

As a matter of fact, my generation has lived most or all of our lives in the Postmodern Age. It would therefore appear that this stage we call "postdictatorship" is simply a microperiod within the greater reaches of postmodernity. Or to put it in other—specifically Uruguayan—terms, postmodernity began when the so-called country of the fat cows thinned down to this scrawny and emaciated present. (I say "emaciated" so as to make a postmodern niche for the *Larousse*, so frequently hyped on Uruguayan TV these days.) Another metaphor for weight reduction is the fact that before the dictatorship the country had an area of 187,000 square kilometers, but now, thanks to technology, one decade later we have only 176,215.

As part of a postmodern world (though not necessarily a postmodern First World, given the business about nonindustrialization and uneven and combined development), Uruguay now prepares to enter the twenty-first century. Let's be clear about this. "Prepares to enter" is a rhetorical means of denying the fact that the twenty-first century is upon us (or soon will be) whether Uruguay likes it or not. That is, the general sweep of history, the national and world economies, and technological and scientific development are carrying the country along by force because, given its sores and mutilations, its shortcomings and lack of awareness, the process is not likely to be voluntary. What I offer here are some preliminary thoughts about the state of our culture and the different projects ("nonprojects" may be a more accurate description) with which our society is currently wrestling. My words are not (and hardly could be in the limited space afforded cultural issues) a detailed or global discussion. Globalizations are in crisis, and postmodernly speaking, the great interpretive and narrative systems have been called into question.

In the midst of our current and very postmodern chaos, there is nevertheless one major metaphor that in my view offers insight—albeit only partial—into the present moment in Uruguayan culture (or should I say Uruguayan cultures?): "The Raft of the *Medusa*." In his painting which bears that title, Théodore Géricault depicted a group of shipwrecked sailors lost on the high seas and drifting aimlessly, although there appear to be signs that salvation is at hand. I know not whether the glad tidings have reached Uruguayan culture(s) or are about to. But what seems obvious (at least from my perspective) is that we are now adrift on a raft, where a host of despairing and

Utopian visions—I note that we inhabit a pluralistic and democratic space—wail and harangue (though never in concert), and what stands out is a cacophony of voices, each concerned with individual salvation. The rudder is in anonymous (or at best, collective) hands, which results in everyone taking command for a while and no one setting a precise or discernible course. What with fragmentation considered something to be celebrated, this may seem both natural and desirable for the pluralistic and free development of culture. But pluralism and democracy are one thing and fragmentation is another, just as precise and productive statements are one thing and authoritarianism another.

In the postmodern postdictatorship of Uruguay, the ship of culture is on the rocks; and as in Géricault's painting and the short story by Uruguayan writer Horacio Quiroga, all we have left is a raft drifting around in circles, abandoned by the gods. Our foundational myths are dead, and today some of them seem grotesque. For the few survivors on this chaotic raft, phrases like "There's no place like Uruguay," "the Athens of the River Plate," "the Switzerland of America," or the "welfare state" are nothing but scuttled sarcasms.

From the Dictatorship to Everyone against Everyone Else

A little over a decade before the end of the second millennium of the history of Western civilization, and a little over a century and a half after we achieved independence—formally speaking, at least—Uruguay has begun to take stock of the first democratic period following the most brutal dictatorship in its history. In that necessarily tentative venture, political ambitions mix with battles over economic models of development or modernization and battles over the wisdom of evaluating the recent past. Serving justice via the referendum and facing the future and forgetting the past are but two of the battle cries or attempts at reflection with which diverse social and ideological groups attempt to rationalize their present daily life.

In the slightly more than three years since our return to democracy, the country (in particular, the cultural community) has witnessed a considerable number of happenings and mishaps. With the period of the dictatorship behind us—and especially of resistance to the dictatorship—our national consensus, once embodied in the National Planning Commission (Comisión Nacional de Programación [CONAPRO]), has all but collapsed. Chief among the diverse factors responsible for this is the fact that Uruguay has entered a new phase. With the actors from the last tragicomedy backstage now, we have begun to play by new rules. Whereas during the dictatorship our motto was "Everyone against them," now it is "Everyone against everyone else." Or part of that "everyone" against some here, others there, and still others somewhere else. The new rules have not simply made rivals of economic and political groups, they have also pitted young against old and men against women. Obviously, in the confrontation between old and new or renewal (known in some quarters as modernization) and restoration, the battle lines were not drawn originally according to age. During the dictatorship, the transgenerational alliance generated by a common enemy allowed for little internal discussion. But once democracy was attained, the tensions of a society marked by unequal age distribution made it clear that the old alliance was dead.

If the spirit of the CONAPRO was "power to the people," what has followed is "I want my share of power": the well-known (and by now trite) metaphor of the piece of pie. To the struggle between restorers and innovators has been added the struggle between young and old and the preexisting struggle between feminists and male chauvinists. As in the struggle involving youth, in the latter men and women could (and still can) be found on both sides. As if that were not sufficient, a local version of the *nouveaux philosophes* has also appeared, climbing onto the bandwagon of the Old Right in their New Right getup. So has a New Left, to test the waters vis-à-vis the Old Left, while together we build the ideological macroconfusion in which we currently find ourselves. Our homegrown new philosophers may not feel confused, and some leftists immune to *perestroika* may not have had their ideological underpinnings shaken (although the ideological macroconfusion appears more widespread on the left than on the right). Nevertheless, what I say applies to the country as a whole—this poor country of ours, where everyone is pulling against everyone else, overseen from backstage during what certain retired actors take to be just an intermission and, above all, watched from the balcony by a population that slips further and further (young and old, men and women alike) toward a local version of the Spaniards' *pasotismo*[8] encompassing the traditional Uruguayan *notemetás* ("don't get involved"), a new fondness for drugs, and continuing emigration.

The struggle to make a buck is rough, and it's routine. And more or less justice, more or less modernization notwithstanding, for many what really matters is putting food on the table however they can (the priorities set by daily life sometimes preclude other options). Clearly, the game (or the drama) of everyone against everyone else has many players; above all, it is played on many stages.

Uruguay on the Raft

When Géricault painted his famous "Raft of the *Medusa*," he did not have Uruguay in mind, but rather the odyssey of the survivors of a shipwreck off the coast of Dakar. I point that out because obvious truths can be instructive. Nevertheless, the painting is a powerful metaphor, especially if one thinks about the cultural community as a space (the raft) shared by young and old, radicals and reactionaries, supporters and opponents of the government—all of them trying to get their hands on the rudder, on the assumption that salvation may be (or may have been) at hand.

The day the democratic government took office, the Angel Rama Foundation was greeted with great fanfare; but then it was forgotten, left to languish. While the sculptures of Agueda di Cancro (one of our most refined and sophisticated artists) are given away as gifts to foreign dignitaries, the president of Uruguay sings the praises of Sylvia Puentes de Oyenhardt, whose work is the antithesis of all di Cancro stands for, aesthetically and ideologically. The old guard of the Left smiles patronizingly at Leo Masliah's fiction, puts its money on realism, and works itself up over certain rebellious young writers. The members of this new literary "underground" yell, use "swear words" (as if that were something new), attack Mario Benedetti, Juan Carlos Onetti, and others, but seldom produce works comparable to Onetti's *El astillero* (*The Shipyard*), Benedetti's *Poemas de la oficina* (*Office Poems*), Ida Vitale's *Cada uno en su noche* (*Each in His Own Night*), Idea Vilariño's *Nocturnos* (*Nocturnes*), or Amanda Berenguer's *La dama de Elche* (*The Lady of Elche*). Even worse—for we all agree that what is outmoded about our elders should be questioned—they keep reinventing the wheel out of ignorance of the history of Uruguayan culture. Meanwhile, certain of their elders continue their traditional practice of squelching and silencing the young. In short—because all this is said very much in passing and really warrants a longer, closer look—between the conservative restoration of a certain Left, the pseudoliberal and mediocre eclecticism of the government, the often simplistic and merely repetitive aggression of some ideologues of the New Right, and the failure of certain young people (some of whom, parenthetically, will never see thirty-five again) to back up their otherwise welcome questioning with proposals of their own, we find ourselves in a chaos unlikely to lead us to land. And that is the worst of it: with some of us wanting to turn back and others wanting to go on, we are getting nowhere at all.

With very few exceptions—Tomás de Mattos may be one—our narrative fiction presents a provincial and atrociously outdated panorama, where nothing promising ever reaches maturity. Our poetry is richer and more interesting, but since no one reads it, its place in general culture is more mythical than real. Despite the visits of foreign troupes to participate in international festivals, our theater as a whole smells of mothballs. Those composers whose works are performed have little cause for optimism as they go on waiting for Montevideo's principal concert hall to rise again from ashes which are now almost two decades old. Our *canto popular, murgas,* and national rock oscillate between the folkloric, import substitution, and a populism less and less appealing to its audience. Uruguayan TV is a perfect postmodern reproduction—a copy that makes Uruguayan culture seem non-existent because almost everything about it is prepackaged. And film? Uruguayan film is another postmodern product, for that signifier has virtually no signified at all; our recently created video industry is still insignificant.

Lest this sound like a litany of disasters, I hasten to note that in spite of everything there have been achievements as well. For example, we could sing the praises of our plastic arts, the most robust part of the local cultural scene. However, my point is that the poverty and bleakness of Uruguayan culture—not to speak of education, an essential part of culture—are partly the result of the lack of a thoroughgoing debate that might stimulate our creativity and national imagination. And by debate I mean not a trivial polemic about whether this author is worth more than that one, but a comprehensive review of our diverse positions—an appraisal of our cultural history which does not begin in 1945, 1930, or 1900. I mean the intellectual debate about Uruguayan culture which is still not under way. Or, to be more precise, which is under way fundamentally among a few social scientists, historians, and political scientists—in academic circles but not in the open space we all need because this country has had more than its share of ghettoes.

It's true that we are paying the price of more than a decade of dictatorship and the repeated errors of our present system of education. It's true that neither our elders, our children, nor we ourselves have studied the history of Uruguayan culture systematically. It's true that there has never been a course in Uruguayan cultural history, at the secondary or university level, that offered our youth a chance to learn who or what Larrañaga, Vázquez y Vega, Alicia Goyena, and the Ateneo were. Or Figari, Fabini, Sambuccetti, Gradín, Blanes Viale, "el Flaco" Cleanto, the Conventillo del Medio Mundo, Angel Falco, Susana Soca, "el Loro" Collazo and his Troupe Ateniense ("Athenian Troupe"). Or Cluzeau Mortet, Villamajó, *planismo,* L. S. Garini, the Línea Maginot ("Maginot Line"), Felisberto Hernández, the Carro del Chaná, Luisa Luisi, etc., etc., etc.[9] I deliberately mention very well known names along with others barely remembered (if at all) because all are a part of Uruguayan culture(s). On this raft of ours, the only history we recall is that of the shipwreck; and out of ignorance we may end up returning to situations that are all too familiar. On this raft of ours, there is lots of yelling but no discussion. The government warns us against looking back, even as it repeatedly recalls the nineteenth-century Battle of Carpintería[10] and the emergence of the so-called traditional parties. We are asked to attend to the present, to bring the country up-to-date; but the period prior to 1973 is regarded as a lost paradise. Perhaps because we are on the periphery of the postmodern world; perhaps because the banks and the capital of late capitalism can underwrite those contemporary temples known as shopping centers, where one goes to worship Benetton and Levi and to wonder at the objects used in the cult to those deities; perhaps because it doesn't matter—because nothing matters or seems to matter in today's Uruguay except the careful cult to one's own sect, magazine, party, or movement—we will have to keep shouting at one another, everyone against everyone else, until we get to the twenty-first century and history has left us definitively behind. Or until the next dictatorship generates a new mission and some mythical gods that at present we can neither create nor conceive of.

   In conclusion—and as proof that the atmosphere of the postdictatorship is what it is, especially for the young—it's worth noting that in Montevideo today, our young people write graffiti on the walls that read, "Some are born lucky and others are born in Uruguay." It's true that other young people call for freedom, work, get married, and struggle for a living and for the country. But the crisis is great, and it's widespread. The despair of the young—that rhetorically overworked "future of all societies"—is where it's at, and some of them have already begun to emigrate again. Which leads me back to the first part of this essay, written in 1986. Only this time the metaphor of necessary bridges points not to the coming back together of a country but to the despair of a society that in peacetime has not been able to build a space big enough for everyone.

March 1986/November 1988

Notes

1   For other aspects of my views on the topic of exile see "¿Trasterrados o desterrados?" *Actualidades* 6 (1980–82):79–85, and "La crítica literaria uruguaya, el exilio y la producción de conocimientos," *Ideologies and Literatures,* 2d cycle, no. 4, 224–41.

2   José Emilio Pacheco, "Seres entre dos aguas, marginales de ayer y mañana: es esto lo que hicieron de nosotros." From the poem entitled "Transparencia de los enigmas," in *No me preguntes como pasa el tiempo* (Mexico: Joaquin Mortiz, 1969), trans. Alistair

Reid as *Don't Ask Me How the Time Goes By* (New York: Columbia University Press, 1978), 10. (Note that the Spanish expression *estar entre dos aguas* is roughly the equivalent of "to sit on the fence"; thus, were Pacheco's aquatic imagery not central to the author's discussion here, his verse might more accurately be rendered as "Creatures caught on the fence" [TRANS.].)

3   Ruben Yáñez, "Teatro en exilio," *Metamorfosis* 5 (2) and 6 (1) (1984–85):41–42.

4   Ernesto González Bermejo, *Las manos en el fuego* (Montevideo: Banda Oriental, 1985), 281.

5   Edward Said, "Opponents, Audiences, Constituencies and Community," *Critical Inquiry* 9 (1) (1982):24.

6   Terry Eagleton, *The Function of Criticism* (London: Verso, 1984).

7   For the most part, part 2 of this essay reproduces my article "La cultura uruguaya en la 'Balsa de la Medusa,'" published in *Brecha* (Montevideo), November 11, 1988.

8   A neologism derived from the poker player's "I pass" (*paso*) and alluding to a type of political indifference or apathy which refuses, as it were, to "take part in the game" [TRANS.].

9   Father Larrañaga, a nineteenth-century naturalist, was also Artigas's first secretary. Vázquez y Vega was a nineteenth-century statesman. Alicia Goyena was a prominent educator; the Ateneo was a learned society important in the late nineteenth century. Figari and Blanes Viale were painters; Fabini, Sambucetti, and Cluzeau Mortet were musicians; Gradín was a soccer player; "el Flaco" Cleanto was a comic-strip character popular during the 1960s. The Conventillo del Medio Mundo was a well-known residence and gathering place for the working classes of the Barrio Sur, the black section of Montevideo. Angel Falco, Susana Soca, L. S. Garini, Felisberto Hernández, and Luisa Luisi were all writers. "El Loro" Collazo was the leader of a famous *murga*, the Troupe Ateniense. Villamajó was an arquitect; *planismo* was a movement in modern Uruguayan painting; the Línea Maginot was a radio program popular during World War 2. Finally, the Carro del Chaná, a perennial prizewinner in the Carnival parade, is a float sponsored by the producers of a popular brand of Uruguayan coffee [TRANS.].

10   It was during this battle, which took place on September 19, 1836, that the warring factions later to become Uruguay's Blanco and Colorado parties first wore their traditional symbols [TRANS.].

Uruguay: Redemocratization, Culture, Return from Exile (Is It Possible to Go Home Again?)

Alvaro Barros-Lémez

❂

> As a kid in school
> I was taught this song:
> You were born in Montevideo
> near a river like a sea.
> Don't look for a prettier place
> because you'll never find it.
>
> . . .
>
> I looked for prettier places
> —and though I did find them—
> I never did love them as much
> as I love my city.
> —Quintín Cabrera,
> "Yo nací en Montevideo"

With the years of the dictatorship behind us, the cultural community is faced with a tremendous challenge—that of reconstructing and creating at the same time. Reconstructing because until we get back a context, we cannot undertake the essential task of developing a minimal framework within which to examine the multiple meanings violated during the previous period. Creating because we also need to understand the new reality prevailing in Uruguay, and thus the forms and modalities through which that same community will gradually reinsert its productions into its social context, interpret the facts of its everyday existence, become an integral culture again—that is, a set of cohesive cultural assets—and an integral social entity.

All this points to a series of pressing needs: for an analysis of postdictatorship Uruguay in all its multifaceted complexity; for an assessment of the national situation during the years 1973–84; for incorporating not just the culture of resistance but also the culture generated within or under the tutelage of the dictatorial regime, and the cultures developed by different communities of Uruguayan exiles; and just as crucial, for a detailed and scrupulously honest examination of conditions in Uruguay prior to the 1973 coup. A renovated culture, up-to-date with today's Uruguay but informed by all the aforementioned elements (as well as the accomplishments and discoveries these last decades have spawned in other latitudes and settings), will imply a new and serious commitment in the creative and the individual, even more than the "personal," spheres to the principal lines of social struggle in the country—a joining of forces aimed at achieving true democratization of creation and universal access to the products of meaning.

To some extent, even those who agree that this is needed have different views, interpretations, and analyses regarding the means by which we should proceed, the forms the struggle should take, and the demands it will make on us. There is also more than one reading of the national situation. And as if that weren't enough, the arduous task of restructuring civil society implies overcoming, or incorporating, all the false, exaggerated, idealized, or frozen images of "Uruguayan reality" that were created (out of real or imagined need) throughout the years of repression, prison, and exile. What emerges from all the preceding is one of the most complex symptomatologies our society has exhibited in the little over a century and a half of Uruguay's existence as an independent nation (in a formal sense).

Now, in all matters concerning culture and the creation of meanings, the *whens* are as critical as the *hows*. The same poem or work of fiction, musical event, theatrical performance, film, work of criticism, or other cultural project that may have had some value (whether broad and massive or minor and limited) during the years of the dictatorship either inside or outside the country is looked upon today with different eyes, from a different perspective, with different critical baggage and a different sense of where it might fit into the larger picture.

But that is not all. Cultural products—and here I refer particularly to those that emerged in exile—which once perhaps both served a purpose in international campaigns of solidarity and anchored members of the exile community to their "suspended" homeland may very well fail to meet current needs. And they may clash violently with the vision, the analysis, and the experience of those living within our borders, both then and now. In other words, the need for broadened horizons that engendered the cultural product in the first place no longer exists; so that now, that same product may strike us as hollow, false, inauthentic, and contradictory to the vital experience of readers, spectators, or participants in the comings and goings of their society.

Also, the same cultural object that sought to express a given need and tended to achieve a given effect—that was realized in such and such a way, taking into account this or that circumstance—today, as part of a reality known as 1986, inside the country, may be greeted and treated harshly by the critics, considered an error (or a horror), and may even cause tensions we could call grave. Beyond certain identifiable and comprehensible shared characteristics, the differences between what the country and its people looked like from the outside and what they look like from the inside can generate areas of friction, or splits within the country, that are not easily dealt with. If we add to all this the enormous diversity of ideological and analytical perspectives regarding the remote past, recent past, present, and future that can evolve out of manifestly shared intentions and declaredly parallel commitments, obviously the degree of responsibility and the amount of time required to repair the social fabric will be even greater.

The reconquest of Uruguayan culture will be a long and arduous process. Dismantling the offensive and defensive scaffolding created in contexts as dissimilar as prison, the underground struggle, and exile (not to mention apathy, collaborationism, and refusal to take a stand), with the numerous variables each of these permit, will require not just a collective team effort but also an enormous willingness to listen, to let others talk, to form new opinions and let go of old ones we once considered conclusive and irreversible. A complicated assignment, no doubt. No doubt an essential one, too.

Healing the rift between society and culture (a rift created and programmed by the enemies of culture old and new, but no less a product of our own auditory-olfactory difficulties and of our simplistic treatment of reality as something univalent and immutable), creating a new framework, a new context, and a new relationship between the common citizen and cultural workers: that would seem to be the great task before us. The longer we delay, the more conflicts we will generate. The more times we walk by the mirror without looking at ourselves, without stopping in front of it and telling it and ourselves all the things we should, the harder it will be to build those new roads and find our way home.

❂

In "Uruguay: una literatura sin fronteras" ("Uruguay: A Literature without Borders"), I divided the years of the dictatorship into four periods.[1] For a clearer understanding of what has happened since, I should add another three.

The first period extends from the internal elections held by the political parties that were not proscribed (November 28, 1982) to the national elections of November 27, 1984; important milestones during that period were May 1, 1983, the rally at the Obelisk (November 1983), the national strike of January 1984, the freeing of political prisoners at different points throughout 1984 (some as a result of agreements reached during the meetings at the Club Naval) and the successive events of the electoral campaign itself, with the detention of Wilson Ferreira and the liberation of Líber Seregni.

The second period begins with the national elections of November 27, 1984, and includes the retirement of dictator General Gregorio Alvarez (February 12, 1985), the reopening of Parliament (February 15), the inauguration of President Sanguinetti (March 1), the legalization of all the proscribed parties, political groups, and trade unions (March 2), and the freeing of the last political prisoners (during the entire month of March).

The third period encompasses the current process of democratic recovery, which is considered to have begun in February–March 1985.

Now, within this framework, what has "redemocratization" meant for Uruguay in concrete terms? Above all, it has meant a clear and obvious freedom of action on all levels, which, even for many who participated in the fall of the dictatorship, is still hard to get used to. Along with that, a *continuismo,* or "continuism," in different aspects of everyday life, in particular in the area of economics and public finance. We are still under the thumb of international banking interests, and the neoliberal economic model that guides the economy has not changed since the military first applied it. Also, while the great majority of Uruguayans still expect the newly restored judiciary to deal with individuals who were responsible for abuses and violations of human rights, the executive branch has systematically prevented this from happening. In the same vein, scores of the disappeared have yet to be accounted for. In essence, the military, police, and civilian cadres of the dictatorship remain intact.

In the area of education, which was devastated by the military, there have been several proposals for reform and recovery, but to date none has gotten past the stage of good intentions. Except for the rehiring of some faculty and administrative officials dismissed by the dictatorship, the government has opted for a masked version of the same continuism to which I just referred— a combination of inaction, legalized repression, inertia, and limited functioning due to lack of funds.

In the political sphere, the first twelve months of elected government have been marked by clashes among political parties, between the executive and the legislative branches, between the executive and the judicial branches, between the unions and the executive branch, and between the unions and the "traditional" parties.

In this context (summarily described and undoubtedly deficient in many respects) with so many continuist aspects, with a crisis in the area of economics and public finance for which no solution is possible under current policies, with hundreds of thousands of Uruguayans still outside the country and others leaving or leaving again, a first conclusion seems unavoidable. Uruguay is not yet fertile ground for her own children—among them, those who wish to contribute in the area of culture. Nevertheless, this statement would fall short of the mark if I failed to point out that many who have returned (whether from prison, exile, or "insile") are trying to participate significantly in intellectual life, tackle the problems I have mentioned, and share the difficult task of reactivation.

❂

To what extent is cultural production an active and integral part of Uruguayan society today? I will now examine some aspects I touched upon in "Uruguay: una literatura sin fronteras."

In the field of the dramatic arts (traditionally one of Uruguay's strengths), the first year of redemocratization was quite poor. The return of theater people from exile, the freedom to choose which works to perform, and the presence of touring troupes from abroad did not bring about an improvement in the overall quality of productions, the creativity of playwrights, or the participation of audiences—a few clearly successful plays and theater groups being the exception rather than the rule. I anticipate a long-awaited revival in the near future, primarily because of an increased interest in theater on the part of young people and the belief, shared by many working in the field, that 1985 was a year for getting back into shape, repaying old debts, and getting to know the country again.

As to the mass media, the proliferation of political weeklies that was already a trend during the years of the dictatorship, primarily from 1980 on, has continued despite some closings (*Opinar, Correo de los Viernes, Asamblea*, etc.). Those remaining (*Aquí, Las Bases, La Juventud, Búsqueda, Jaque, La Democracia*) were joined in 1985 by *Compañero, El Popular, Alternativa Socialista, Brecha*, and *Opinión*, as well as by the monthly *Zeta*. All these publications have literary, or at least cultural, sections, albeit much less significant than their counterparts in the years before the dictatorship. The same is true of the daily press (*El Dia, El País, Mundocolor, La Hora, Ultimas Noticias, La Mañana, El Diario*), which now devotes far less space to cultural and literary topics than it did in the early seventies. The sales volume of dailies has decreased enormously, and the weeklies have not sold in proportionately greater numbers, except in very exceptional instances directly related to important events.

As regards film, national production is just as lacking, if not more so, than it was fifteen years ago. Most of the few Uruguayan films that premiered in 1985 were produced outside the country or are valuable primarily because they document the final years of the dictatorship. A positive change can be seen, however, in the growth of the organization known as Cinemateca Uruguaya. Originally created as a *ciné-club,* since the years of the dictatorship it has developed into a cultural enterprise that has six movie theaters under its control as well as sole responsibility for the distribution of "alternative films," including those of the developed countries. With more than twenty thousand permanent subscribers, it has succeeded in lowering the cost of tickets to fixed sums that allow moviegoers to attend its screenings frequently. On the commercial circuit, a number of old theaters closed during the sixties and seventies have been renovated and reopened. There has also been a proliferation of "minitheaters," the majority of which show X-rated films.

For Uruguayan *canto popular,* enormously vigorous and influential during the years of the dictatorship, 1985 has been a year of reflection and self-searching. Many artists have lowered their level of production notably. Their public appearances have been fewer and their songs have been aired on the radio much less frequently. Only within the context of Carnival has there been a certain renaissance, linked to the dances and other activities that are part of that traditional celebration.[2] Nevertheless, internationally known figures who were banned under the dictatorship, including Silvio Rodríguez, Mercedes Sosa, and Joan Manuel Serrat, played to huge audiences at their open-air performances.

Specifically as regards the book industry, of the twenty publishing houses that maintained a high level of production before the dictatorship, only two remain: Arca and Ediciones de la Banda Oriental. Others such as De la Plaza, Zanocchi, and Edisur publish either political texts or texts that target specific audiences. To date, the only publishing house created as part of a search for new paths is Monte Sexto, although three or four more are slated to appear in 1986 with the same avowed intentions.

Economically, the repressive policies of the dictatorship had tremendous implications for the book industry. To the disappearance of publishing houses I should add the waning size of the reading public due to both reduced buying power and diminished interest—the latter in response to a market that for years offered nothing but best-sellers or texts that had the blessing of the regime. As a direct result, editions that used to average three thousand copies now average five hundred to a thousand. The book with the highest sales volume for 1985, Ernesto González Bermejo's *Las manos en el fuego* (*Hands in the Fire,* a testimonial novel based on the experience of Tupamaro guerrilla leader David Cámpora),³ sold a little over four thousand copies between September and December in a total of three editions: one of a thousand copies, and two of two thousand each. In other words, publishers prefer to keep their costs high (assuming a greater per-unit cost, the fewer the copies printed) rather than take a chance on large editions, even though the latter would be cheaper in the long run.

Thematically, neither the expected avalanche of texts long hidden away in drawers nor the expected flood of testimonial literature about the years of the dictatorship has materialized. There have been two other trends: texts written by former prisoners and texts written by returning exiles. Among the former, Mauricio Rosencof has undoubtedly been the most widely publicized, as a playwright and a narrator. Among the latter, Mario Benedetti and Eduardo Galeano figured among the most popular for 1985. Even though Benedetti has not returned definitively, preferring instead to divide his time between Spain and Uruguay, the appearance in Montevideo of texts originally published elsewhere seems aimed at repairing links of creative continuity that were broken as a result of the censorship and repression of the last decade. Galeano's case is similar.

Arca Editorial has published Benedetti's *Escritos políticos (1971–1973)* (*Political Writings*) and *Preguntas al azar* (*Random Questions*).⁴ The latter is a collection of Benedetti's work over the last five years, including the series "El Sur también existe" ("There is a South Too"), which served as the basis for a recital presented not long ago in Montevideo by Joan Manuel Serrat. Arca also republished, with further modifications, an earlier revised edition (1967) of Benedetti's *Esta mañana y otros cuentos* (*This Morning and Other Stories*), first published in Montevideo by Editorial Alfa in 1949.

Arca has published *Días y noches de amor y de guerra* (*Days and Nights of Love and War*),⁵ by Eduardo Galeano, adding only a journalistic epilogue (an interview that appeared in the weekly *Aquí* in March 1984). His *Vagamundo,* which first came out in Buenos Aires in 1973, has been republished; and Arca also plans to publish a third title, a revised edition of *Contraseña* (*Password*).⁶ Although works by other writers who lived in exile have not yet appeared in Uruguay (except in the political realm, with works by Rodney

Arismendi, Zelmar Michelini, and others), it seems clear that the repairing of broken links will continue for the next several years.

As regards subject matter directly related to the years of the dictatorship, the collected correspondence of political prisoners Raul Sendic and Leon Lev has been published.[7] So have *Las manos en el fuego* (referred to above), *Araújo: Vivir hasta el mañana* (*Araújo: To Live until Tomorrow*), and a volume of short stories about events and characters from prison, *Esta empecinada flor: relatos de la cárcel* (*This Obstinate Flower: Prison Stories*), by Claudio Invernizzi.[8] Several more volumes are slated for publication in 1986. Nevertheless, of all the books presented at the twenty-sixth Feria Nacional de Libros y Grabados (National Book and Art Fair)—and there were not that many—the most significant were those just mentioned, plus editions of works by recently deceased fiction writer Mario Arregui.

Three books containing texts written in exile have also appeared: *La nostalgia tiene bolsillo* (*Nostalgia Has a Pocket*), by Leo Harari; *Las voces distantes: muestra de los creadores uruguayos de la diáspora* (*Distant Voices: A Sampling of Uruguayan Writers of the Diaspora*); and a third, which, while published in Sweden, was clearly aimed at the Uruguayan market, *Fuera de fronteras: escritores del exilio uruguayo* (*Beyond Our Borders: Uruguayan Writers in Exile*).[9] I am not sure whether a fourth book, *El libro de Eis* (*Eis's Book*),[10] was written inside or outside Uruguay, but its author, Milton Schinca, was exiled in Mexico.

Special mention is also due the publishing activity of the Angel Rama Foundation, its only activity to date. In the twelve months since the elected government took office, four volumes of texts by and about Rama have appeared. The first three contain works by Rama himself: *La ciudad letrada* (*The Learned City*), *Las máscaras democráticas del modernismo* (*The Democratic Masks of Modernism*), and *Tierra sin mapa* (*Uncharted Territory*).[11] The fourth volume, *Cronología y bibliografía general de Angel Rama* (*Chronology and General Bibliography of Angel Rama*),[12] is in two parts, the first by Professor Carina Blixen and the second by myself.

One additional comment seems necessary in the light of what I said a moment ago. Besides the few works that deal explicitly with the years of the dictatorship, a number of other texts have appeared, written by authors who for one reason or another were unable to publish during those years. Among these are works by Mario Arregui, Jorge Sclavo, Matilde Bianchi, and Hugo Giovanetti. But perhaps it is too soon to expect writers or publishers to produce the long-awaited spate of books on that topic. Writing about the dictatorship may be possible only after the currently confused political situation has grown more intelligible, the reading public has gotten over the impact of its first few years of regained freedom, and subject matter has settled back into the context of everyday "normality."

Returning briefly to the writers who lived and worked outside the country, it is worth noting that of the fifty-seven whose work is included in *Las voces distantes*,[13] four died in exile (most recently, Carlos Martínez Moreno), half have returned to Uruguay, and the rest have yet to return, have no intention of doing so, or have arranged to divide their time between Uruguay and some other place of residence.

○

With the preceding in mind, I turn now to a matter of extreme relevance for which many of us, as critics, are responsible. What has been the role (if any) of cultural and literary criticism in this "redemocratized" country? An obvious and enormous decline in the level of critical analysis, specifically in the areas mentioned, is both the tip of an iceberg and something essential to an understanding of the currently conflictive Uruguayan scene. What I see as being true of cultural criticism is not paralleled—at least, not to the same degree—in any other area of knowledge, be it politics, history, sociology, medicine, or whatever. So as better to see the road, let us clear away a little of the underbrush.

Unfortunately, two of our old national scourges are more in evidence than ever: *amiguismo* ("cronyism") and *perismo* (what we might call "yes, but-ism"), the former to such a degree that "critics" from this or that faction, fraternity, or "mafia" often concern themselves exclusively with their own while ignoring works or writers belonging to other groups or to none at all. From a variety of pulpits, potshots are aimed not so much at specific works as at their creators or their subject matter, with irrelevant anecdotes and sometimes outright gossip serving as the basis for personal attacks. Publication notices in the press focus on the subjective to the exclusion of the substantive, as critics place their "analytical tools" (???) at the service of their feelings: love or hate, friendship or animosity.

I say "publication notices" because what masquerades as critical discourse today is not much more than that. To tell the truth, there is little by way of textual analysis, background information, and consideration of context. Very little, in fact. The rest is "silenceable." Of course, if the writer in question belongs to the clan, the clique, the group, the gang, or if he happens to have power of any kind, he will be praised. If dealing in dithyrambs is impossible, vagueness will suffice and his life will be spared. Everything has some value. If not, the problem can be solved with an interview; no scalpels allowed, just a few witticisms. Controversy? Just drawing room chatter and arguments over nothing. Real controversy? Maybe someday.

In any case, the avalanche of superficialities (in a milieu where serious searching is scarcer than hen's teeth), the you-and-me brand of cronyism, and the nasty neighborhood barroom variety of "yes, butism" are—just like Johnny Walker—"still going strong." Instead of criticism that educates and broadens, we deal on the level of cosmetics, typographical errors, and outer wrappings. Cheap jokes have found their way in, along with racy remarks and sarcastic, flip answers. Or lacking those, gratuitous diatribes and would-be solid sentences poised over a huge, disproportionate void. "Agility" seems to have destroyed serious, serene analysis aimed at achieving depth. We have been inundated by cultural "slapstick." That many-edged sword known as gossip has taken the place of ideas and discussion of ideas, and "speed of execution" seems to have displaced reflection and study. The previously mentioned rare exceptions only serve to confirm the rule. By dwelling on this desolate landscape I do not mean to denigrate the future. Clearly these problems will be overcome. Of course all this will change. Undoubtedly things will improve. Meanwhile, amid the "wild uproar" of this Carnival season, each of us goes on sniping, as Gila once put it, "all snug and warm" in our respective minitrenches.

The paths to be followed are not these. After years of repression and triteness—two sides of the same coin—the recovery of democratic spaces demands that we exercise other options, undertake other searches involving other kinds of effort. The first of these is serious criticism, not machine guns loaded with half-buried hate, ill-disguised envy, gussied-up chronyism, or "you-do-for-me—I'll-do-for-you" deals, but precisely the opposite: the training of new generations; a real identification of the cultural with the general context of Uruguayan society both present and future; an ongoing process that will require learning and teaching, research and participation.

Of course, that will mean work, time, reading new things, listening to people and understanding them, in the street and in the corner café: diverse actions in a society where crisis has reached such gigantic proportions that no return to the past is possible. And nevertheless, voices can still be heard clamoring for the Montevideo of the Generation of '45, that "happy Arcadia" full of so-called parricides[14] from April to November, and beachgoers from December to March. A futile wish, as far as both society and culture are concerned. There is no going back to that Uruguay, or to that Montevideo. We have to build a different future just as we have to build a different country, as Alfredo Zitarrosa's song goes, "from the bottom up." Until now, cultural criticism, and literary criticism in particular, either has not seen that or has not been willing to do it. If this does not change, if we do not begin to live in our country as it really is, we will contribute little to those searches and cleanups even if we forget, with our backs to the mirror, that laurels wither and fade.

We all recognize that the night has ended. Now the new day demands that we look at the sun, turn toward it, get back our bearings, incorporate what helped us defend ourselves during the hardest times—and live today and tomorrow face-to-face with the future. For only that will guarantee us a present free of prejudice and a future free of backsliding, even if we hold on to everything we learned about survival so painfully, the hard way, during those years when our Uruguayan "we" was destroyed—that is, "we" the unit that encompasses an entire people, in each and every one of its circumstances.

I conclude these hastily written reflections with the words of Walt Whitman, a poet long influential on our multifaceted continent:

Now I will do nothing but listen,
To accrue what I hear into this song, to let sounds contribute toward it.

I hear bravuras of birds, bustle of growing wheat, gossip of flames, clack
    of sticks cooking my meals,
I hear the sound I love, the sound of the human voice,
I hear all sounds running together, combined, fused or following,
Sounds of the city and sounds out of the city, sounds of the day and
    night.[15]

March 1986

Notes

1   Alvaro Barros-Lémez, "Uruguay: una literatura sin fronteras," *Revista de Crítica Literaria Latinoamericana* 9 (17):195–206. See also the prologue to *Las voces distantes: muestra de los creadores uruguayos de la diáspora* (Montevideo: Monte Sexto, 1985). (The four periods referred to are as follows: [1] from the coup [June 27, 1976] to the onset of massive repression in late 1976, [2] from late 1976 to the reappearance of a visible internal opposition in late 1978, [3] from late 1978 until the plebiscite on the military's draft constitution [November 1980], and [4] from the November 1980 plebiscite to the internal elections held by the political parties on November 28, 1982 [TRANS.].)

2   The 1986 Carnival texts warrant a study of their own. Our first Carnival under democracy brought with it an excessive amount of pamphleteering that was not very well received.

3   Ernesto González Bermejo, *Las manos en el fuego* (Montevideo: Banda Oriental, 1985).

4 Mario Benedetti, *Escritos políticos (1971–73)* (Montevideo: Arca, 1985); Benedetti, *Preguntas al azar* (Montevideo: Arca, 1985).

5 Eduardo Galeano, *Días y noches de amor y de guerra* (Montevideo: Arca, 1985). Originally, this book, which won the Casa de las Américas prize for testimonial literature, was published by Casa de las Américas in Havana in 1978; there was also a Spanish edition (Barcelona: Editorial Laia, 1978).

6 Eduardo Galeano, *Vagamundo* (Montevideo: Arca, 1985), first published in Buenos Aires (Crisis, 1973); Galeano, *Contraseña* (Montevideo: Arca, 1986). This was a modified version of an earlier book with the same title (Buenos Aires: Ediciones del Sol, 1985).

7 Raúl Sendic, *Cartas desde la prisión* (Montevideo: Zanocchi Editor, 1985); Leon Lev, *Cartas desde mi celda* (Montevideo: Ediciones de la Puerta, 1985).

8 Alvaro Barros-Lémez, *Araújo: Vivir hasta el mañana* (Montevideo: Monte Sexto, 1985); Claudio Invernizzi, *Esta empecinada flor: relatos de la cárcel* (Montevideo: Ediciones de Las Bases, 1986).

9 Leo Harari, *La nostalgia tiene bolsillo* (Montevideo: Zanocchi Editor, 1985); Alvaro Barros-Lémez, ed., *Las voces distantes: muestra de los creadores uruguayos de la diáspora* (Montevideo: Monte Sexto: 1985); María Gianelli, Fernando Beramendi, and Ana Luisa Valdés, eds., *Fuera de fronteras: escritores del exilio uruguayo* (Stockholm: Nordan-Comunidad, 1985).

10 Milton Schinca, *El libro de Eis* (Montevideo: Arca, 1985).

11 Angel Rama, *La ciudad letrada* (Montevideo: Fundación Angel Rama, 1985), originally published in the United States (Hanover, N.H.: Ediciones del Norte, 1984); Rama, *Las máscaras democráticas del modernismo* (Montevideo: Fundación Angel Rama, 1985); Rama, *Tierra sin mapa* (Montevideo: Fundación Angel Rama, 1985), original edition (Montevideo: Ediciones Asir, 1961).

12 Carina Blixen and Alvaro Barros-Lémez, *Cronología y bibliografía general de Angel Rama* (Montevideo: Fundación Angel Rama, 1986).

13 See Barros-Lémez, ed., *Las voces distantes*.

14 Because of their severely critical attitude toward the two generations which preceded them [TRANS.].

15 Walt Whitman, "Songs of Myself," in *Leaves of Grass* (Boston: Small, Maynard, 1899), 51.

Uruguay, Inside and Out
Jorge Ruffinelli

✪

I n addition to having plunged the country into economic decline, stifled
public freedoms in order to govern, and repressed its inhabitants by
maiming their bodies, the military dictatorship under which Uruguay
languished from June 27, 1973, to March 1, 1985, holds the dubious honor
of having aggravated an inherited and already critical problem: emigration.
The slow exodus which sapped our energy, especially from 1965 on, swelled
to dramatic and painful dimensions as blatantly political considerations—
persecution, a reign of terror, the suspension of constitutional guarantees—
overshadowed economic ones. With the installation of a de facto regime, national development and the flowering of Uruguayan culture became things
of the past or at best, vague aspirations for a distant future. Today, owing
largely to the passive resistance of a society in which military ideology never
enjoyed civilian support (and was roundly rejected as soon as the 1980
plebiscite gave us an opportunity to express ourselves), that distant future
seems once again to be within our reach.

✪

Uruguay has just emerged from twelve tragic years during which its intellectual cadres were hard hit and decimated along with the rest of its population.
Survival in less hazardous terms than those presented by prison, torture, and
death was to be found either in an attitude of inner exile—a kind of passive
resistance in which the song movement known as *canto popular* afforded
practically the only escape valve—or in the literal exile that scattered professionals, journalists, artists, and writers alike into a diaspora. For the most part
(organized emigration to Australia being an exception with characteristics of
its own), those exiled intellectual cadres gravitated toward metropolitan

centers in Latin America, the United States, and Europe. During the 1970s, internal mobility in Latin America reached new heights, although countries like Mexico, having received waves of immigrants from the Spanish Republic and Central America, already possessed structures capable of accommodating such groups temporarily and sometimes permanently.

Our educational and cultural heritage emigrated along with us, endured in the process, struggled, and grew richer and more diverse. Angel Rama commented perceptively on the transformation of intellectual production in relation to the exiled writer's reading public:

> The exiled writer functions vis-à-vis three potential audiences which, familiar though they may be, exist under different conditions: his major audience in the country or culture in which he resides temporarily; the similarly broad audience in his country of origin that he hopes to go on addressing; and notwithstanding the efforts of dictatorships to limit circulation of his message, the audience comprised of his fellow countrymen in exile, which exists apart from that of his country of origin because of the new situations it must face.[1]

The Floodwaters Recede

A basic problem arises for the writer to the extent that those audiences (especially those of his homeland and his home in exile) have differing cultural codes—different languages and values, for example—and the circumstances surrounding writing and publishing force him to choose one set over the other. Generally speaking, I would venture to say that writers and artists have continued producing for their national audiences, even while broadening their frames of reference to encompass things they construe to be more broadly Latin American. Perhaps the most distinctly native-sounding voices are those which have blurred around the edges as their exiled owners moved about and readapted to their new surroundings—none of which implies the "denationalization" of discourse, unless we somehow start issuing naturalization papers for stylistic traits. In any case, literature written inside Uruguay at the same time was in an analogous situation, albeit opposite in meaning, inasmuch as restricted freedom of expression brought with it the "denaturalization" of spontaneous discourse.

What happened, then, when the floodwaters receded and conditions for the production of Uruguayan literature inside and outside the country were normalized—relatively speaking of course, since what is normal in 1985 bears no resemblance to what was normal in 1973 when the coup d'état transformed the country? Perhaps I should put the question differently. What can and should our present attitude be toward the reappraisal and reconstruction of culture, taking into consideration the return of freedom and the reality of a country both changed and unchanging? An ample political space has opened up in Uruguay, bringing with it for writers who remained there a degree of freedom of expression unknown during the twelve years of the dictatorship, and for writers who went into exile the possibility of rejoining their "natural" audience. Even the semantic category of "exile" loses its meaning.

However, the situation is more complex than is suggested by these terms—these formulas to which we often fall prey—chiefly because the economic, and in some sense political, conditions that gave rise to emigration continue to exist, sometimes to an even greater degree. Thus, the "deterritorialized" country comprised of Uruguayans living outside Uruguay will continue to exist as well, in an indefinite sense, for an unforeseeable future, in incredibly complex and conflictive forms (which we will have to integrate into Uruguayan culture through a major stretch of the imagination, lest we lose them needlessly).

What is happening in general terms can also be observed more specifically in the diverse attitudes of our writers and artists concerning the possibility of return. While some have gone back to Uruguay seeking reinstatement into the social and cultural reality from which they were absent for over a decade, others have chosen not to return for the time being (and perhaps never will). Where circumstances permit, still others have carried on their personal and professional lives both in their country of origin and in the countries where they put down roots in exile, going back and forth as dictated by the demands of profession and family or by the wariness with which they regard a democracy as yet incompletely consolidated. Uruguayan culture has never before found itself in this situation, at least not as broadly and categorically. For that reason, when it comes time to think about reconstructing a culture deeply wounded by factors foreign to its own dynamics we have no precedents to cling to.

A Proposal for Reconstruction

Having said this, I offer the following reflections, conclusions, and proposals for the reconstruction of Uruguayan culture.

Between 1973 and 1985, that culture underwent a schism and a crisis as a result of political repression and exile. Obviously, the dictatorship was not created in a void but must be understood in the light of the failed liberal project and political corruption which preceded it. However, that is beyond the scope of this discussion.

We must acknowledge the existence of a deterritorialized Uruguayan culture, inasmuch as many writers continued producing in exile and their production was almost entirely unknown inside the country. Conversely, only exceptionally and insufficiently did cultural production inside Uruguay transcend our national borders to reach Uruguayan readers abroad. The task of updating our knowledge of Uruguayan culture through a reexamination of these two corpuses, with attention to their differing conditions and contexts, should prove as essential as it will be interesting.

For a long time it was customary to regard such internationally famous authors as Isidore Ducasse, Jules Laforgue, and Jules Supervielle as "the writers that Uruguay gave to France," even while we integrated them artificially into our culture. Actually, a far more cogent case could be made for including as part of our common heritage the work of our exiled writers, who never abandoned our language and values notwithstanding all the mediating factors to which I have referred. In any future assessment of Uruguayan culture, the production and unique experience of exile and emigration should be considered no less ours than anything generated and published inside the country.

Even then, we must rethink our culture within productive parameters that to date have gone unnoticed, perhaps because they constituted, or were regarded as, isolated cases rather than a phenomenon peculiar to a period. We must remember, for example, that many of the historical novels of Eduardo Acevedo Díaz, one of the founders of our literary nationalism, were written and published in Argentina. And that Horacio Quiroga wrote his best works in Misiones and published them in Buenos Aires. Other names abound, among them Enrique Amorim, Juan Carlos Onetti, and Felisberto Hernández. In Spanish America as a whole, books written or published far from the "old homestead" are legion: *Cien años de soledad* (*One Hundred Years of Solitude*), *La ciudad y los perros* (translated into English as *Time and the Hero*), *Rayuela* (*Hopscotch*), *Yo, el Supremo* (*I, the Supreme*), *Terra nostra, Palinuro de México* (*Palinuro of Mexico*). There is not the slightest doubt that these works or others I might mention belong legitimately to the national culture of their respective authors. If I may digress momentarily, I would like to point out that Latin American literature has given rise in large part to a culture that is deterritorialized in national terms, and that this culture owes its discernible outlines—indeed, its very name—to the critical thought that has accompanied it from its origins and served as its great unifying force.

A first step in the spiritual and material reconstruction of our literary culture might be to gather and foster awareness of the wealth of bibliographic material that informs it, through projects undertaken concurrently at diverse centers of cultural activity: the National University, the press, publishing houses, literary magazines, book fairs, and so on. In this connection we have a great precedent to fall back on—namely, the splendid accomplishments of the Generation of '45 from the late 1950s onward. Excellent coverage of cultural issues being an extraordinary and almost unique feature of Latin American journalism, particularly during the 1960s, the work of these writers served as a vehicle for the understanding and dissemination of Uruguay's outstanding contributions to critical thought, poetry, fiction, theater, music, and the visual arts. Virtually nonexistent until then, the publishing industry was given a major boost, while magazines, the literary pages of dailies and weeklies (especially those of *Marcha*), and the National Book and Art Fair founded and directed for the last twenty-six years by Nancy Bacelo were proof that a small country could produce, reproduce, and sustain the instruments of a great culture.

Conditions Today

Today our point of departure is a radically different and critical situation. Dismantled by the dictatorship and the rightist governments which preceded it, the National University lacks the budgetary resources necessary to fund increased research in the humanities and the arts or to give new impetus to publishing once (in the 1960s) a very respectable part of its operations.

Activity at the commercial presses first dwindled, then ceased; and today, the few that remain operate under such critical infrastructural constraints that the price of books has become prohibitive for the average reader. Chief among these constraints are the high costs of production and an appreciable decrease in the size of the reading public. Between 1968 and 1972, the average size of editions was three to five thousand copies. From 1982 to 1986, editions have averaged about five hundred copies each. A decline in income, continuous inflation, the rising costs of paper, ink, and energy, emigration (which has reduced the number of actual readers), and an overriding concern with economics and politics have brought about an overall decline in the size of the reading public to levels which the ailing book industry finds nonviable.

As a genre, generational literary journals have disappeared almost entirely, although in some cases they have been transformed. Given the sparseness of the current periodical scene, a case worth mentioning in this connection is that of *Maldoror*, which has become a vehicle for specialized literary studies with recent issues dedicated to reception theory and to the theoretical writings of Gérard Genette and Jacques Derrida. There is a pressing need for new generational journals through which new writers might gain visibility.

Since the creation of a number of weeklies in 1983, some of which still exist, political journalism has flourished. Unfortunately, we still cannot speak of a comparably broad, rigorous, and systematic cultural space within the press. Criticism tends to be sporadic and is of little importance in the key places where the country's problems are discussed; while scores of self-styled "critics" publish occasional reviews, major figures of the stature of Alberto Zum Felde, Angel Rama, and Emir Rodríguez Monegal—to mention three of our literary giants of the past—are singularly lacking.

The perspectives for the immediate future are not very auspicious. After twelve years of repression and exile, Uruguay's cultural projects have been lost and nothing has been proposed by way of replacement. At present, in fact, the prospect of an organic, integrated, vital national culture—one which expresses our needs, fears, and hopes for the future—seems further away than ever. In any event, we should keep in mind that the meaning of culture can only be that which its intellectual cadres choose to give it. And that there as elsewhere, life is always beginning anew.

March 1986

Notes

This essay was also published in *Brecha* (Montevideo), May 2, 1986, 29. No mention was made there of its presentation at the Maryland symposium.

1   Angel Rama, "La riesgosa navegación del escritor exiliado," *Nueva Sociedad* 35:10.

Contributors

✪

Saúl Sosnowski is Chair, Department of Spanish and Portuguese, and Director, Latin American Studies Center, University of Maryland. He is the author of *Borges y la Cabala: la búsqueda del Verbo* and *La orilla inminente: escritores judíos argentinos.*

Louise Popkin is a professional translator and a member of the American Translators' Association and the American Literary Translators' Association. She is a lecturer in Spanish at the Harvard University Division of Continuing Education. Her translations of Latin American prose, poetry, and drama have appeared in literary journals and anthologies. She is the author of *The Theater of Rafael Alberti.*

Hugo Achugar is Professor of Latin American Literature, Universidad de la República, Montevideo. His recent books of criticism include *Poesía y sociedad: Uruguay, 1880–1911* and *La biblioteca en ruinas: ensayos sobre literatura/s en América Latina.* Recent books of poetry include *Las mariposas tropicales, Todo lo que es sólido se disuelve en el aire,* and *Orfeo en el salón de la memoria.*

Alvaro Barros-Lémez is Professor of Journalism, Universidad de la República, Montevideo, and Director, Editorial Monte Sexto. His scholarly works include *Abraxas en el país de las pesadillas: la narrativa de Samuel Dashiell Hammett, La obra cuentística de Javier de Viana,* and *Angel Rama: Bibliografía general anotada.* He has also edited anthologies and published book-length interviews with major political figures.

Amanda Berenguer is a poet and critic. Her earlier poetry was collected in *Poesía (1949–79).* More recent books include *Identidad de ciertas frutas, La dama de Elche,* and *El monstruo incesante: (expedición de caza).*

Lisa Block de Behar is Professor of Literary Theory and Linguistics, Instituto de Profesores Artigas, and Professor of Semiotics, Universidad de la República, Montevideo. Recent scholarly works include *Una retorica del silencio, Al margen de Borges,* and *Dos medios entre dos medios: sobre la representación y sus dualidades.*

Hiber Conteris is Chair, Division of Modern Languages, Alfred University, Alfred, New York. He is Professor of Latin American Literature and author of plays, novels, and short stories. His recent works of fiction include *El diez por ciento de vida, La cifra anonima: cuatro relatos de prisión, Información sobre la ruta uno,* and *La diana en el crepúsculo.*

José Pedro Díaz is Professor of French Literature and Research Methodology, Universidad de la República, Montevideo. His critical works include *Gustavo Adolfo Bécquer: vida y poesia, El espectáculo imaginario* (2 vols.) and *Novela y sociedad*. Works of fiction include *Los fuegos de San Telmo* and *Partes de Naufragios*.

Eduardo Galeano is a journalist and author of fiction and essays. Some of his best-known titles are *Las venas abiertas de América Latina, Días y noches de amor y de guerra, Contraseña, Memoria del fuego* (3 vols.), *El libro de los abrazos*, and *Nosotros decimos no*.

Edy Kaufman is Professor of Political Science and Director, Truman Institute for International Peace, Hebrew University, Jerusalem. His major publications include *Uruguay in Transition: From Civilian to Military Rule, Israel-Latin American Relations* (with Y. Shapira and J. Barromi), and *Crisis in Allende's Chile: New Perspectives*.

Leo Masliah is best known as a composer, lyricist, performer, and humorist. As such, he has produced over a dozen cassettes of original compositions, including "Persianas," "Extraños en tu casa," "Falta un vidrio," and "I lique roc." He is also a prolific author of poems, plays, short stories, and novels. Publications include *Teléfonos públicos, La tortuga y otros cuentos, Historia transversal de Floreal Menéndez, Zanahorias, Tarjeta roja*.

Carina Perelli is Professor of Sociology and Political Science, Universidad de la República, Montevideo, and cofounder and codirector of a research institute, Peitho, in Montevideo. Major publications include *De mitos y memorias políticas: la represión, el miedo y después* (with J. Rial) and *Gobierno y política en Montevideo* (with F. Filgueira and S. Rubino).

Teresa Porzecanski is Professor of Cultural Anthropology and Director, School of Social Work, Universidad de la República, Montevideo. She is also a poet, essayist, and writer of fiction. Recent scholarly works include *Curanderos y canibales: ensayos antropológicos sobre guaraníes, charrúas, terenas, bororos y adivinos* and *Rituales: ensayos antropológicos sobre Umbanda, ciencias sociales y mitologías*. Her recent works of fiction include *Invención de los soles, Una novela erótica, Ciudad impune*, and *La respiración es una fragua*.

Juan Rial is Professor of Political Science, Universidad de la República, Montevideo, and cofounder and codirector of a research institute, Peitho, in Montevideo. His major publications include *De mitos y memorias políticas: la represión, el miedo y después* (with C. Perelli), *Partidos políticos, democracia y autoritarismo* (2 vols.), *Uruguay, elecciones de 1984: sistema electoral y resultados*, and *Las fuerzas armadas: ¿soldados-políticos garantes de la democracia?*

Mauricio Rosencof is best known as a playwright and journalist, but he has also published poetry and fiction. Some of his best-known plays are *Las ranas, Los caballos, El saco de Antonio, El combate del establo, El hijo que espera*. Journalistic works include *La rebelión de los cañeros* and his memoirs of prison life, *Memorias del calabozo* (3 vols., with E. Fernández Huidobro).

Jorge Ruffinelli is Professor of Latin American Literature and editor-in-chief of the literary journal *Nuevo Texto Critico*, Stanford University. Major critical works include *José Revueltas, ficción, política y verdad, Crítica en Marcha, Las infamias de la inteligencia burguesa, La escritura invisible*, and *Poesía y descolonización*.

Martin Weinstein is Professor of Political Science, William Paterson College, Wayne, New Jersey. Major publications include *Uruguay: The Politics of Failure* and *Uruguay: Democracy at the Crossroads*.

Ruben Yáñez is Professor of the Philosophy of Education, Universidad de la República, Montevideo. Also an actor and theater director, he served as artistic director of the independent theater group "El Galpón" from 1971 to 1990. He is the author of numerous journal articles in addition to his book *Democracia y laicidad*.

Library of Congress Cataloging-in-Publication Data
Represión, exilio y democracia. English.
Repression, exile, and democracy : Uruguayan culture / editors,
Saúl Sosnowski and Louise B. Popkin ; translated from the Spanish by
Louise B. Popkin.
p. cm. — (Latin America in translation/en traducción/em
tradução)
Translation of : Represión, exilio y democracia. College Park,
U.S.A. : Universidad de Maryland ; Montevideo : Ediciones de la
Banda Oriental, 1987.
Includes bibliographical references and index.
ISBN 0-8223-1258-1 (hard). — ISBN 0-8223-1268-9 (pbk.)
1. Uruguay—Politics and government—1973– —Congresses.
2. Authoritarianism—Uruguay—History—20th century—Congresses.
3. Politics and culture—Uruguay—History—20th century—Congresses.
4. Uruguay—Cultural policy—Congresses. 5. Uruguay—Intellectual
life—20th century—Congresses. 6. Arts—Censorship—Uruguay—
History—20th century—Congresses. 7. Civil rights—Uruguay—
History—20th century—Congresses. I. Sosnowski, Saúl.
II. Popkin, Louise B. III. Title. IV. Series.
F2729.R4613   1993
306.2'09895—dc20   92-10650 CIP